D1034140

SALES
LETTERS
THAT
SIZZLE

Herschell Gordon Lewis

Printed on recyclable paper

NTC Business Books

a division of *NTC Publishing Group* • Lincolnwood, Illinois USA

MOHAWK VALLEY COMMUNITY COLLEGE LIBRARY

Library of Congress Cataloging-in-Publication Data

Lewis, Herschell Gordon
    Sales letters that sizzle: all the hooks, lines, and sinkers you'll
ever need to close sales/Herschell Gordon Lewis
        p.   cm.
    ISBN 0-8442-3547-4
    1. Sales letters. 2. Direct marketing. I. Title.
HF5730.L48   1995
658.8'1—dc20   94–16176
                                               CIP

Published by NTC Business Books, a division of NTC Publishing Group
4255 West Touhy Avenue
Lincolnwood (Chicago), Illinois 60646–1975, U.S.A.
© 1995 by NTC Publishing Group. All rights reserved.
No part of this book may be reproduced, stored in a retrieval system,
or transmitted in any form or by any means,
electronic, mechanical, photocopying, recording or otherwise,
without the prior permission of NTC Publishing Group.
Manufactured in the United States of America.

4 5 6 7 8 9 BC 9 8 7 6 5 4 3 2 1

HF
5730
L48
1995

Contents

Chapter 3   22
The Most Effective Ways to Grab Your Reader's Attention: *What's on Top? And What's in the Middle?*

Chapter 4   46
What's at the End? *How to Close with a Bang, Not a Whimper*

Chapter 5
Envelopes: *That Crucial, Very First Impression*   56

PART II   79
Your Library of Letter-Openings

Chapter 6   81
The Importance of the Opening

Acknowledgments

I'm indebted to Messrs. Henry Hoke II and Henry Hoke III, past and present publishers of the distinguished publication *Direct Marketing*, for allowing me to test in the pages of that magazine many of the concepts described in this book.

Such giants and pioneers of force-communication as Richard Benson, Betty Ann Jones, the Jennings family, Richard Hamilton, Guy Crossley, Susan Wiles, Bob Stupak, Ira Martel, David Madigan, Christi Ashby, Marcia Aubrey, and Jeffrey Nagel have contributed more than they know, by allowing me to experiment . . . and then reporting candidly on the results of those experiments.

The talented writer Carol Nelson, who graciously read and commented on much of this text, helped me prevent some of the self-canceling and downright stupid statements authors often make without such help. My son Bob keeps me amply supplied with letters, brilliant and strange, I'd never see if it weren't for his eagle-eye.

Of course I'm forever indebted to Anne Knudsen, Richard Hagle, and the super-competent editorial staff at NTC Books. They accepted components—and arguments for inclusion or exclusion—I probably wouldn't have accepted had our roles been reversed.

To Jonah Gitlitz, Karen Burns, Valerie Naster, and other executives of the Direct Marketing Association I offer thanks for making it possible for me to bounce ideas off the most critical of all audiences: professionals who attend the DMA conferences and, with luck, my sessions.

But all other acknowledgments are trivial when compared with my debt to the person who has made my life both orderly and deliriously happy—my wife Margo—whose brilliant suggestions, encouragement, and assistance are on the same stratospheric plane as her tireless pursuit of examples and her uncompromising proofreading.

Foreword

This book is about the most common tool—no, the most common weapon—any communicator can have in his or her arsenal.

Letters.

I don't care who you are. I don't care how exalted or miserable your professional or personal circumstances are. I don't care whether you have a string of advanced university degrees or are borderline literate. I don't care how old you are, what color you are, what religion you practice, or how happy or sad your domestic situation is.

You write letters.

How do I know that? Because everybody writes letters. Oh, the fax machine has taken over some of the more instantaneous communications, but have you noticed that faxes are more and more letter-like? And they should be, because letters are the best of two worlds: They enable you to communicate personally, and they enable you to put your best foot forward.

That's the second edge of the sword. Haven't you looked at a letter and thought, "What an imbecile!" or "She doesn't know what she's talking about" or "This guy is just showing off" or "What does that have to do with me?"

Have you built a file of letters—letters that grabbed you, letters that left you cold, letters you know at once are a band-aid over a lie, letters in which the writer is showing off, letters you wish you'd written, letters causing you to wonder about the writer's literacy, letters that don't match or explain or justify the offer, letters that bring a stupid offer to life, letters letters letters? If not, why not start?

Put yourself in the position of the person sending the letter instead of the person getting it, and you'll see the significance of knowing how to write an effective sales letter.

If you're thinking, "I don't write letters like that. I have people around me who do things like that". . . then I pity you. The people around you can make an ass out of you (or your organization); or they can pass you on the far turn because they begin to learn bits and pieces of letter-writing psychology you don't think you have to know; or when, sooner or later, you have to create a letter, you're trapped in ancient rhetoric or primitive devices or obfuscatory phrasing.

Now, there's a word—*obfuscatory*. It helps me make a point that otherwise would be —well, it would be obfuscatory.

Suppose, for a moment, we're looking for the master key to effective letter writing. It isn't cleverness. It isn't a massive vocabulary. It isn't thorough product knowledge.

In fact, those three elements can <u>suppress</u> response.

Cleverness too often becomes the end instead of the means. . .and in this Age of Skepticism we all know that cleverness for the sake of cleverness may well be a liability rather than an asset.

Massive vocabulary? Heck, effective letter-writing often depends on vocabulary <u>suppression</u>. People who know the big words usually know the smaller, clearer words, too. If I write here and now that big words can be obfuscatory, I'll bet many of the readers of this distinguished publication will have to look up that word—<u>if they choose to</u>. What have I proved? That I know a big word? Bully for me! But better for me if I'd skipped *obfuscatory* and relied on a more dependable term, *confusing*. . .or said that many people aren't sure what some big words actually mean and subliminally resent the arrogance of a writer who uses them to show off.

Thorough product knowledge too often brings results skewed 180 degrees from the effect we're after, because regurgitating product knowledge is 180 degrees skewed from the master key to effective letter-writing. I, as prospective buyer or inquirer or donor, care far less about what something is than about what it will do for me. Letters loaded with product knowledge usually are also loaded with corporate arrogance, a "me"-centered message which leaves the reader as reader, not as an involved participant. (An early tip: If you have to include product specifications, put them on a separate enclosure and refer to them in the letter.)

So the master key is writing in a style and mode that matches the reader's demographic, psychological, and attitudinal position of the moment.

Not easy, you say? Wonderful. If it were easy, anybody could do what we can do.

This book isn't as huge as I'd like it to be, and it's considerably bigger than the publisher wants it to be. I can make just one promise: It should help generate professional, reader-oriented sales letters that don't depend on cleverness or big vocabularies or product knowledge meaningless to the reader.

Along the way, you'll see tips about envelopes and overlines and the "p.s." and some of the other accoutrements that can make an in-the-mail appeal successful.

Go out and grab. And when you've grabbed, think like a pit bull: You don't let go.

The 21st century will be a communications century. Are you ready? Then let's go!

Herschell Gordon Lewis
Plantation, Florida

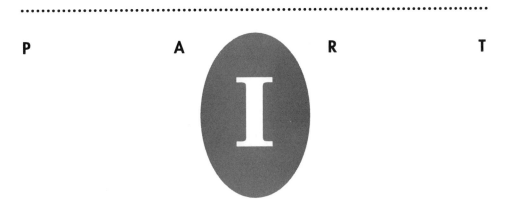

Rules and Tools: "Tricks of the Trade"

How easy it is!

Part I of this book shows you how easy it is—not just to understand all the devices you'll ever need to write sales letters that communicate your sales message to your prospects effectively and persuasively—but to <u>use</u> them, starting today.

"Tricks of the trade" at first glance may seem to be the wrong title. "Trade" implies a craft, and effective, persuasive letters are the private domain of people self-called "creatives" who think great thoughts and turn clever phrases. Right?

Nah. There <u>are</u> those rare individuals who have innate talent, who do create truly memorable messages that dazzle us with their inventiveness <u>and</u>

salesmanship. But more often than not, the people who call themselves "creatives" are called other things when their rhetorical pearls turn out to be "faux-pearls."

If you're reading this book, you already know why the two adjectives "creative" and "effective" aren't always applicable to the same person: Too many writers concentrate on "being creative" instead of using the rules and tools of effective sales communication. And being able to apply these rules and tools is a craft.

That's what this part of this book is about: the craft of communicating convincingly to a potential customer. The five chapters that follow explain how and when to use the devices effective communicators use to sell.

How about "Tricks"?

We live in the Age of Skepticism. Our best targets are bombarded by hundreds of messages every day, many written by "creatives" who muddy the water instead of clarifying it.

Our targets have become wary. So we "trick" them into reading our message . . . and responding to it.

Hold it! That doesn't mean tricking them into making a positive decision by overstating or misrepresenting. We're communicators, not cunning thieves. When you misrepresent, you run a double gauntlet:

1. Many of your prime prospects will see through the charade, and your message will end up in the garbage.
2. Of those few naive souls who are duped by false claims and promises, when you make one sale you also eventually make one enemy—for life. That enemy, no longer naive, despises not only you but your legitimate competitors whom you've tarred with your word-brush. So they hate you too.

Ah, but if your trickery results in a prospect's reading your message instead of a competitor's without misrepresentation, then you're a genuine professional.

And it's easy . . . because the rules and techniques are easy.

That's not just a promise. It's a guarantee. It's what Part I will help you do.

The Basic Rules of
Successful Letter-Writing

Everybody writes letters. Everybody. From the day we write our first job-hunting letter to the day we write our retirement valedictory, we create letters. This is a twenty-first-century guidebook to the most primitive element in direct response communication—and the most sophisticated element in direct response communication.

They're the same. The most primitive element in direct response is the letter. The most sophisticated element in direct response is the letter.

Ads may be written by a committee; various sets of hands tinker and alter, so a finished ad or brochure may be a hybrid product the writer who started it doesn't even recognize.

Not so with letters. They're one person's statement.

This tends to be true not only of two-paragraph notes but of four-page and eight-page direct mail epics. Why? Because a letter is—or at least should be—a single, coherent statement. A copy chief might say, "Rewrite this section," but the writer who starts it usually is the writer who finishes it.

If you've bought this book, obviously I don't have to convince *you* how important letters are. You wouldn't be reading this if you didn't share my view that the letter is <u>the primary element</u> in a multi-component mailing and <u>the only criterion of success</u> when the letter is the only component.

As so many letters say: Frankly, I'm puzzled. I'm puzzled to see so many writers and art directors fussing over inconsequential details of brochures, or insisting on die-cuts and six-color printing, while paying no attention to the message. They're paying attention to production, not message—form, not substance—and they pay <u>no</u> attention to the letter.

Three "Little" Elements That Produce Big Results

I can name three principal reasons why many letters fail and others succeed. By "succeed" I mean <u>pull response</u>. That's how we keep score. Remember these three little elements and you can sleep-read through the rest of this book because if you can write a letter that doesn't violate them, you're home free.

The first reason will make sense to you if you have any sense of salesmanship:

 The letter should be a single coherent statement.

Don't misinterpret this. By "a single coherent statement" I don't mean mindlessly repeating the same words over and over again. I do mean thinking, before sitting down to write:

 What am I trying to convince the reader to do?

What am I trying to convince the reader to do? Write down the specific imperative as a note on the side. Then build your sales argument around that core, that nucleus, that essence. Weave your pattern. <u>Don't</u> rush at the reader like a bowling bowl, unless your offer is implicitly so attractive, so terrific, that just announcing it is the best salesmanship.

When you think in terms of a single coherent statement, you force yourself to be specific. This can make a gigantic difference in the pulling power of your message, and I'll tell you why:

Specifics outpull generalizations.

Here's the difference between the world of specific communication and the typical conventional advertising agency: An ad agency can claim success if the recipient "recalls" its ad. A letter can't claim success if the recipient recalls it; the letter can claim success only if the recipient performs a positive act as the result of having read it.

Specifics sell. Generalities don't sell. And regardless of what you may have heard from some of the philosophers who <u>don't</u> earn their living by matching wits with the great unwashed public, the purpose of <u>any</u> direct response message is to convince the reader, viewer, or listener to perform a positive act, as the direct result of having absorbed the message.

So if you want that phone to ring . . . if you want that mail to come through the door . . . if you want those people out there to say, "I want that," here's the second reason why some letters fail and others succeed:

  Get to the point.

Get to the point. Don't dawdle. Don't try to be subtle, because subtlety will cost you some response. Subtlety suppresses response. Cleverness for the sake of cleverness suppresses response. In-jokes suppress response. Starting in super-low gear suppresses response. So: Get to the point!

And how, you ask, can you be sure you're getting to the point?

Here's a little help for you: Four short opening phrases whose benefit will be obvious to you when you start using them. They <u>force</u> you to get to the point. No professional communicator can write one of these and then <u>not</u> follow up with specifics that get to the point.

1. *"For example. . ."*

When you say, "For example. . ." after making a statement, you <u>force</u> yourself to give an example. You <u>force</u> yourself to get to the point, no matter how loose and nonspecific your argument may have been before that.

2. *"Why? Because. . ."*

This technique has the advantage of dismantling the skepticism your target may be erecting. Internally or externally, that person may

THE WALL STREET JOURNAL.

World Financial Center, 200 Liberty Street, New York, NY 10281

Dear Reader:

On a beautiful late spring afternoon, twenty-five years ago, two young men graduated from the same college. They were very much alike, these two young men. Both had been better than average students, both were personable and both—as young college graduates are—were filled with ambitious dreams for the future.

Recently, these men returned to their college for their 25th reunion.

They were still very much alike. Both were happily married. Both had three children. And both, it turned out, had gone to work for the same Midwestern manufacturing company after graduation, and were still there.

But there was a difference. One of the men was manager of a small department of that company. The other was its president.

What Made The Difference

Have you ever wondered, as I have, what makes this kind of difference in people's lives? It isn't a native intelligence or talent or dedication. It isn't that one person wants success and the other doesn't.

The difference lies in what each person knows and how he or she makes use of that knowledge.

And that is why I am writing to you and to people like you about The Wall Street Journal. For that is the whole purpose of The Journal: to give its readers knowledge—knowledge that they can use in business.

A Publication Unlike Any Other

You see, The Wall Street Journal is a unique publication. It's the country's only national business daily. Each business day, it is put together by the world's largest staff of business-news experts.

Each business day, The Journal's pages include a broad range of information of interest and significance to business-minded people, no matter where it comes from. Not just stocks and finance, but anything and everything in the whole, fast-moving world of business...The Wall Street Journal gives you all the business news you need—when you need it.

Knowledge Is Power

Right now, I am looking at page one of The Journal, the best-read front page in America. It combines all the important news of the day with in-depth feature reporting. Every phase of business news is covered. I see articles on new taxes, inflation, business forecasts, gas prices, politics. I see major stories from Washington, Berlin, Tokyo, the Middle East. I see item after item that can affect you, your job, your future.

(over, please)

FIG. 1–1 This surely is one of the longest-running and most famous subscription letters of all time. Over the years *The Wall Street Journal* has mailed it to me a dozen times or more. The one niggling question: Isn't this letter, whose point is that a subscription to this publication can make a profound career difference, inadvertently aimed at junior executives?

And there is page after page inside The Journal, filled with fascinating and significant information that's useful to you. The Marketplace section gives you insights into how consumers are thinking and spending. How companies compete for market share. There is daily coverage of law, technology, media and marketing. Plus daily features on the challenges of managing smaller companies.

The Journal is also the single best source for news and statistics about your money. In the Money & Investing section there are helpful charts, easy-to-scan market quotations, plus "Abreast of the Market," "Heard on the Street" and "Your Money Matters," three of America's most influential and carefully read investment columns.

If you have never read The Wall Street Journal, you cannot imagine how useful it can be to you.

A Money-Saving Subscription

Put our statements to the proof by subscribing for the next 13 weeks for just $44. This is among the shortest subscription terms we offer—and a perfect way to get acquainted with The Journal.

Or you may prefer to take advantage of our better buy—one year for $149. You save over $40 off the cover price of The Journal.

Simply fill out the enclosed order card and mail it in the postage-paid envelope provided. And here's The Journal's guarantee: should The Journal not measure up to your expectations, you may cancel this arrangement at any point and receive a refund for the undelivered portion of your subscription.

If you feel as we do that this is a fair and reasonable proposition, then you will want to find out without delay if The Wall Street Journal can do for you what it is doing for millions of readers. So please mail the enclosed order card now, and we will start serving you immediately.

About those two college classmates I mention at the beginning of this letter: they were graduated from college together and together got started in the business world. So what made their lives in business different?

Knowledge. Useful knowledge. And its application.

An Investment In Success

I cannot promise you that success will be instantly yours if you start reading The Wall Street Journal. But I can guarantee that you will find The Journal always interesting, always reliable, and always useful.

Sincerely,

Peter R. Kann
Publisher

PRK: id
Encs.

P.S. It's important to note that The Journal's subscription price may be tax deductible. Ask your tax advisor.

AMERICAN EXPRESS
TRAVEL RELATED SERVICES COMPANY, INC.

Phillip Riese
Executive Vice President

Ms. Margo E. Lewis
340 N. Fig Tree Ln.
Fort Lauderdl, FL 33317-2561

Dear Ms. Lewis:

The road to financial success has many milestones
marking how far you've come. Becoming an American
Express® Cardmember is one such milestone.

You are now cordially invited to apply for the American
Express Card.

As you may know, Cardmembership is accorded only to
those who have achieved a certain measure of financial
success. That's because -- unlike credit cards -- <u>we do
not set a spending limit in advance</u>. Instead, your
purchases with the American Express Card are approved
based on your ability to pay as demonstrated by your
personal resources and your past spending and payment
patterns.

<u>Now, you can easily apply for the Card by completing
this short form and signing your name</u>. Simply reply by
the date on the enclosed application form and if you
qualify, all the benefits of Cardmembership may be
yours.

For example, you pay no interest with the American
Express Card. None. <u>That's because the American
Express Card is a charge card, not a credit card</u>.
Since you pay your bill in full each month, all you pay
is the $55 annual fee. With most credit cards, if you
carry over an unpaid balance from one month to the next
-- even one dollar -- you pay interest on that balance
as well as on any new purchases. Even purchases you pay
for in full. Result: The American Express Card could
easily save you hundreds of dollars a year in credit
card interest.

Cardmembership also signifies that you merit an
unrivaled level of personal service. We're here for you

(over, please)

FIG. 1–2 This is another famous letter that has become part of American folklore. Many people know and recite the line, "As you may know, Cardmembership is accorded only to those who have achieved a certain measure of financial success." (My wife and I both have had American Express cards for years. Each of us gets this letter once or twice every year, which suggests a serious deficiency in the company's database.)

24 hours a day, 365 days a year. From a simple question about a bill to obtaining medical or legal referrals when you're away from home, you'll find the Card to be an invaluable asset.

<u>We've even made it easy for you to apply</u>. Just return the enclosed short application form, and provided that you meet all the necessary requirements, and as long as any account you may have with us remains in good standing, the Card will arrive in just a few weeks.

I greatly look forward to welcoming you as a Cardmember.

Sincerely,

Phillip Riess

P.S. Understandably, how fast we are able to process your application depends on how quickly you return it to us. Please respond by the date on the enclosed form.

be asking, "Why?" By asking the question on his or her behalf, you seem to place yourself in the position of your target individual. You establish that wonderful word, *rapport*—and you <u>force</u> yourself to be specific. This construction has terrific power.

3. *"The reason is. . ."*

Once again you <u>force</u> yourself to be specific by going a step beyond trying to make a point without offering evidence. Evidence is by its very nature specific. Evidence by its very nature gets to the point.

4. *"I have something you want."*

This is the easiest of all. If I say to you, "I have something you want," what is your immediate reaction? Right! Your immediate reaction is, "What is it?" I've grabbed your interest by involving you, and while I have your interest, I <u>force</u> myself to get to the point.

Do you run the risk of the individual saying, "No, that isn't what I want"? Certainly not. We're dealing in <u>force</u>-communication. We take the reader by the hand and lead him or her through the maze. We're in command. Any reader who resists our command—who mutinies—deserves to be left behind while the smarter, more astute readers are enjoying the benefits of whatever we've convinced them to do. Serves them right.

And anyway, we're writing for our best targets. In theory, if in a mass mailing the list selection is decent, or if in a one-to-one mailing we've done even a modicum of homework, when we say, "I have something you want," it *is* something the recipient should want.

Now the third element:

 Tell the reader what to do.

You can see how easy the three elements are. You can see how logical the three elements are. You can see how basic the three elements are. So why, oh, why, do so many writers ignore all three?

My answer is: Too many writers don't understand what our function is. We're salespeople. Yes, I know that hurts. We'd rather be called "creatives." (I'll settle for "creative salespeople," but that's my final offer.)

Who Are We?

In the second half of this book is a cold-blooded analysis of 100 different ways to begin a sales letter. Number 91: "Who are we?"

Who, indeed? Who are *you*?

No, not your actual person; the *persona* you project in a letter. Are you casual or severe? Are you pedantic or a plain ol' country boy or gal? You're in command, because you're the one writing the letter.

In a multipart business mailing, the letter is the identifying component. Who are you? P.T. Barnum? Dale Carnegie? Zeus? Uriah Heep? Good Sam? Florence Nightingale? J.P. Morgan? Lucrezia Borgia? Albert Einstein? The Emperor Tiberius? Socrates? Nostradamus?

Who are you?

The letter is your projected image. The recipient's <u>psychological</u> reaction is to that image; how deeply the psychological reaction colors the physical reaction to the offer is a matter of percentages . . . but the percentage is never zero.

This shows once again that the letter has a profound effect on that mystical ingredient, *rapport*. Whatever your offer, whatever your proposition, whatever miracle you represent, the offer alone can't establish rapport; if it could, mailers wouldn't need letters because other enclosures spell out the offer.

Can you see the significance of choosing a letter opening that mirrors the person you're trying to be?

Who <u>are</u> you?

Albert Einstein once might have begun a letter to someone with "I have a free gift for you." <u>The image of</u> Albert Einstein never would. Maybe P.T. Barnum once said to somebody, "It's late and I'm tired but I have to tell you this" but <u>the image of</u> P.T. Barnum doesn't say that. The statement is in perfect sync with the image of Florence Nightingale.

(Did Lucrezia Borgia ever say, "Visualize this scenario"? Probably.)

Once you've decided who you are, the next key is to stay in character. This becomes a simple matter. Choose the right opening. Then remember who you are and don't take off your costume or your mask until the show is over!

2

10 Easy-to-Use Tips
to Showcase Your Message

A well-written sales or direct response letter is an amalgam of sales psychology, word manipulation, and mechanical application.

I'm no longer surprised to see communications professionals failing to take advantage of mechanical procedures a reasonably bright eight-year-old can implement. They're victims of a vertical education that excludes the mechanics of force-communication—and victims of a professional indoctrination founded on the regrettable concept that communication is effective if it accomplishes self-glorification.

So the ten tips described in this chapter are surprisingly easy to apply. . .and, I hope, surprisingly obvious to the astute communicator. I say this with confidence because they aren't abstruse philosophical notions; they're mechanical devices, instant tools designed not to replace imagination but to showcase imagination properly.

Tip Number 1: *Keep your first sentence short.*

The first sentence is your indicator to the reader. It's an early warning, and your target forms a quick impression: The letter is going to be easy to read or is going to be hard slogging.

The short first sentence isn't an absolute, invariable law. It's just a good idea most of the time and because it's a good idea most of the time, as well as an easy idea to implement, it's on this list.

Which opener is most likely to grab and shake the reader? This. . .

> I want 1½ minutes of your time.

. . . or this . . .

> If you'll give me 1½ minutes of your time, in turn I'll give you information about an opportunity you probably never thought would be available to you in today's marketplace.

No contest. You won't have any problem activating this tool if you say to yourself as your fingers poise to generate that crucial first sentence: If I were speaking instead of writing, to someone who has no reason to respect my position, what would I use as an opener?

Tip Number 2: *No paragraphs longer than seven lines.*

I suggested this concept to an assemblage of copywriters. I guess I shouldn't have been surprised to get the question, "But what if a paragraph has to be longer than seven lines?"

The question reminded me of my own complaint when I was writing one of my earlier books. I said to my wife, "I've written considerably more than one hundred thousand words, and the book isn't finished." Her answer cut the Gordian knot. She said, "Yes, it is."

So my own answer to the question, "What if a paragraph has to be longer than seven lines?": No paragraph has to be longer than seven lines. Break up the text. One paragraph becomes two, three, or four, and reader fatigue vanishes.

Tip Number 3: *Single space the letter; double space between paragraphs.*

This notion is even easier to implement than the first two. It's based on ease of readership. Manuscripts and news releases traditionally are double-spaced, but that's because an editor needs the space between the lines to write in blue-pencil chicken-scratch.

A letter should set itself up for easy reading; a double-spaced letter not only is harder to read, but double-spacing balloons every aspect. A two-page letter becomes four pages, and an eight-page letter—well, don't even think about it. Worse, the page has an overall gray look because the space between paragraphs is identical to the space within paragraphs. Emphasizing points is a lot harder to do.

A suggestion, if you disagree on grounds of tradition rather than reader attention: Type out your next letter both ways. Ask 50 people which one is easier to read. If you're really scientific, ask those people questions based on reader comprehension.

Tip Number 4: *Break every page (except the last) in the middle of a sentence.*

What this tip means is: In a letter longer than one page, don't end a paragraph at the bottom of any page except the last; break in the middle of a sentence.

Newspapers have known this for a hundred years. Readers demand completeness. So a newspaper story on page one may have the legend "Continued on page 14, column 2"—and the reader is more likely to turn to page 14 if that break comes in mid-sentence, so the reader doesn't have even a vestige of completeness.

If you've ended a paragraph at the bottom of the page, the reader has a reason to read on only if he or she already has a firm interest in what you're selling. Leaving the reader hanging in mid-sentence maintains the writer's command. The reader is your captive until the end of the sentence—on the next page.

This is the force-communication parallel to a motion picture on the Late Show. The show doesn't open with credits and titles; it opens with action. Once you've seen the first five minutes, it's too late to switch channels because you've already missed the opening of the film on the competing channel; it started with action too.

Tip Number 5: *Don't sneak up on the reader.*

An inverse way to word this tip might be, "Fire a big gun to start the battle." We're in the Age of Skepticism, and letter openings such as this one betray a 1930s selling attitude:

> This story begins around the turn of the century, when times were peaceful and big fortunes could be made.
>
> Way back then, someone took a look at a contraption a lot of people still called a horseless carriage, and they said, "Gee, wouldn't it be great if we could start these vehicles without cranking them by hand? Old Silas broke his arm cranking his machine, and the danged thing never would go."

I agree—it isn't dull. As this type of opening goes, it's more intriguing than most. I agree. Now read the next paragraph:

> Half a century later, a guy named Alan Shepard climbed into a different contraption, and a lot of smoke came out of the bottom end. Wham! Within a couple of minutes our first astronaut was not only out of sight, he'd made history.

Now I'm not so pleased. It's obvious at last: we aren't talking about starters or storage batteries, and we aren't talking about outer space. We still don't know what we *are* supposed to be talking about, and we're deep into the letter.

Just for the sake of history, I'll tell you. This writer is selling vacations. It could have been any of 10,000 other possibilities, including aardvarks and Zoroastrian texts.

Firing your biggest gun first is a good idea because you can't miss. As the letter opens, you're at point-blank range, and you may never have this advantage over your target prospect again.

Tip Number 6: *Never again start a letter with "Dear Sir" or "Dear Madame."*

Why not? Because these are nineteenth-century techniques. They suggest stiff-necked, old-fashioned pomposity. Warming up the reader, establishing rapport with him or her, is one of the great hurdles we face. A greeting such as "Dear Sir" or "Dear Madame" adds sandbags to the obstacle when we should be shoveling sand away.

In this unisex age, I occasionally see "Dear Sir or Madame." This is the kind of opening we might expect from a bill collector.

The mail order industry has pretty much settled on some version of the words "Dear Friend" as a neutral substitute when we can't personalize the opening. Depending on the list, you can move in closer:

"Dear Fellow Member"
"Dear Executive"
"Dear Colleague"
"Dear World Traveler"
"Dear Collector"
"Dear Tennis Nut" (you can see the benefit of <u>equivalence</u> in greetings when you add a word—"Dear *Fellow* Tennis Nut").

A nit-picking question: Should we put a comma or should we put a colon after the greeting?

Business letter-writing classes teach colon, not comma, but under most circumstances of the late 1990s I disagree—conditionally. The colon suggests a respect for the reader, but it also maintains an arm's-length relationship. Today we're after that magical word *rapport*. I often make the comma/colon decision based on whether or not I'll indent each paragraph. Indenting is less formal, which makes the comma more logical.

Some strong usable substitutes for the old-fashioned opening gain their strength from suggesting the communication is limited to a special-interest group:

"Good Morning!"
"To the Sophisticated Handful of Homeowners Who Demand Pure Water:"
"This Private Notification Is Limited to Executives Earning More Than $50,000 a Year."
"Information for Administrators Only."

The close isn't as crucial as the opening, but here's a tip: Don't close with "Yours truly."

"Yours truly" isn't as stiffly formal as the "Dear Sir" or "Gentlemen" that often begins a letter in which we see it. But you know what it is? Antiquity without polish.

Antiquity *with* polish is a standard and often elegant selling technique. "Your servant, sir" is an example of this writing style—which had better match in *all* components, or you'll look dumb.

You'll find "Sincerely" (*not* "Sincerely yours") as the close on most letters; business-to-business often uses "Cordially" on the theory that "Sincerely" is more emotional a close than the text justifies.

Attacking "Sincerely" is like breaking a butterfly on the rack: Why do it? But if you're doggedly determined to improve the close of your letter, try adding another pinch of salesmanship:

"Yours for more vigorous health"
"For the Board of Directors"
"For your friends at *[NAME OF COMPANY]*"
"Bless you, my dear friend" (fund raising only, please)

Tip Number 7: *Use an overline, if it isn't stupid.*

The overline, a potentially valuable element in mass mailings, warrants its own chapter in this book. (See Chapter 3.)

In force-communication, creative rules and mechanical rules are so tightly linked that we sometimes can't separate them.

Here's an example in a test of an identical message:

• One version has a typewritten overline
• One version has a typeset overline.
• One version has a handwritten overline.
• One version has no overline.

Which probably will bring heavier response?

Although I'll cancel part of this opinion in Chapter 3, my fast vote is for the letter with the handwritten overline. Why? Because my experience has been that a letter with a handwritten overline is read more thoroughly by the person who gets it.

You can position the overline toward the right edge, or if you have a neatness complex, you can center it.

But here you have another opportunity to relate mechanical rules to creative rules. I prefer having the overline on the right. Why? Because of this rule:

 Perfect balance detracts from the impact of your message.

Can you see how art direction, which can have a set of goals completely different from the goals of the communicator, can damage the communicator's message?

If perfect balance detracts from the impact of your message, how does this knowledge affect your decision whether to type or handwrite your overline?

Let's follow a logical path here. To begin, we can formulate a rule:

 A handwritten overline tends to outpull a typewritten overline.

Why? Because the typewritten overline has less contrast with the rest of the letter. . . and it more closely parallels perfect balance than a handwritten overline.

This is the stuff obsolescence is made of.

Let's suppose you agree with me. We all start following this rule. We all start writing letters with handwritten overlines. My secret system is no longer a secret. Instead, it becomes the standard procedure. Anyone who *doesn't* use a handwritten overline is regarded as ignorant. Then what happens?

By the turn of the century we all will run afoul of a broader rule:

 Sameness equals boredom. Overuse equals abuse.

So sameness has produced boredom, and our first rule doesn't work anymore.

You know the second half of this equation: Overuse equals abuse. By overusing a rule we accelerate the evolutionary process. Marketing isn't a stagnant pool. The water is always running from that great, fresh spring in the heavens. We have to keep our wits about us.

So the rules are fluid. We can't sit back year after year and apply the same ones. If we do, we'll suddenly find we're twenty years out of date.

Tip Number 8: *A p.s. should reinforce a key selling motivator.*

Stated more fully: If you include a p.s., it should reinforce one of the key selling motivators or mention an extra benefit—one that doesn't require explanation. So this p.s.:

> Don't you agree this is a wonderful and unique opportunity? I urge you to respond without delay, because delay can be costly to you.

adds nothing to the power of the letter. This p.s. does add power:

> If you want this special private discount, be sure to mail the postage-free card or call my personal toll-free phone number within the next 10 days. I'd hate to see you miss out.

The various faces, benefits, and perils of the p.s. will be covered in Chapter 4. In general, a p.s. is second only to the overline in its position as being more likely to be read than the text of the letter. Mailers have many tests showing that what's in the p.s. can actually pull the reader into the letter . . . or push the reader away.

The postscript is standard in direct response mass mailings; in one-to-one mailings, the key is <u>pertinence</u>. If your p.s. causes the recipient to think he or she is one of a mob of people getting a mass mailing, wow, have you goofed!

Tip Number 9: *Experiment with marginal notes.*

Marginal notes are a specialty. Not every letter benefits from them, and this suggests you decide, based on the tone of the letter, whether or not they'll be beneficial.

When you do use them, the rules for marginal notes are even tighter than they are for overlines. Two of them, in my opinion, are absolute:

1. Handwrite everything.
2. Use no more than four or five words for each marginal note.

Marginal notes draw their power from appearing to be a spontaneous outburst of enthusiasm. The writer is so excited, so enthusiastic, he or she bubbles over.

Handwritten bubbling-over has verisimilitude, the appearance of truth. Typed bubbling-over looks contrived. We fight like tigers to avoid a contrived look, so why take the risk?

The four- or five-word maximum is a good idea mechanically as well as creatively. When you limit yourself to four or five words, you can write big enough to grab the reader's eye the way you should. There's no handwritten marginal message that can't be transmitted in four or five words, <u>maximum</u>.

Don't put a whole bunch of marginal notes together on the same page. Remember the broad rule: Sameness equals boredom. Overuse equals abuse.

Some "boiler-plate" marginal notes:

Here's your FREE bonus!
Read this *extra*-carefully"
Save 50 percent

Don't be afraid to use hand-drawn arrows, lines, brackets, or even stars for emphasis. You're creating the impression of spontaneous enthusiasm.

Marginal notes, along with handwritten overlines, should be in a second color. What color? Don't consider any color other than the one in which you print the signature, usually process blue. (Why should it be in the same color as the signature? Because you're trying to project an effect—the writer is going over the letter before signing it. He or she has pen in hand, and this pen—the one that signs the letter—is the same one that writes the marginal notes.)

If the whole letter, including signature, is printed in one color, you don't have any decision to make.

For heaven's sake, don't have an overline and marginal comments in beautiful calligraphy, and then have an illegible scrawl for a signature at the end of the letter. The writing should match.

An extra tip: There <u>never</u> is an excuse for an illegible signature on a letter. It may give ego-satisfaction to an executive, but it drains intimacy out of the communication.

The one thing worse than an illegible signature: an illegible signature with no name typed below it.

Tip Number 10: *Use letters to test.*

The letter is the most logical testing instrument in a direct mail package. Testing one brochure against another is expensive, even if all the changes are in the black plate. Testing response devices such as order forms often gives muddy results because this type of test isn't always logical.

But letters! The writer becomes a hero because his four-page letter outpulled the one-page letter—or vice versa. The writer can create letters with different flavors to test the five great motivators of our era (<u>Fear, Exclusivity, Greed, Guilt,</u> and <u>Need for Approval</u>) against one another . . . or test one of these against the "soft" motivators (<u>Convenience</u> and <u>Pleasure</u>).

Best of all, letter tests are cheap. It costs next to nothing to print two versions of the letter instead of one.

While you're at it, consider testing a tinted paper stock against white. The text has to be identical, or you destroy the purity of results. Color psychology is itself one of the creative aspects of communication.

Following these 10 little tips can result in a quick spurt in the effectiveness of your letter-writing. A suggestion: Print just the 10 tips on a small sheet of paper, and keep it visible when you're writing. If one of them jogs loose an effective thought, you're already ahead.

The Most Effective Ways to Grab Your Reader's Attention

What's on Top?
And What's in the Middle?

Until the mid-1970s, a letter was a letter. Gimmickry and tampering with the standardized format—date, greeting, text—weren't considered, because nobody had yet thought of new <u>and effective</u> ways to grab and shake the reader's attention.

The overline came into its own when experiments revealed two results:

1. A properly constructed overline is the most-read part of the letter. This is both natural and expected because the overline is the first element the reader sees. The consequence: The reader's reaction to the overline determines whether that individual will continue reading.
2. Considerably more significant: a letter with an overline will outpull the identical letter with no overline.

The First Law of Overlines: Don't Synopsize the Offer

As you can see from some of the samples reproduced in this book, the <u>mechanical</u> choice of overline techniques is unlimited. Want to have one giant word, wet in 120-point type? Why not? Want a handwritten message? Why not? Want a heading and subhead, as though the letter is an ad? Why not? The space is available. . .and the mechanical constraint is subject only to the creative constraint—The First Law of Overlines:

 The overline should generate or enhance the reader's desire to keep reading. This means the overline should *not* synopsize the offer.

Too many overlines summarize the offer, <u>before</u> the reader is conditioned to accept the premise. So an overline with the words:

Save 20% on your automobile insurance!

isn't as effective as:

Put an extra $100 a year in your pocket!

Figure 3-1 is an example of an overline that synopsizes the offer. If the writer needs five handwritten lines, warning flags should go up.

Figure 3.2 is an example of an overline that says nothing but establishes a receptive attitude.

When should you? When shouldn't you?

With one exception, overlines have little place in one-to-one correspondence. That's because they're implicitly "pitchy." They're suggesting an offer, which puts the writer in a selling posture.

What's the one exception? When the writer wants the reader to feel he/she is reading over the letter before mailing it and has a spontaneous burst of enthusiasm. So this type of overline would be handwritten and not look "produced."

WWF

World Wildlife Fund

This letter deals with today's most critical environmental problem ... your support will entitle you to your new wildlife calendar ... with full-color photos of the wildlife you are helping us save ...

Dear Friend,

   The problem simply stated is this:

   "Without firing a shot, we may kill one-fifth of all species of life on this planet in the next 20 years."

   You see, years ago, rain forests circled the earth in abundance from South America to Africa, Malaysia, and Indonesia. Yet in the time it takes you to read this sentence, another eight acres of rain forest will have been bulldozed and burned off the face of the earth.

   Why should we care about the fate of these forests thousands of miles away?

   Because not only do they provide food and shelter to at least half the world's species of wildlife, these tropical forests are also the world's largest "pharmaceutical factory" -- the sole source of lifesaving medicines like quinine, man's most potent weapon against malaria. Hundreds of thousands of people owe their lives today to these precious plants, shrubs, and trees. What would we do without them?

   Commercial exploitation and growing population demands will speed destruction of rain forests as well as oceans, grasslands, lakes, and wetlands. Pleading ignorance of these vital and fragile ecosystems can only spell global disaster. What can you do?

   You can accept this invitation to support World Wildlife Fund. We have a plan for survival. We need your help to make it succeed.

(over, please)

World Wildlife Fund & The Conservation Foundation
1250 Twenty-Fourth Street, NW   Washington, DC 20037   USA   202/293-4800   Telex: 64505 PANDA
Incorporating The Conservation Foundation. Affiliated with World Wide Fund for Nature.

♻ Printed on recycled paper

FIG. 3-1   Does the handwritten overline add any impact? Don't, in fact, terms such as *entitle* and *full-color* damage any sense of urgency? By synopsizing what's in the letter, the writer <u>reduces</u> the recipient's inclination to read the text.

Thanks for asking for more information about the properties of InterCoastal Communities!

Welcome to a new carefree life in sunny Florida!

When we at InterCoastal say, "Luxury is affordable," we can show you many, many hundreds of delighted homeowners who can prove it. We know: When you move here, you want the living to be easy. You want to wake up happy and go to bed happy. You want to have the kind of lifestyle you've worked years to enjoy.

You and I think alike: We want life to be satisfying. That's what has made the name InterCoastal synonymous with "The Good Life." The colorful book you have in your hands, with its many inserts, gives you a wide choice of locations. Each InterCoastal Community has something special to offer you. Each has its own personality.

But every one of our communities is dedicated to affordable luxury. You can live like a king for far less than you've ever thought possible.

Why strain your budget? Why live in a tiny, poorly-located home out in the wilderness? That isn't what you deserve. You want to be proud to show your home and your neighborhood to friends and relatives who visit. HERE'S YOUR OPPORTUNITY!

This opportunity is yours right now. I say this because even we, with all our locations and homebuilding knowledge, can't control spiraling costs. In my opinion you'll never have a more favorable time to get so much home for your dollar.

Here's my suggestion: Look through the enclosed information. Then call my office. We'll arrange for you to stay one or two nights in a "host home" at the community of your choice. That way, you can get the full flavor without having to make a commitment in advance. To reserve your host home, send a $30 deposit for each night you want to stay. Your deposit is returned in full when you get here, so your stay is free.

(Our toll-free number for all information: 1-800-525-0050.)

It's a pleasure to welcome you to the pleasant world of InterCoastal. As my friend George Gobel says, "You just can't find places like this no more."

With every good wish,

Ned Allen, President

P.S. If you can make your decision quickly, we'll have a special extra bonus-benefit for you. Call and ask us about it.

FIG. 3–2 What strength the three handwritten words—"Thanks! And Welcome!"— add to this letter. In a smaller size, the words would have seemed less spontaneous. . .ergo, less effective.

The most effective and most common overlines are those on mass mailings because the recipient either has no prior relationship with the sender or, as a prior customer, has the standard buyer-to-vendor relationship.

Rules and Techniques of Overline Writing

A handwritten overline is an unequalled attention-getting device for any letter. Except for huge bold handwriting as a greeting or just after the greeting (see Figures 3-3 and 3-4 for examples of this; also see no. 69 in chapter 9) the handwritten overline is the <u>most-read</u> element of the letter. The reader's eye goes there first. That's what gives it strength... and that's what makes it so dangerous. As an attention-getting device, in the Age of Skepticism, it has a double responsibility:

 First, the overline has to grab and shake the reader's attention.

But don't give away your message in the overline. I read this overline on the letter in a fat, heavily-produced mailing.

> If you've driven accident-free for the past three years, you can save 10 percent to 20 percent on your automobile insurance.

I'd have said, ". . . let me show you how to save. . ." rather than ". . . you can save . . ." But my objection to this overline isn't based on one little refinement; it's based on this: Instead of improving reading, comprehension, and pre-acceptance, these words blunted my interest and lost me as a reader. Too much too soon.

The purpose of the overline parallels the purpose of envelope copy. Envelope copy is like a kamikaze dive, with one purpose only: to convince the reader to open the envelope. That's it. If the writer tries to go beyond this purpose, chances are envelope copy will be weaker, not stronger. (See Chapter 5.)

Similarly, the overline has one purpose only: to get the reader into the letter, with more enthusiasm or anticipation than the writer can generate without the overline.

In my opinion, "This is a private offer" or "Do you qualify?" are stronger overlines than the "accident-free" wording. Years ago, college

COMMUNITY FEDERAL SAVINGS
and LOAN ASSOCIATION
OF THE PALM BEACHES

POST OFFICE DRAWER 10673 RIVIERA BEACH, FLORIDA 33404-1673

We can't make your property taxes go away...
but we can help you avoid the nasty October surprise.

Dear Homeowner:

Wham !!

That's the sound of a taxpayer being hit between the eyes with the annual property tax bill.

This is the time of year when we dig deep into our pockets to pay the tax. Even as we pay it, we know we'll get another one next year --- probably even higher. Wham!

But this year's blow can be cushioned, and next year's won't even be felt, if you put us to work for you. We'll lend you the money for this year's taxes and set up a monthly escrow program for next year's. No problem, because your mortgage loan is with us.

Here's how it works:

1.   You call us or drop in. If you already have your tax bill, tell us the amount; if you don't have it yet, we'll prearrange a loan so the money will be there when the bill comes in.

2.   For this year's tax, there'll be a small increase in your payments, to cover the new loan.

3.   For next year's tax, you won't have to worry about suddenly having to come up with a big lump sum, because you'll already have provided for the tax with our easy monthly escrow program. When you get your tax bill, it already will have been paid.

You needn't fill out a million papers to get this going. You can drop off the bottom portion of this letter next time you're in any of our offices; or you can mail it in the envelope I've enclosed; or you can phone us in Palm Beach County at 845-3200 and in Martin County at 283-5200. I do suggest you not wait too long, because much as we all dislike tax bills, they have to be paid, and delays cause penalties making the tax bite even greater.

I'm delighted to be able to offer you this service. I hope you'll take advantage of it and end forever the annual "Wham!" of your property tax bill.

Sincerely,

Pat F. Snow, Jr.
Senior Vice President

P.S. Once Community Federal is handling your tax bill, you'll be able to cover most annual increases by simply adjusting next year's amount. We're your savings and loan and we intend to prove it every day!

FIG. 3–3 This early 1980s example was one of the first letters to use a single hand-written expletive as its opener. Mailed to a sedate group of bank customers, it far outpulled the previous conventional letter. (Also see Fig. 3–4.)

The Most Effective Ways to Grab Your Reader's Attention **27**

Klasek Letter Company

Creative Direct Mail Advertising

```
Mr. Herschell Gordon Lewis
Box 15725
Plantation, FL 33318

Dear Mr. Beechwood:
```

w h a t ! !

```
You're not Mr. Beechwood?

We know that, Mr. Lewis.

This is just our way of making a point.  You see, sometimes so-called
"personalized" letters
                    do
                  f u n n y y y

things  like  this.  Evenrunwordstogethersotheydon'tmakemuchsense...

Terrible, isn't it?  Sure, sometimes it's funny...unless it happens
to be the letters you sent out to a prospect or customer.

So, that's our point...If you're dissatisfied with your current direct
mail production services ... or even if you're not ... and whether
you need personalized letters or complete direct mail services -- from
creative concepts through printing and mailing -- you might give me
a call at (314) 772-6245.

Sincerely,
```

Frank J. Deptula

```
Frank J. Deptula
Director of Marketing


P.S.  Use the enclosed postage-FREE card and put an "X" after your
      name.  We'll send you our free publications on "How to Do
      Effective Direct Mail."
```

901-909 So. Grand Ave. St. Louis, Missouri 63103 314-772-6245

FIG. 3–4 One of the cleverest uses of a single handwritten word under the greeting is this one—"What!!"—acknowledging that the name is Lewis, not Beechwood. The letter gets overly cute in the later paragraphs, but what a grabber! Who can put it aside unread?

courses in advertising dismissed <u>outdoor</u> advertising with a single direction: "No message longer than fifteen words." We might revive this suggestion today for overlines.

Now let's add the second responsibility:

 The overline should make the reader eager to continue reading.

This eliminates overlines that tell too much. It eliminates overlines that steal the selling argument from the letter itself.

So an overline such as this one, even though it's short—

Save twenty percent on automobile insurance

is <u>less</u> effective than this overline:

Just mail the card and you'll save $100 to $200

because the first overline makes it unnecessary for the recipient to read the letter, while the second overline impels the recipient to read the letter.

Even though both are handwritten and both promise benefit, the first tells too much, and it violates the second responsibility of a valid overline.

Printed Legends and Pictures

The technique of having <u>something</u> before the greeting has become so widespread that many professional letter-writers wouldn't consider sending out a mass mailing without it.

Note the qualifier: <u>mass</u> mailings. In one-to-one correspondence, handwriting maintains the personalized aspect; a printed legend or a picture doesn't.

Figure 3-5 shows a five-paragraph pre-greeting message. Is it too much? The decision lies in the hands of those who get the letter. Certainly it's readable, lyrical, and provocative.

Figure 3-6, on the other hand, can provoke derisory laughter: "Luxuriate in a more restful sleep night after night . . . with Slumberwool"—and the illustration is a sheep, hooves and all, which suggests

You look out your window, past your gardener, who is busily pruning the lemon, cherry, and fig trees...amidst the splendor of gardenias, hibiscus, and hollyhocks.

The sky is clear blue. The sea is a deeper blue, sparkling with sunlight.

A gentle breeze comes drifting in from the ocean, clean and refreshing, as your maid brings you breakfast in bed.

For a moment, you think you have died and gone to heaven.

But this paradise is real. And affordable. In fact, it costs only half as much to live this dream lifestyle...as it would to stay in your own home!

Dear Reader,

I'd like to send you a FREE copy of a unique—and invaluable—report.

It's called **The 5 Best Retirement Destinations in the World.** And it tells you about the best places in the world for retirement living.

In one of the places included in this report, gentle sea breezes keep the climate nearly perfect, with mild temperatures year-round.

You'll find cliffs, hidden coves with secluded beaches, rolling hills, and high mountains nearby dotted with picturesque villages.

In this place, you can buy a beautiful villa, complete with lavish gardens, marble floors, and hand-painted tiles, for about *half* what you would pay for an average house in your home town. (Or you can rent an ocean-front apartment for as little as $340 month.)...

...you'll pay 30% less for groceries than you probably would back home...

over, please

1

FIG. 3–5 The pre-greeting message occupies two thirds of the first page. Too much? Opinion: Not at all, because the way this is laid out increases the possibility the letter will be read. . .and isn't that why writers use such devices?

SLUMBERWOOL,USA
908 Stewart Street
Madison, WI 53713

Luxuriate in a more restful sleep night after night...
with Slumberwool

Put this New Zealand lambswool sleeper cushion to the test on your bed for 30 nights—at no risk.

Dear Friend:

For years, New Zealand has kept a secret from the rest of the world. It's the secret to a luxuriously deep sleep.

But, we don't think it's fair to keep this secret to ourselves any longer. That's why we're importing Slumberwool to the U.S. for you to try. It's a lush, deep pile cushion of lambswool that slips between your mattress and bottom sheet -- for the ultimate in nighttime comfort.

Experience the luxury of a deep, restful "Slumberwool sleep" -- at our risk.

Sink into the thick, baby-soft lambswool pile and drift off into a sound sleep. You'll awaken to realize Slumberwool is all we say it is...and more. But, since this is the first time Slumberwool is available in the U.S., we want you to become properly acquainted with all its benefits.

That's why we're inviting you to try Slumberwool on your <u>own</u> bed for 30 nights -- at no risk. So, you'll see for yourself just how remarkably rested and refreshed you'll feel after sleeping on Slumberwool.

Then, if you're not absolutely delighted, we'll refund your money in full <u>plus</u> return postage. We'll even pick up Slumberwool at your home or office. That's how certain <u>we</u> are you won't want to spend one more night <u>without</u> Slumberwool, once you try it.

Slumberwool eases uncomfortable pressure points -- and helps you fall asleep faster.

The Slumberwool fleece actually contours itself to your body and cushions away irritating pressure points at your hips, elbows, shoulders and knees. So, you can relax and sink into a sounder sleep -- without tossing and turning all night.

Clinical research actually bears this out. According to a recent study published in the Medical Journal of Australia (1/21/84), "The subjects... reported feeling better in the morning, sleeping better than usual, and experiencing less than usual tossing and turning when sleeping on the woolen underlay."

What's more, even though Slumberwool is no "miracle cure" for arthritis and back

(over, please)

FIG. 3–6 Would <u>you</u> put this on your bed for 30 nights? Illustration should agree with what we're selling, and this "pre-cushion" photograph of an entire animal makes the selling argument—well, it makes it funny.

a considerable risk to the next lines, "Put this New Zealand lambswool sleeper cushion to the test on your bed for 30 nights—at no risk." No risk? With that thing on my bed?

Figure 3-7 (Studebaker) exemplifies an early experiment with one of the newest techniques, the "Rebus" letter, in which pictures break up the text.

Figure 3-8 (Shutterbug) combines three readership-enhancing elements—a handwritten overline; marginal notes; and a picture.

"Johnson Boxes"

The origin of the term *Johnson Box* is murky, although many knowledgeable historians of the writing craft attribute it to Frank Johnson, who used it in subscription promotions in the 1970s.

A Johnson Box is a typed legend above the greeting. It's usually centered and "boxed" with a border of asterisks or stars.

Figure 3-9 shows a classic Johnson Box, exemplifying the pro and the con of this technique. Pro: Someone who might not read the letter sees the Johnson Box, thinks, "Oh, I might be interested in that," and then does read the letter. Con: Someone the letter might convince to buy insurance sees the pitch before a logical sales argument has a chance to make a point, thinks, "Oh, I'm not interested in that," and tosses the letter unread into the wastebasket.

Figure 3-10 is considerably more intriguing and considerably more likely to induce the recipient to keep reading.

I admit, I'm not a fan of Johnson Boxes. It's because almost every one seems to parallel the overline which said, "Save 20% on auto insurance." Almost every one removes suspense rather than heighten it. Almost every one uses a closing line before the sales argument even begins.

A typical Johnson Box (Figure 3-11) says, "Here's a bet you can't lose. . .on a motivational poster program that's a proven winner!"

See what's wrong here? The writer has given away the point of the letter before making the point. The reader quickly says, "I don't want a motivational poster program." And the reader is right because we've leaped into the close without pitching any benefit. Visualize the letter without the Johnson Box and see how it leaps to life. When I say "Get to the point," I don't mean "Start with the close."

STUDEBAKER-WORTHINGTON
LEASING CORP.

100 JERICHO QUADRANGLE • JERICHO, N.Y. 11753
(800) 645-7242 • (516) 938-5460

Studebaker-Worthington has a powerful new sales tool for you, absolutely FREE

Good Morning,

FREE VIDEO

We've just completed a NEW VIDEO called "How to Close More Sales with Leasing". It's unique in the world of equipment leasing. It doesn't just tell you how to use leasing. It shows you.

Viewing this video can be a VERY profitable 10 minutes for your salespeople. You know as well as I do -- maybe better than I do -- how most salespeople avoid recommending what they don't fully understand.

We've seen case after case in which this all-too-common situation -- the customer saying, "Yeah, I'll let you know... I need to think about it" --- can be transformed into this sit-

uation --- the customer saying, "You've got a deal." The difference is the dealer's ability to use leasing to close sales.

Our video shows you and your staff how leasing not only can replace price-cutting as the logical way to save a sale. It also improves the whole profit picture, from thin to thick.

I want to send this video to you, FREE. Why? Because Studebaker-Worthington wants to be your leasing company. Any help we give you helps us too. And we've spent a lot of time and money producing a professional training video that shows you how to close more sales and bigger sales, and how to make more profit on each sale.

As a suggestion: Show this video to everyone on your sales staff, every couple of months. The triple impact of example, sound and selling techniques make video the ideal way of cementing the information in anyone's mind. It's a powerful memory-enhancer.

continued...

FIG. 3-7 This was one of the first examples of a "rebus" letter (named after the Egyptian pictogram). It used "stock" art, but later examples used photographs, cartoons, and custom-designed graphics.

The Most Effective Ways to Grab Your Reader's Attention **33**

shutterbug®

I'll keep this open for you for 30 days. Please read.

Dear Fellow Photographer,

     I was reading an article about night photography in a recent issue of SHUTTERBUG.

     I've been publisher of this magazine (and of course a photographer) for years, but I admit — I never even thought about using a red or blue filter for night shots. The whole idea is exciting, and it's one I'd <u>never</u> have seen if I hadn't been reading SHUTTERBUG.

Blue filter = "Cold" effect

     Another article was about shooting portraits <u>outside</u>, using natural settings. We've all done that, but this article told me when to shoot from a lower angle to solve a reflection problem I often encounter.

Ilford mgII Paper, filtered at 2.5

     This same article told me (and all SHUTTERBUG) readers) how to make a black and white outdoor portrait shot. It specified which paper to use to hold soft skin tones and still get high contrast.

     Like all the articles in SHUTTERBUG, the descriptions were so clear a beginner could follow them easily. And the subject was so useful a professional could benefit from them. (We have letters to prove it.)

<u>Will You Look at a Free Issue?</u>

     I invite you to become a subscriber to SHUTTERBUG, at a very special price ... far, far below the cover price.

     Please, before you make a quick decision to toss this mailing into the wastebasket, understand what I'm offering you. Yes, I want you to become a subscriber. No, I don't want you to decide — yes or no — until you've seen a sample issue.

     I'll tell you why: I can sit here all day, writing about SHUTTERBUG, and not be able to transmit a fraction of what you can expect to find in the pages of this magazine.

FIG. 3–8 A subscription test of various approaches and formats made this the "winner" in terms of bringing the highest percentage of response: a letter combining a handwritten overline, marginal notes, and a photograph.

AAA LIFE INSURANCE COMPANY

```
* * * * * * * * * * * * * * * * * * * * * * * * * * * *
*                                                      *
*    Here's great news for AAA members between         *
*    45 and 75!  You can now buy between $2,000         *
*    and $10,000 in life insurance -- at a very         *
*    affordable cost.  And as a AAA member --           *
*    you can't be turned down for this policy ...       *
*    even if you're in poor health.  You are            *
*    guaranteed this insurance.                          *
*                                                      *
* * * * * * * * * * * * * * * * * * * * * * * * * * * *
```

Dear Member:

    What I said above really <u>is</u> good news! It's so good that I urge you to send in your application and payment today -- to be certain you beat the reply date shown on your application.

    I'm talking about our <u>AAA Guaranteed Life</u> insurance policy. It has so many great features I'll have trouble describing them all in this letter. So I better start right now. Here's a brief listing of advantages this policy brings you:

    √ You buy it by mail -- with no medical exam and no questions to answer about your health.

    √ It insures you for your entire life. (At age 100, you receive the full policy amount.) You can't be canceled because of age or poor health.

    √ You never get a rate increase either because of age or health. And the amount of your insurance is never reduced because of age or health.

    √ You can't be turned down for <u>any</u> reason -- as long as you're a AAA member and between 45 and 75. Even if you have cancer or heart trouble -- even if you have a dangerous occupation or hobby. We guarantee to accept your application.

    √ Pays benefits for death due to illness or injury. In order to guarantee your acceptance, death benefits payable for natural causes are reduced during the first two years you own the plan -- paying 125% of the annual premium in the

Over, please

AAA Life Insurance Company • Administration and Service Center • Dodge at 33rd • Omaha, Nebraska 68175

FIG. 3-9 Does the "Johnson Box" at the top of page one of this four-page letter help or damage the possibility of response? One can make an argument both ways. As a general rule, a provocative message is more likely to bring the reader into the main message than a synopsis of what the letter holds because rapport hasn't been established and sales points haven't been developed.

CATFANCY®

TRUE OR FALSE

1. Cats cannot be leash trained.
2. Kittens from the same litter can have different fathers.
3. Any medicine that is safe for humans is also safe for cats.
4. Cats can help people heal.

Dear Friend:

So much has been said and written about cats over the years that it's hard to separate fact from fiction. Just where do you go for the truth?

For over 26 years many thousands of cat lovers like you have relied upon CAT FANCY magazine to explode the myths, define the facts and explain it all in terms that are easy to understand.

And now, for a limited time, you can get this truth-packed publication at a very special introductory rate:

1 Full year (12 issues) for Only $11.99
That's 50% Off the regular price!

Yes, it's true. CAT FANCY, the world's most popular magazine about cats and kittens will be coming to your home each month at HALF PRICE. <u>We guarantee this is the best rate available.</u> And along with a great bargain, you'll be getting the most up-to-date information on cat care, health, nutrition and safety.

Do you sometimes wonder why your cat acts the way it does? CAT FANCY's behavior experts will answer your questions and help you better understand your cat. For example, did you know...

Cats will drink more water if you place the bowl well away from the food dish.

It's normal for an adult cat to sleep an average of 18 hours a day.

You can often tell what mood your cat is in from the position of its ears and tail.

P.O. BOX 52864, BOULDER, CO 80322-2864

FIG. 3–10 Who can resist a quiz like this, especially in a mailing targeted to a specific interest-group? This message <u>forces</u> readership. (The answers, at the bottom of page 2: 1-F; 2-T; 3-F; 4-T.)

```
* * * * * * * * * * * * * * * * * * *
*                                   *
*   HERE'S A BET YOU CAN'T LOSE ... *
*                                   *
*   ON A MOTIVATIONAL POSTER PROGRAM*
*   THAT'S A PROVEN WINNER!         *
*                                   *
* * * * * * * * * * * * * * * * * * *
```

Dear Executive:

    I have a small bet that I'd like to make with you -- a bet that you simply can't lose!

    It has to do with a subject that I know is of great importance to you: motivating your employees, day in and day out, to do the best possible job for you and your company.

                Here's the bet: right now, while it's close at hand, display the enclosed HERMAN ® Poster somewhere in your office. Don't say anything about it to your employees -- just watch their reactions when they see it, and listen to their comments.

                I'll wager, in fact I'll guarantee, that eight out of ten will smile, three out of five will chuckle, and at least one or two will <u>say</u> something favorable about the poster.

    If you don't get this kind of reaction, then the laugh's on me -- and the bet won't cost you a penny. But I'm confident that even this one HERMAN Poster will have a positive impact on your employees' attitudes -- and that you'll want to keep these outstanding posters coming in the weeks and months ahead, beginning with <u>four FREE weekly issues</u>!

    To do so, you need only drop the enclosed "HERMAN Poster Certificate" in the mail. (It's postage-paid for your convenience.) That's all there is to it.

    But once you've begun using your new posters ... and seen how much your employees enjoy and respond to them ... I'm sure you'll appreciate why HERMAN is <u>the most popular motivational poster program in America today</u>.

    So, take me up on my bet, won't you? And take advantage of our Special Introductory Offer at the same time. We'll start you with as many copies of

                          (over, please)

CLEMENT COMMUNICATIONS, INC.
Leaders in Management-Employee Communications

Concord Industrial Park · Concordville, Pennsylvania 19331 · 1-800-345-8101

FIG. 3-11 This typical Johnson Box adds nothing and certainly must turn off some who might have read the letter. Without an explanation of benefits, who wants a motivational poster program?

The Most Effective Ways to Grab Your Reader's Attention **37**

UNITED STATES HISTORICAL SOCIETY

ANTIQUE ARMS COMMITTEE

R. L. WILSON	LES LINE	MICHAEL KORDA	MEL TORMÉ	KEN WARNER	JEFFERY BELCHER
Chairman	Editor	Editor-in-Chief	Entertainer	Editor	Chief Gunsmith
Author/Historian	Audubon Magazine	Simon & Schuster, Inc.	Antique Firearms Collector	Gun Digest	Society of Arms & Armour

You are invited to own a pistol
of remarkable beauty and
historical importance - the
gold decorated Buffalo Bill
Centennial Pistol.

Dear Friend:

A hundred years ago, a Pony Express rider galloped madly
toward his destination. A band of howling Indians cut him off.
Amid a volley of shots and arrows, he escaped to safety.

No sooner had he disappeared from view than the Deadwood
Stage thundered past, its driver firing round after round from
his trusty Colt at the marauding Indians, led by the stony-faced
Chief Iron Tail.

Any onlooker, watching the wide open action, responded in
the only logical way: he applauded.

The event was Buffalo Bill's Wild West Show. The date
was almost exactly a century ago. The Pony Express,
the Deadwood Stage, Chief Iron Tail and incredible
crack-shot Annie Oakley packed the house for
performance after performance, all over the world.

But the star of stars was Colonel William Cody
himself -- Buffalo Bill, who already was a legend as
a buffalo hunter, a U.S. Cavalry hero and a government
scout. From 1883 until his death in 1917, the legend
grew as the flamboyant western panjandrum wheeled his
horse and twirled his ivory-handled Colt .44's.

Photographs of Buffalo Bill show him with his constant
companion, his 1860 Army Colt revolver. This pistol probably is
the most famous hand-weapon ever built, and now I invite you to
be one of only 2,500 individuals in the world who own an exact,
<u>working</u> reproduction of the celebrated firearm, the official
Buffalo Bill Centennial pistol.

First and Main Streets • Richmond, Virginia 23219 • (804) 648-4736 • Telex (804) 379-2638 • FAX (804) 648-0002

FIG. 3–12 How much more dramatic the opening of this letter would have been <u>without</u> the five-line "invitation to own a pistol." Yes, that's what's for sale, but introducing the for-sale element dilutes the drama of the opening. Where might those five lines have had a logical home? How about the envelope?

Figure 3-12 shifts the Johnson Box to the right side of the page, but position doesn't keep it from being another example of a Johnson Box that damages the suspense the first sentence of the letter might have generated. Again, visualize the letter <u>minus</u> the giveaway five lines. . . and see how liveliness returns.

If you're going to have a legend above the greeting, write that legend with one goal in mind—to force the reader to continue reading.

What Else Is "In"? Rubber Stamps, for One. Post-it Notes®, for Another.

We've begun to see two powerful devices used together—handwriting and a rubber stamp effect. (See Figures 3-13 and 3-14.) Rubber stamps and post-it notes are <u>in</u>.

A rubber stamp <u>implicity</u> says, "Personal and important." A post-it note <u>implicitly</u> says, "I thought of this after the letter was written and want to be sure you see it."

But some writers who know post-it notes are in don't know how to use them. A mailing that came to me had a post-it note affixed to the front sheet. The message begins:

> Since the invitation enclosed includes several months of
> Smithsonian, I want you to know that we make every issue. . . .

Nope. That's not what post-it notes are for. Figure 3-15 an example of a post-it note whose length is questionable, but whose effectiveness is enhanced tremendously by the technological achievement of personalization on the note.

Figure 3-16 is a simple imperative. The intention is to double the persuasion to read the letter.

Post-it notes are useful in subscription renewal mailings, fund raising, collection letters, and any notification of an expiration date, as the cry of "Wolf!"

What about Highlighting?

We occasionally see a letter that highlights, in yellow or green, specific words, phrases, and sentences.

Even if you never send for things — return this card to receive three free gifts to make you happier, healthier and wealthier

I know you're busy.

I know you have too much to read.

And yet, that's exactly why I want to send you
THREE FREE ISSUES of BOTTOM LINE/PERSONAL --
the magazine for busy people.

Dear Reader:

> In the olden days (actually, not long ago) life was simpler and slower.

When Mom and Dad were born, people took trains, not planes. They didn't
trust cars or roads for long trips. There were no TV's, no computers, no fax
machines, no cellular phones. Nobody ever heard of cholesterol, crack, junk
bonds, or nuclear energy. Tax rules were understandable.

Then things started changing too fast.

> The world speeded up. Scientific discoveries multiplied. Finance
> and money management became complicated. Rules of sexual relations
> were revised. Staying fit became everyone's No. 1 priority. We
> jogged, walked, and even stopped eating many of the foods that we
> loved. We learned how to use computers and program VCRs.

> Soon we were drowning in a flood of information. It became almost
> impossible to find enough time to be well-informed.

Never mind. I have good news for you...

As more than 400,000 families already know, BOTTOM LINE/PERSONAL seeks
out the new knowledge you need -- and zips it to you regularly twice-a-month
in 16 pages of brief, intelligent, and easy-to-read super-useful form.

There is no fiction, no advertising, no pretty pictures -- just facts,
ideas and advice to help you live better and live smarter -- digested to save
you time.

     *   *   *   *   *   *   *

But I am NOT asking you to buy anything. I'm NOT asking you to spend
a penny.

All I ask is that you accept some sample issues (three, to be exact) and
see BOTTOM LINE/PERSONAL for yourself. Then, if you like it, buy it -- or
if you don't like it, don't buy it. You're the boss. Sure, this is a *over*

FREE GIFTS NO CONTEST NO PURCHASE NECESSARY

FIG. 3–13 The word to describe heavy handwriting coupled with a rubber stamp:
Excitement. Excitement carries through the pre-greeting message; then,
after "Dear Reader:" the mood slackness momentarily. A suggestion:
Eliminate the "In the olden days. . ." line and the pace continues at a
gallop.

AMERICA'S CIVILWAR

You are there!

Dear Reader,

You are there!

You're there when Admiral Farragut shouts, "Damn the torpedoes!"

You're there when the residents of Gettysburg cower in the corners of their homes, fearfully waiting to discover whether they'll be citizens of the Union or the Confederacy.

You're there to see many observers misrepresent the outcome of the battle between the USS Monitor and the Merrimack.

Ah, you're there at the very shoulder of a tough Union sergeant about to repel Robert E. Lee's last offensive north of the James River at Darbytown, Virginia. You're so close you can see the insignia on the bridle of his horse.

And you're there to see a Union raider you never heard of before, a former Illinois music teacher named Benjamin Grierson, literally dismantle 50 crucial miles of railroad and telegraph lines in Mississippi.

Where are you? In the exciting, exhilarating, colorful pages of a classic magazine unlike any other: AMERICA'S CIVIL WAR.

Should YOU Have This Extraordinary Magazine?
Read On for a Special Private Offer

It's no coincidence that I'm writing, specifically, to you. You have reason for pride, because the source from which your name came to us indicates you're both educated and thoughtful.

We cheerfully admit, AMERICA'S CIVIL WAR isn't for everyone. But it <u>is</u> for you, and I intend to prove that point <u>at no risk to you whatever</u>.

Please consider this proposition:

Six times a year AMERICA'S CIVIL WAR brings you page after page of absolutely fascinating (and absolutely factual) knowledge of the

(over, please)

FIG. 3-14 "You are there!" is provocative without betraying what's in the letter; the rubber stamp adds immediacy and an appeal to greed. Quite properly, the letter begins with the theme of the handwritten line, <u>then</u> validates the "free issue" offer.

DAY-TIMERS, Inc.

> *Mr. Herschell Lewis:*
>
> *Seeing is believing!*
>
> *So please use the enclosed free sample for a full month and ask yourself if it didn't help you work smarter...get more done...and give you more time to yourself.*
>
> *I think you'll answer "Yes" to all!*
>
> *Steve Rowley, President*
> *Day-Timers, Inc.*

Planner/Diary...and cordially invite you to...

...DISCOVER FIRSTHAND THE BENEFITS OF OUR SYSTEM WITH
NO RISK, COMMITMENT, OR OBLIGATION ON YOUR PART.

You've probably known about Day-Timer planners for years...seen them wherever you've traveled...and wondered just how anything that fits into a coat pocket or purse could be so indispensable to more than 4,000,000 men and women around the world, all distinguished by their success.

I know your sample will show you why at once! Suddenly, everything about your job and life is going to be a little easier. You should sense the difference almost immediately:

- *Your days will literally organize themselves*
- *Your schedule will be less wearing*
- *Your "memory" will improve dramatically*
- *Your "To Do" list will be prioritized and help you plan better...short- and long-term*
- *Your output will improve noticeably*
- *Your time off the job will be better, too*

And, at the same time, you'll find that you're no longer forgetting meetings, overlooking details, or having the usual problems keeping track of bills, receipts, and other expenses.

Beyond that—and, perhaps, most importantly—you won't have to change the way you do things to enjoy Day-Timer benefits! That's what makes it great. You're already very good at what you do. Otherwise, you wouldn't have received this note.

So we'll gladly let you manage your work. We'll help manage your time. *And nothing more.* Quickly. Naturally. Effortlessly. Without the paralysis of analysis or creating yet another new job for you!

FIG. 3–15 This post-it note, which conceals a lasered personalization, includes the recipient's name—a near-triumph of technology ("near" because the lasered personalization on the letter doesn't quite match the typeface of the letter itself). Does such a device increase the possibility the recipient will read the letter? Unquestionably. Will improved results be in excess of the additional cost? Only an actual test can answer that question.

United States Committee for

unicef 🅤

United Nations Children's Fund
333 East 38th St., New York, NY 10016

Please be sure to read the important situation report I've enclosed

A Future for Every Child

Dear Friend:

In the ten seconds it took you to open and begin to read this letter, four children died from the effects of malnutrition or disease somewhere in the world.

No statistic can express what it's like to see even one child die that way ... to see a mother sitting hour after hour, leaning her child's body against her own ... to watch the small, feeble head movements that expend all the energy a youngster has left ... to see the panic in a dying tot's innocent eyes ... and then to know in a moment that life is gone.

But I'm not writing this letter simply to describe an all-too-common tragedy.

      I'm writing because, after decades of hard work, <u>UNICEF</u> -- the United Nations Children's Fund -- <u>has identified four simple, low-cost techniques that, if applied, have the potential to cut the yearly child mortality rate in this decade by one third</u>.

These methods work immediately -- even before large-scale solutions like increasing food supply or cleaning up contaminated water can be implemented. They can be put into effect before a single additional bushel of wheat is grown, or before a single new well is dug.

They may depend on <u>what you decide to do</u> by the time you finish reading this letter. You see, putting these simple techniques to work requires the support of UNICEF's programs by people around the world. In our country, it means helping the U.S. Committee for UNICEF contribute to that vital work.

      With your help, millions of children can be given the chance of a lifetime -- the chance to live -- to grow up healthy and strong. Without your help, more children may continue to die painfully, slowly, and needlessly -- children like the four who have died in the past ten seconds.

The first method is called <u>oral rehydration</u>. Most children who die

over, please ...

FIG. 3-16 Any device that increases the one-to-one intention of a fund-raising letter is a worthwhile addition. That's what the note affixed to this letter accomplishes. It transmits no message but says to the reader, "This is from me to you."

I've dabbled with this technique and retired from it. Highlighting does emphasize the words it attacks; but unlike rubber stamps and post-it notes, highlighting <u>damages</u> the impact of the rest of the letter. The reader tends to see only the highlighted portions and ignores completely, as unworthy of attention, any <u>un</u>-highlighted words.

So what happens? The writer highlights too much of the letter. The ploy becomes transparent. The impact disappears.

You know the equation: $E^2 = 0$. When you emphasize everything, you emphasize nothing.

Handwriting within the Letter

If handwriting works for an overline, how about handwriting <u>inside</u> the letter?

This development was experimental in the very late 1970s, fell into disuse in the 1980s, and has become a big winner in the mid-1990s.

The simple rule for handwriting within the letter:

 Don't overdo it.

An example of handwriting well inside the body of the letter:

I want to send you this Premier Issue—free.

If you're worried about reader fatigue—and you shouldn't be, if you break up your letter into chewable bites—an occasional handwritten chunk lets the reader breathe.

In one test to which I was privy, handwriting within the letter well outpulled the identical letter without handwriting.

What about a <u>Totally</u> Handwritten Letter?

Well . . . that's how correspondence began. And after all, if we don't seize the reader's attention, we've lost the battle because our ammunition got wet.

But careful! First of all, computerized handwriting can only go so far. If your letter is more than a few paragraphs, you'll do a better job of avoiding reader fatigue by using <u>some</u> handwriting, together with other devices.

Ah, but how about a handwritten envelope?

Good idea. We'll come to that in Chapter 5.

Conclusion

Are gimmicks good?

What a question! *Per se*, gimmicks—and in this pile I include all the mechanical devices we've looked at, plus stickers and scratch-offs and pads of name and address labels and for that matter sweepstakes—are artifices.

But don't let that throw you. What matters is <u>response</u>—and all of us should applaud, embrace, and vigorously use professionally applied gimmicks that increase response.

What's at the End?

How to Close with a Bang, Not a Whimper

Some years ago, I was involved in a test originated by one of the most alert and sophisticated fund raisers, St. Jude Children's Research Hospital, of Memphis, Tennessee. We tested the identical letter with and without a postscript. The one with the p.s. pulled an astonishing 19 percent better. (At the time, the late Danny Thomas was the spokesperson for St. Jude.)

This was the wording of the p.s.:

> I hope that our own family never suffers the tragedy of losing a child to an incurable disease. At St. Jude, we're fighting to conquer these killers, and one day someone in your own family may live because we succeeded.

So powerful was this p.s. that years later different letters retained this same wording.

The Rule for P.S. Writing

Think for a moment: *Why have a p.s.?*

The question generates its own answer. We put a postscript on a letter so the letter will end with a bang, not a whimper. So a p.s. that does nothing to add to the reader's desire to respond is a waste.

The overline is the most read part of a letter, and the p.s. is next. Automatically the format itself gives us thunderbolts to throw. Let's not take the electricity out of them.

The Postscript Rule is Tip Number 8 described in Chapter 1:

 If you include a p.s., it should reinforce one of the key selling motivators or mention an extra benefit—one which doesn't require explanation.

"Public Domain" Postscripts

If you're unsure what to put into a p.s., here are some "public domain" postscripts you're free to use without fear of damage:

1. To get your [WHATEVER], be sure to call our toll-free number before the expiration date.
2. Don't risk losing out on this exclusive private offer. Use the postage-free envelope I've enclosed. I'll look for it on my desk.
3. An <u>extra</u> bonus! If we hear from you by May 31, we'll include an extra gift.
4. Please don't put this in a drawer thinking you'll get to it later. You'll run the risk of missing an opportunity that may never be repeated.
5. I'm counting on you to stand shoulder-to-shoulder with us. I wouldn't be writing you if I didn't know you're the kind of person who cares. . .and who will do something about it.
6. God bless you for caring.
7. You take no risk whatsoever. Our [service/product] is unconditionally guaranteed.
8. Much as I'd like to, I can't send you another reminder of this offer. Electronic curbs mean this is the <u>only</u> notification I can send you, so please respond as quickly as possible. Thanks.

That word *Thanks* is a safe and reader-friendly way to end a p.s.

```
Lotus Freelance Graphics 2.0
for Windows Upgrade .........................Sugg. Retail Price: $150
AddImpact!™ for Windows  ......................Sugg. Retail Price $149
                                            Total Retail Value: $299
```

FOR A LIMITED TIME ONLY $99!
YOU SAVE $200!

```
Don't wait...order Freelance Graphics and get FREE AddImpact! TODAY!
```

<u>HERE'S HOW TO ORDER:</u>

<u>CALL</u> us toll free at 1-800-622-7006, or
<u>MAIL</u> us the enclosed ORDER CARD in the
postage-paid envelope provided, or
<u>FAX</u> your order at 1-908-370-7046

```
We look forward to serving you!

Sincerely,
```

[signature: Adam Shaffer]

```
Adam Shaffer
Director, MicroShopper
```

```
P.S. As always, order with complete confidence. I'm positive that
     you'll find Freelance Graphics the easiest presentation package
     you've used. If you're not completely satisfied, return it within
     60 days and we'll refund your money. NO QUESTIONS ASKED.
```

MicroSHOPPER
1720 OAK STREET P.O. BOX 341 LAKEWOOD, NJ 08701
PHONE 1-800-622-7006 FAX 1-908-370-7046

FIG. 4–1 Recapitulating the guarantee in the p.s. is safe and effective. Those last three words in caps, "NO QUESTIONS ASKED," had to help convince some readers to take a chance and order the software.

you the Premiere Issue of THE INDUSTRY to examine free!

If you like it, continue your Charter Subscription, and receive 25 more issues (26 total) for just $57, our low introductory price. (You save $21 off the cover price. You pay less than the cost of one expense account lunch.)

If you decide THE INDUSTRY is not for you, return our invoice marked "cancel," owe nothing, and keep the free Premiere Issue.

With all of THE INDUSTRY to gain and absolutely nothing to lose, shouldn't you at least take a look? I trust you will, and I look forward to welcoming you...

To the bold new business magazine of inside news and information for the movie-music-publishing-TV-magazine-advertising-and-fashion Industry...

To the hot new magazine that serves up leaks, leads, scoops, and secrets you can use to your benefit...

To the new magazine you'll turn to every other week as your must-read journal of the Industry...

Welcome -- to THE INDUSTRY!

Sincerely,

Patricia Hart

Patricia Hart
for THE INDUSTRY

PH:ksa

P.S. This free issue offer is good for a limited time only.
Mail today to take advantage, using the postage-paid
envelope provided. Supplies of the Premiere Issue
are limited. Act now!

FIG. 4-2 What might you have written differently in this p.s.? Even without knowing what's in the letter proper, you'd have replaced "for a limited time only" with a specific number of days. . .and scratched "Supplies of the Premiere Issue are limited" in favor of "I only have a handful of the Premiere Issue, and one of them has your name on it."

to what's best and guard you against what's dubious -- or downright dangerous. Issue after issue is crammed with information you can rely on absolutely. The straight facts. Impartial. Authoritative.

- <u>Tips</u> on selecting and preparing food, complete with recipes and sometimes whole menus. (Recently, for example, a Special Report on beef: how to buy and use the lean and healthy cuts.)

- <u>Recommendations of good choices</u>. (Find out the 100 frozen dinners that can fit most easily into a nutritious diet.)

- <u>Warnings</u> about products and practices to avoid. (Yes, you can overdose on vitamin C and end up with diarrhea!)

- <u>Advice</u> on exercise and diet programs with full analyses of the pros and cons. (Even drastic weight-loss regimens like Oprah's could be okay with strict doctor supervision.)

Simply and engagingly written, free of medical jargon, studded with helpful charts, the Tufts Diet & Nutrition Letter covers every aspect of nutrition from adolescent anorexia to the special concerns of seniors (a surprising finding: more older men who live alone eat better than do women).

It questions what needs questioning -- such as organic foods; are they worth the extra cost? And it explains what needs explaining -- such as why you can have a cholesterol reading above 200 and be fine, or a reading below 200 and yet be in trouble.

But above all the Tufts Letter is always aware that nutrition is not just science. It's nourishment for the soul and senses ... one of life's greatest pleasures, meant to be enjoyed. For example, in a study of frozen dinners that was picked up by the press from coast to coast, the Diet & Nutrition Letter not only compared the nutrients and costs, but had a panel of connoisseurs to judge the dishes for taste.

The freshest news ... the most trustworthy knowledge ... the soundest advice about the key ingredient in any plan for a healthier and happier life: nutrition. All concentrated in a lively newsletter you'll want to read at once every month, and keep for reference in months to come.

See for yourself. See how much the Tufts Diet & Nutrition Letter can give you -- and how much it can save you. <u>Save you money</u> you might otherwise spend unnecessarily. <u>Save you time</u> with checklists for your shopping. <u>Save you from worrying</u> whether you're doing the right things. You will be.

Just return the "Let's see" reply form today -- and see.

Sincerely,

Stanley Gershoff

Stanley N. Gershoff
Dean, Tufts School of Nutrition

SNG:acg

P.S. Remember, your FREE issue request puts you under no obligation to subscribe. You'll enjoy substantial savings off our regular subscription rate if you do, but if not you need only return our bill marked "Cancel," and keep your free copy.

FIG. 4–3 Many standard postscripts begin with that word "Remember." Nothing wrong with it, but neither is it an excitement-builder, especially in a p.s. like this one, altogether too tranquil and negative. Why not end with a bang instead of a whimper, such as, "Before you take that next tablet of Vitamin C or put some skim-milk Ricotta cheese on your plate, why not have all the facts, pro and con? Your FREE issue request brings you these and a lot of others, and you don't risk a dime."

Experiments, Good and Bad

Depending on other enclosures—and on budget—a handwritten p.s. on a separate sheet of paper can be remarkably effective because it adds a separate emphasis and still carries the "P.S." label.

If you try this, keep the piece of paper small—I'd say 4" x 6" (10 x 15 cm) maximum. Blue ink on cheap paper, please, or overproduction causes you to lose the p.s. effect.

Obviously, if you do this, you won't have a conventional p.s. on the letter proper.

Another experiment is a p.s. so long that it dwarfs the letter. I've seen this a couple of times, but I've never seen a mailer repeat it, which confirms my own negative view of such a procedure.

A gigantic p.s. doesn't just violate the Postscript Rule. . .it destroys it. The p.s. isn't really a p.s., and reader interest leaks out the bottom instead of being sharpened and honed.

May I suggest: If you can't read the p.s. without taking a breath, you've written too much.

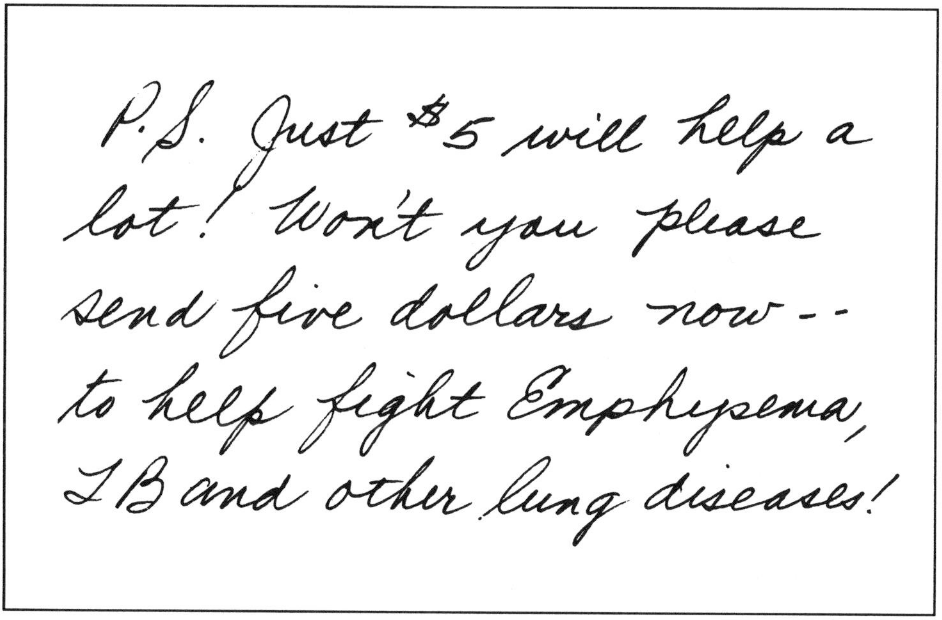

> *P.S. Just $5 will help a lot! Won't you please send five dollars now -- to help fight Emphysema, TB and other lung diseases!*

FIG. 4–4 Is it a p.s. or isn't it? This is a separate enclosure in a fund-raising mailing. The extra "kick" is considerably stronger than the same words would have been in a conventional postscript.

One P.S. per Customer, Please

Here's another rule, and it couldn't be simpler:

 If you enclose two letters in your mailing, don't put a p.s. on more than one of them.

When might you have two letters? In subscription mailings, for example. The second letter, which some direct marketers call the "lift" letter, is also called the "publisher's" letter.

A typical mailing has a letter, a brochure, and—as an option—a validating enclosure. Often the second letter is the validating enclosure. Why not? It's easy to write and it's inexpensive to produce. If you're using a second letter in your mailing, please observe one logical rule:

 No matter how long that first letter is, keep the second letter down to one page.

And assuming the first letter has a p.s., you're exposing the <u>device</u> as a device if you put a p.s. on the second letter.

Two Postscripts? No Postscripts?

We've all seen letters with a p.s. and then a p.p.s. Cute, huh?

Ugh.

The concept of a p.p.s. betrays insecurity. "Oh, God, I really haven't done a strong enough selling job."

Probably true—but the key reason to have no more than one p.s. is our old friend, the equation: $E^2 = 0$. When you emphasize everything, you emphasize nothing. Two postscripts are weaker than one because emphasis is split. (Figure 4-5 exemplifies this point. You can see for yourself how the second p.s. damages impact.)

What about having *no* p.s.?

I've read statements by professional copywriters that every letter should have a p.s. What these writers mean is that every letter they write has a p.s.

The rule isn't invariable. I can envision many business-to business

Enclosed on the yellow rate card is our price schedule. We've studied the competition, tried to understand why they charge the way they do and have come out with a rate card that works for every size of direct marketer. However, it doesn't contain the padding and fluff we felt were unnecessary elements in getting the job done.

You see, we're straight forward, to the point kind of people. And have worked hard at keeping...

The Way We Do Business Simple, Concise, Clear, and Direct.

(Which, by the way, are the four important elements used in writing good marketing pieces.)

How does it all work? A call comes in on the DID lines. Your company name is displayed on phone terminal. The operator is then able to answer the phone the way you have specified. Your computer screen is pulled up where the information is correctly inputted. In fact, recently we received an order from a gentleman for one of our clients where the last name consisted of all consonants. Our client called back saying that this name was not a possibility. So we called the client's customer to verify. Indeed it was right. Now, they often change their database from the correct data our operators obtain.

All of <u>your customer information is kept strictly confidential.</u> Only with your permission do we tell others you're our client of anything about your customers.

We'd be happy to answer any questions you might have and pledge ourselves to serving you in excellence. It will be like you've hired a whole office staff without the hassles of taxes and payroll and training. In other words, more of your energies will be put towards doing what you do best. As an astute entrepreneur once put it, "You need to **work on** your business, **not in** it."

It's easy to start. Just call 1-800-825-6585 and ask for Brian or Stacey. You'll be glad you did.

Sincerely,

Stacey

Stacey Adams

P.S. If you'd like to see how much money will stay in your bank account, send a copy of last months billing from your current service bureau. We'll run a spreadsheet showing you the savings, lock you in at those prices and fax the answer back to you.

P.P.S. We're able to offer you the diversity, complexity and sophistication of the big service bureaus but for a friendly, affordable price.

please go to next page...

FIG. 4–5 The P.S. on this letter suffers from lack of an apostrophe in "last month's billing". . .and "please go to next page" is laughable, since this is the last page of the letter. But the biggest problem is with the P.P.S. It not only adds nothing to the sales argument; by splitting interest and attention, it detracts from the basic P.S.

Plus you'll get the best of Chopin, Brahms, Liszt, Gershwin, and more.

If you're ready for <u>Mozart</u> right now,
say <u>YES</u>...

If you already <u>know</u> that you want <u>Mozart</u> in your collection, just choose the "YES" sticker on your RISK-FREE Offer Certificate enclosed in this letter. Then, we'll send you <u>Mozart</u> for a 10-day free audition so you can try it before you buy it — without risk or commitment. If you enjoy every minute of this magnificent music as much as we think you will, it's yours at our Special Introductory Price of just $7.99 for two double-length cassettes or two compact discs.

Future albums will come, one every month or so, for the same 10-day free audition. Each two-cassette album will cost just $17.99. Each two-compact disc album will cost just $19.99. A shipping and handling charge will be added to each shipment. Keep only the albums you want — there is no minimum to purchase and you may cancel at any time simply by notifying us.

If you still need to be convinced,
say <u>MAYBE</u>...

Choose the "MAYBE" sticker and we'll send you <u>Mozart</u> for a completely RISK-FREE try <u>before</u> you buy! Listen to it for 10 full days in your own home. Then decide. If you don't love <u>Mozart</u>, just send it back and owe absolutely nothing. It's that simple.

If you decide to keep <u>Mozart</u>, pay the low Special Introductory Price. Then you'll receive future albums under the terms described above!

If this sound like a great deal to you, you're right. It's an absolutely painless way to round out your music collection with the classics from GREAT COMPOSERS. Don't hesitate — this offer's too good to pass up!

Sincerely,

Steven L. Janas
President

L/CMP293

P.S. Remember, if you're ready for <u>Mozart</u> right now, say YES! But, if you're still not sure, choose the "MAYBE" sticker! It's your chance to give classical music a try before you buy. No record store can make you such an RISK-FREE offer. Return your certificate today!

FIG. 4–6 Three exclamation points in this p.s. Now read it again: Three exclamation points in this p.s.! Those exclamation points do force excitement, even though the reader knows they're an artifice. This call to action is a classic postscript.

circumstances in which a postscript gives the letter a "bulk-mailing" look. If, after writing a p.s., you re-read your letter and are uneasy because it seems to lose personalization at the end, eliminate the p.s. and incorporate its message into the letter proper.

Many a letter has benefited by shifting the p.s. upward to become the final paragraph.

This gives us another imperative:

 If you move the p.s. up into the letter and agree the letter is stronger, it's a signal your p.s. wasn't so hot to begin with. Try again.

A polished p.s. is more than a work of art . . . it's a terrific sales closer. If you've been dismissing the p.s. as a necessary but not very significant chore, give this element more respect and it, in turn, will give you more response.

5

Envelopes

That Crucial, Very First Impression

"Who looks at the envelope?"

The answer, of course, is: <u>Everybody</u>.

I think it's strange that the most obvious, most visible, and potentially most effective attention-getter a piece of mail has is also—too often—the most overlooked element.

The circumstance is exactly the same as that old riddle about a tree falling in the forest and nobody hearing it. Has it really made a sound?

If we mail the most brilliantly written, most beautifully produced letter ever written and nobody opens the envelope, have we really exposed prospects to this package?

The first issue here is whether we should put any legend at all on the envelope. Many battle-scarred direct response veterans will tell you that envelope copy is a "must"—it always helps.

Uh-uh.

Envelope copy is *always* worthy of testing. Sometimes it gives response a huge boost; sometimes it suppresses response; sometimes changing a word or two, or changing a printed message to handwritten, or adding a rubber stamp effect can have a dramatic impact on results.

Many mailers, especially in the financial world, feel envelope copy isn't dignified. It costs them image. Sometimes, they're right, but companies can drown in their own image. What matters is whether your mailing gets the phone or the cash register ringing. (That's one benefit of a handwritten envelope: It can crack the otherwise impenetrable secretarial barrier, where the most clever or most highly produced printed message still winds up in the circular file. See Figures 5-1 and 5-2.)

On the other end we have full-color custom-converted envelopes that cost as much as the rest of the mailing. Are they worth the extra money?

Some mailers in the world of publishing insist they have to compete with the giants by covering every millimeter of the envelope with color separations and tint-blocks and screaming type. This attitude is the result of an analysis by art directors, not by marketers, because the only way to determine whether custom-converted envelopes work for you is to test them against less lavish envelopes with the same copy.

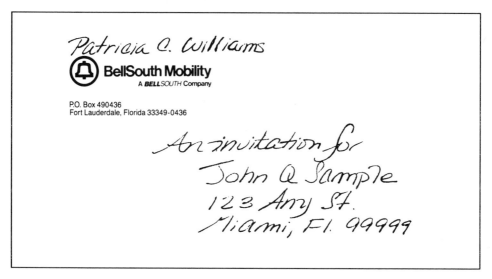

FIG. 5–1 An absolute way to crack the secretarial barrier is a handwritten envelope. Many printers and lettershops have computerized typefaces that replicate handwriting; this one is <u>actual</u> handwriting, accomplished by a battery of students with good penmanship.

FIG. 5–2 This mailer loads up the envelope with color and a gigantic "FREE!" It's eye-catching, but before you start custom-converting envelopes and printing them in full color, be sure the additional response is worth the additional expense. . .especially since sometimes less on an envelope is more.

My own philosophy (which I certainly don't try to superimpose on you) is to spend your money to reach more people, not to win art directors' awards.

Envelope Sizes

The uninitiated, hearing terms such as *Number 10* and *Baronial* and *Jumbo*, think of exotic envelope sizes. They aren't. These three are the most common sizes.

A number 10 is the standard business envelope. Actual dimensions are 4⅛" x 9½". Smaller standard "commercial" sizes run from no. 9 (3⅞" x 8⅞") down to no. 6¼ (3½" x 6"). Bigger "commercial" sizes run from no. 11 (4½" x 10⅜") up to no. 14 (5" x 11½").

The 6" x 9" is a standard "booklet" envelope. Other sizes run upward, the most common being 7" x 10", 10" x 13", and of course 9" x 12". Other envelope types are "announcement" envelopes, ranging from the A-2 size (4⅜" x 5¾") through A-10 (6" x 9½"); "catalog" envelopes, ranging from 5½" x 7½" through 12" x 15½"; and specialty envelopes such as remittance, teller, policy, and coin envelopes.

The difference between many of these types is the position, shape, and size of the flaps. Within each category, the two standard colors are white and manila (kraft).

The choice is wide; yet many mailers opt for custom-converted envelopes. Actually, in a mailing of 50,000 pieces or more, the difference between a custom size and a standard envelope is nominal.

Does this mean a mailer should arbitrarily choose a size? Hardly. It means testing standard sizes should yield information that can lead to a response-increasing decision.

The First Rule of Envelope Copy

Let's introduce The First Rule of Envelope Copy:

 Put a promotional legend on a one-to-one piece of correspondence only when you're reasonably certain the recipient is unlikely to open the envelope unless you add a dramatic "Open me!" imperative.

I'll tell you <u>two</u> reasons why this Rule isn't a truism:

1. You have to have a modicum of professional astuteness to know when your letter probably won't reach its target unless you add an incentive.
2. A legend on a one-to-one envelope from an unknown source may get that envelope opened, but the attitude of the recipient is unlikely to be condescending or skeptical.

So if you're writing to someone who knows you, decide: Is my name in the upper left corner ample incentive to keep me out of the wastebasket?

The Second Rule of Envelope Copy

The physical purpose of an envelope is to keep the components from spilling out onto the street. But the psychological purpose?

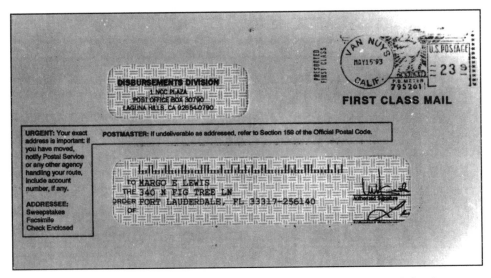

DISBURSEMENTS DIVISION
1 NCC PLAZA
POST OFFICE BOX 30790
LAGUNA HILLS, CA 92654-0790

PRESORTED
FIRST CLASS

VAN NUYS
MAY 15 '93
CALIF

U.S. POSTAGE
P.B. METER
795261

= 23 ½

FIRST CLASS MAIL

URGENT: Your exact address is important: if you have moved, notify Postal Service or any other agency handling your route, include account number, if any.

ADDRESSEE:
Sweepstakes
Facsimile
Check Enclosed

POSTMASTER: If undeliverable as addressed, refer to Section 159 of the Official Postal Code.

TO MARGO E LEWIS
THE 340 N FIG TREE LN
ORDER FORT LAUDERDALE, FL 33317-256140
OF

Authorized Signature

FIG. 5-3 A check? No, a sweepstakes with a 900 number. Meanwhile, the envelope serves its purpose: It gets opened.

That's the Second Rule of Envelope Copy:

 The only purpose of the carrier envelope is to induce the recipient to open it.

That makes your basic decision easy: Will the legend I've put on this envelope induce the recipient to open it?

Dilettantes, beginners, and even professionals who haven't been privy to the results of envelope treatment tests tend to ignore envelopes altogether: "All we're talking about is a handful of words, and how important can a handful of words be?"

Others have read somewhere that envelopes with imperative copy pull better than envelopes without copy. So they come bumbling into the arena, with envelope copy guaranteed to induce catalepsy. Or they'll show off all the big words they know. Or they'll art-direct it instead of paying attention to the supreme rule of all force-communications, the Clarity Commandment:

 When you choose words and phrases for force-communication, clarity is paramount. Don't let any other component of the commnications mix interfere with it.

15825 Shady Grove Rd., Suite 140
Rockville, Maryland 20850

DO NOT FORWARD

POSTMASTER: IF UNDELIVERABLE AS ADDRESSED, PLEASE HANDLE IN
CONFORMANCE WITH REGULATIONS AS SPECIFIED IN SECTION NO. 694
OF THE UNITED STATES POSTAL SERVICE DOMESTIC MAIL MANUAL.

```
Margo Lewis
P.O. Box 15725
Plantation, FL 33318-5725
```

11001 Wilcrest Suite 200
Houston, TX 77099

2000.00 FINE OR 5 YRS. IMPRISONMENT
or both for any person who interferes with or obstructs
delivery of this letter or otherwise violates § 18 United
States Code   1702 et seq.

SEE TIT. 18 SEC. 1708 U.S. CODE
Theft of U.S. Mail is punishable by fines of up to
$2000 or 5 years in prison or both.

FIRST CLASS

PRIVATE BUSINESS USE   BUY US SAVINGS BONDS

```
CLAIM # 17012A4014
PROFESSIONAL VIDEO CORP
HERSCHELL LEWIS
920 N FIG TREE LN
FT LAUDERDALE, FL   33317
```

FIG. 5–4, Many who see these envelopes will open them, expecting some sort of
FIG. 5–5. government message. Actually, what the envelope copy says on 5–4 is
redundant, since this is third class mail and the post office doesn't forward third class mail. Fig. 5–5 is first class presort; its copy simply says
what everybody already knows: Opening mail addressed to another
person is a no-no.

The Clarity Commandment doesn't just pertain to envelopes. It
pertains to every facet of every component of every message.

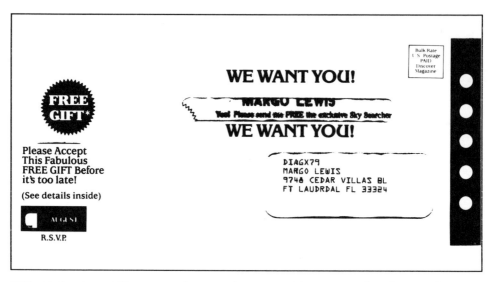

FIG. 5–6 Four different windows. . .the irresistible "Free Gift" (damaged by an asterisk). . .double personalization. The envelope commands: Open me.

Obfuscation and Complication = Negation

An envelope announcing a professional seminar has this legend on the envelope:

> Learn to unravel the mysteries of multiple regression, factor and cluster analysis, and how to apply them on the job—at once.

Sent to a vertical list of statistical analysts, no problem. But this mailing was addressed to me. What's my pre-opening reaction? What's the attitude of the typical recipient?

(Incidently, putting words like *learn* on the envelope can damage response, because *learn* seems like work. *Find out* or *Discover* is a better word. And *at once*—that's too imperative. *Fast* has no "I command you" overtone.)

New Developments in Envelopes

Is anything new in envelopes? Can anything be new in a medium already peopled with many standard sizes and after several hundred years of experimentation?

Experimentation hasn't ended. . .certainly not in colors and windows and paper stocks.

One of the newest and most dynamic and most successful techniques involves the envelope. It's called a "freemium."

A freemium differs from a premium. When you mention a premium on the envelope, the person who gets your mail has to do something to get that premium. But a _freemium_ is enclosed then and there.

The freemium usually involves a <u>second</u> window on the envelope, through which it shows. Because the very nature of mailings requires flatness (unless the mailer goes to unusual packaging), refrigerator magnets are among the most popular freemiums.

A typical freemium envelope shows the magnet with a legend printed on the envelope saying something such as, "Keep the enclosed refrigerator magnet with our compliments." We may hate the refrigerator magnets, but we open the envelope to get at the freemium. And while we're doing it, we read the message. (See Figure 5-7.)

Staying in sync with the Clarity Commandment, an astute mailer customizes the window to show us the freemium. <u>Saying</u> the freemium is inside is in no way as powerful as <u>showing</u> us the freemium.

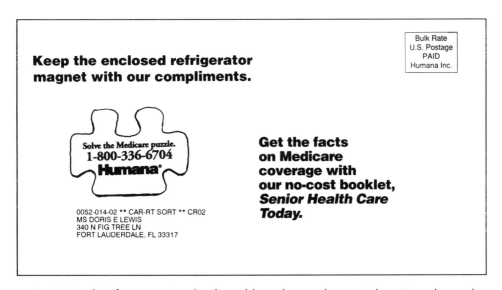

FIG. 5–7 The "freemium" is clearly visible in the envelope window. Even those who have no use for a refrigerator magnet are more likely to open the envelope than they would be if it had no freemium; and the attitude at the moment of opening is more likely to be positive.

(Instead of a refrigerator magnet, think of a nickel or a dime, and you'll understand why showing it is light-years better than saying it's inside.)

Speaking of "Free"...

If you're after <u>safe</u> envelope copy—not <u>brilliant</u> envelope copy, because brilliance has the unpleasant knack of alienating as many people as it attracts—it's hard to go wrong with barnacled but dependable terms such as "Free" or "Private Information" or "Advance Copy Enclosed."

Hard but not impossible.

I'm looking at a double-window envelope, addressed to my wife. Each window has a glassine sleeve, so this mailer—a fund raiser—spent more than the necessary minimum amount of money. The legend on the envelope:

> Your free decal is enclosed

What's wrong with that? The answer lies in realization of a double mismatch of terminology and target: (1) the word *decal* has a *zero* class-quotient; (2) in our bracket, who wants a decal?

If this had been addressed to Nintendo owners or sign-ups for the Ronald McDonald Breakfast Club, *decal* might be a motivator. Kids love to put decals on their bikes and desks and walls. For an upscale sell, *decal* has about as much appeal as, "Your imitation cubic zirconium is enclosed."

Now: What substitute legend <u>might</u> this mailer have chosen?

One substitution leaps to mind quickly: *emblem* instead of *decal*. That's easy. We're matching terminology to recipient, a basic tenet of communication.

Another substitution becomes available when (or more probably, <u>if</u>) we open the envelope. These are the first two paragraphs of the letter:

> A shipwrecked sailor was struggling in the water. The shore was near, but his strength was almost spent.
> Suddenly there was a friendly presence in the water—a strong, sleek body that buoyed him up, escorted him to shallow water, and saved his life.

What if these two paragraphs, replicated in typewriter face, were on the envelope, with two additional words. . .

(Continued inside.)

I don't want a load of hate mail from supporters of this organization who do stick those decals on their cars and boats and bikes. But my point is absolute: The envelope has to say, to the unexpecting recipient: "Open me." And the word "Free" says just that. Don't corrupt it with something your target regards as worthless.

When you have that durable word *Free* in your pocket and know how to use it (which means even a rudimentary understanding of what causes people to react positively or negatively), you're in a secure psychological area. An example of can't-miss envelope copy (from a cigar company):

GIVE THIS MAN A
FREE SPORTS
WATCH AND A BOX
OF <u>FRESH</u> CIGARS!

Whoever wrote that, I salute you. You weren't being cute or tricky, and you understood the difference in rapport generation between attracting the reader and blurting at the reader. How many writers would, thoughtlessly, have left out the key and written serviceable but uninspired envelope copy such as . . .

FREE!
SPORTS WATCH
AND A BOX OF CIGARS

. . . copy which loses impact because the typical recipient doesn't <u>accept</u> (ergo, believe) it because the typical writer just doesn't think of the jolly but scalpel-delicate "Give this man"?

A bizarre use of the word "Free" (Figure 5-8)—an envelope on which is imprinted:

"In Germany,
MEN CHANGE THEIR UNDERWEAR
on an average of
ONCE EVERY 7 DAYS"

FIG. 5-8 Does this strange envelope treatment mean we can get a free pair of 7-day-used German underwear? No, thanks.

Immediately under these words, in a circular window, is the word *Free*.

No, thanks.

The Third and Fourth Rules of Envelope Copy

The trend toward heavy envelope copy has led to overkill . . . which damages response. The Third Rule of Envelope Copy can help avoid overkill:

 If your offer requires explanation, <u>do not</u> spill your guts on the envelope.

The Fourth Rule of Envelope Copy is founded on a psychological truism: In marketing, asking questions can help formulate attitudes. Questions are as valuable and as underrated a weapon as we marketers have in our arsenal. The Rule:

 When dealing in controversy or when uncertain of the recipient's attitude or prejudices, asking a question on the envelope is less likely to generate antagonism than making a flat, positive statement. The same information can be transmitted.

Asking a question on the envelope has power. The question we always have to ask, before creating a question for the envelope: "What's the attitude at the moment of opening . . . have we built sufficient interest to overcome hostility or the fear that a mailer is breaking and entering my private domain?"

Questions are gaining in popularity, and that's good, because questions automatically involve the reader. A popular ploy with publications has been to load up the envelope with a laundry list of questions, assuming that at least one of them will be provocative enough to induce each recipient to open the envelope. One such envelope had this list of questions:

> What do you do if you're locked out of your hotel room—naked?
> Why do dogs bark?
> Can a man be killed by ants?
> How do homing pigeons find their way home?
> What is the effect of headache remedies on radishes?
> How can you get a free subscription to Smithsonian magazine?

Opinions, please: How many recipients think this list of questions helps get the envelope opened? How many think this list damages the possibility of getting the envelope opened?

I side with the majority, and I'll tell you why: The envelope no longer is provocative. It says too much. We bank robbers have an old saying: Wait until you're <u>outside</u> the bank before taking off your mask.

The Fifth Rule of Envelope Copy

Here's another one-sentence rule that can prevent the negative results of overkill. The Fifth Rule of Envelope Copy:

 Saying too much on the envelope can damage response.

What you put on that envelope should encourage the recipient to open it. . .not give away the story inside the envelope.

Example: An envelope has two messages on its face. The first one says—

Inside: Tax Reduction Kit.

Good copy. Now consider the <u>second</u> piece of copy, an ostensible rubber stamp:

"Our tax-free funds can help lower your tax bill. See inside."

As you know from previous chapters, I'm a fan of rubber stamps, so I object when a mailer uses them without thinking. This envelope says too much. I suggest this mailer put "Inside: Tax Reduction Kit" in a rubber stamp effect and put that other legend where it belongs—in the wastebasket.

A minor peripheral point: If you're using a rubber stamp effect, don't just set the type in Stencil. Make a real rubber stamp, for three to five dollars. Stamp that thing on plain paper until you get the effect you want, then make a line shot, and it'll look like what it is—a real rubber stamp. If you're printing in two colors, make it 50% red, 50% black.

Don't draw the conclusion that it's the <u>number</u> of words that determines whether or not an envelope says too much. It's the thrust.

How Database Can Enhance Envelope Copy

I'll make a point here in favor of database, which I often attack because it's so misused and abused: The more certain you are of exactly who your target is, the more specifics you can pile onto the envelope.

That's because your database isolates those whose (a) professional credentials or (b) specified field of interest or (c) prior buying habits qualify them for a closely targeted envelope message.

After all, <u>exclusivity</u> is one of the great motivators of our time. Specifics and exclusivity entwine well together.

Speaking of exclusivity . . .

Words like *Preferred* and *Priority* have as much impact as *Personal* in today's marketplace (with one exception: a handwritten envelope marked *Personal*), without the twin dangers accompanying "Personal"—objection to an assumption of a relationship and recognition of "Personal" as an attention-getting ploy.

Challenging the Recipient

How far should an envelope challenge go? What's the difference between these three legends, all of which really say the same thing?

—Enclosed: Quick test.
—Enclosed: Quick quiz.
—Your opinion, please.

Our role as rudimentary psychologists is never on the line as much as when we're figuring out what, if anything, to put on that envelope. Who are our targets? The problem we face is that our most sophisticated targets, the ones most able to buy what we're selling, are the ones most likely to resent being asked to take a test. The difference between a test and a quiz is light-years. A test puts the tester on a plane far above the testee, who fears being shown up as a fool.

So quiz is safe, and opinion or ballot are even safer because opinion and ballot put the person to whom you're writing in a position of supremacy. which would you rather do, vote or take a test?

So a fund-raising organization puts on its envelope:

You have been selected to participate in an important survey on America's National Parks.

What if the envelope had said, "You have been selected to participate in a test regarding America's National Parks"? The typical recipient would cry, "Why me?"

Sophisticated recipients know this envelope copy is a ploy to get the envelope opened so they will be exposed to a fund-raising message. Less sophisticated recipients' interest can be piqued because they feel opinions mean something. The mailer can't lose because knowing the purpose doesn't kill off the possibility of response.

But envelope copy that's obviously self-serving runs a far more dangerous course. An organization dedicated to the preservation of wildlife has this on the envelope:

May we list you as a grass roots supporter of protection for endangered wildlife? ❑ Yes   ❑ No

A half-wit oyster could see through this one.

Figure 5-9 shows "speed formats." Speed formats openly intend to establish a *trompe-l'oeil* (fool the eye) effect. They aren't as popular as they were in the late 1980s because of a rule we've already discussed:

Sameness = boredom
Overuse = abuse

FIG. 5–9 These are typical of speed formats. Many commercial printers have their
A, B, C, D. own proprietary version, the common denominator being an intent to
look "official," impersonating Express Mail and Federal Express.

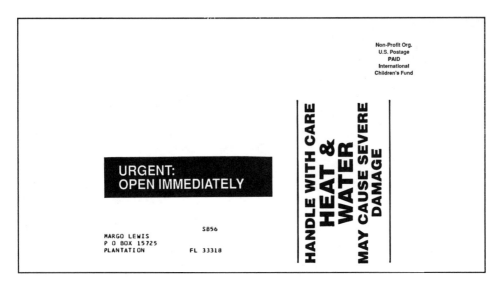

FIG. 5–10 In a red reverse, "Urgent: Open Immediately" is commanding enough to get this envelope opened; the "HANDLE WITH CARE" legend adds a second provocative message.

But they haven't disappeared, and the very nature of waning means they'll wax again. By crying urgent (with hidden third-class mail indicia), speed formats can be an effective way of crying "Wolf!"

(For a description of the cry of "Wolf!" and the cry of "Fire!" as letter openings, see the next section, numbers 14 for "Fire!" and 64 for "Wolf!")

Speed formats have a fast burnout rate. A little psychological rule:

 The more exciting a message is, the faster it wears out.

Figure 5-10 is an example of "Urgent" without using a speed format.

Do the Enclosures Back up the Promise on the Envelope?

The more exciting the message on the envelope, the more likely it is to violate the Sixth Rule of Envelope Copy:

When the reader thinks you are not telling the truth about one point, he extends that opinion to include your entire sales argument. He rejects even those statements which are true.

An example of a violation of the Sixth Rule is an envelope housing an offer for compact disks. On the envelope is this wording:

> Due to the exclusive nature of this special membership offer, please respond immediately

Okay, they've used some trigger words—<u>exclusive</u> and <u>special</u> and <u>immediately</u>. They had a free shot at <u>charter</u>, but they didn't use it. Now, what makes me think this is just another mundane offer to sell me some CDs or videos?

In the upper right corner are those betrayal words: "Bulk rate." How can an exclusive special be offered in bulk? Mailers have options for that upper right corner. Keep the pieces in sync.

Worse is the one that says "Personal and Confidential"—and up in that deadly corner, even though it's a stamp, are the words "Bulk

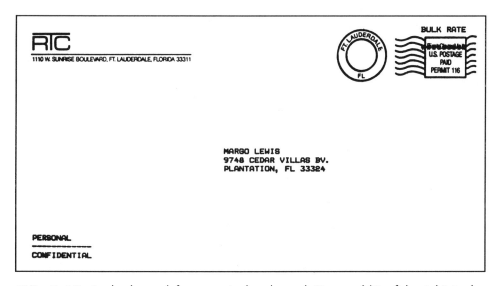

FIG. 5-11 In the lower left corner is the legend "Personal/Confidential." In the upper right corner, "First Class" is crossed out and "Bulk Rate" printed in. What a mismatch, especially since third class stamps are available, attractive, and often misrecognized as first class stamps.

FIG. 5-12 What possesses some mailers? This envelope uses a rubber "Important" stamp. . .and is addressed to "Resident."

Rate." (See Figure 5-11.) I've had mailings with "Personal and Confidential" addressed to "H.G. Lewis or current resident." Mutual of Omaha sent one, marked "important," just to "Resident." (See Figure 5-12.)

<u>Don't</u> waste the word *Important*. It's not only cheap, thoughtless chest-thumping writing, but it isn't effective selling. We're in the Age of Skepticism, remember?

The Seventh and Eighth Rules of Envelope Copy

Wild claims of superiority are the basis of the Seventh Rule of Envelope Copy. The seventh is a key that can unlock a lot of response for you, if you've been wondering why your communications just don't seem to connect:

 Even if your claim of superiority is true, it means nothing to the reader unless it relates to him. Don't thump out "Me Tarzan!" unless the person reading your communication is Jane.

The Eighth Rule of Envelope Copy should give you pause if you've been inclined to empty the basket of superlatives, or to scream "Wolf!" or "Fire!" on the envelope when no wolf is in the neighborhood and the only fire is in the fireplace:

 Calling something "important" when your best readers will know it isn't important will cost you some business you otherwise might have had.

Save that word *important* for something important.

Does Humor Work on Envelopes?

I'm usually not a fan of humor, but my disdain doesn't extend to envelopes. Why? Because of the overriding Second Rule of Envelope Copy: The only purpose of an outer envelope is to get the recipient to open it.

An overnight courier service gets lighthearted . . . and you can see how this lightheartedness generates a receptive mood:

Stepping barefoot on a bee.
Trusting a salesman who says "Trust me."
Giving your important shipments to a carrier who doesn't know
    where those shipments are every single minute.

Then the tiny punchline:

Name three ways to get stung.

Actually, that third bullet is a weak one because it loses its humor, is too long, and makes a more trivial point than losing a shipment or being late.

The Ninth Rule of Envelope Copy

The Ninth rule of Envelope Copy is somewhat more abstruse than any of the other eight:

Mr. John Q. Sample
President
ABC Company
123 Main Street
Anytown, NJ 99999

John Q. Sample
President
ABC Company
123 Main Street
Anytown, NJ 99999-1234

"Have you seen the latest issue of the 'Journal'? It's all 'John Sample this, John Sample that' and nothing about us."

Ms. Margo Lewis
Communicomp
Box 15725
Fort Lauderdale, Florida 33318

"This will just take a minute. It's Margo Lewis with something more important to say."

MYSTERY

6550 East 30th Street
P.O. Box 6309
Indianapolis, IN 46206-6309

BULK RATE
U.S. POSTAGE
PAID
PERMIT NO. 601

You're wanted at the scene of the crime...

MURDER BY MAIL

FREE GIFT WITH MEMBERSHIP!

"Honey, aren't you dying to know where Gordon Lewis finds all these great mysteries?"

JL400 00734022841
MR. GORDON LEWIS
PO BOX 15725
FT LAUDERDALE, FL 33318-5725

**FIG. 5–13
A, B, C, D.** Here are four envelopes, from four different mailers, each one using the combination of a cartoon and personalization in the caption. What begins as an impressive novelty becomes a ho-hum "Here's another one" because of the psychological equation: Sameness = boredom. The saving grace: Each of these represents a different business venture. It's unlikely the same person will see all four or many of the dozens of others using this same device.

  Don't imply a demand for a commitment on the envelope.

An example is an envelope that says:

> Introducing the socially responsible Visa Card.

I don't want a socially responsible Visa Card. That means every derelict in town will knock at my door, asking to use my card. This wording is a turnoff. Compare it with this:

> Something wonderful is about to happen to your phone line. Now there's a long-distance phone company that helps you save forests, animals, rivers and children—just by talking on the telephone. And it won't cost you a penny more.

See the difference? The second example is a parallel message, but disarming rather than challenging to the point of annoyance.

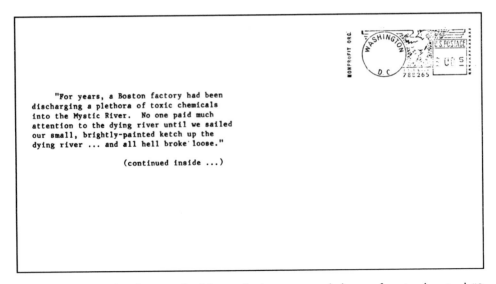

FIG. 5–14 So this factory "had been discharging a plethora of toxic chemicals"? How many recipients don't know the word *plethora*? Showing off your mammoth vocabulary on the envelope can be a costly mistake.

Conclusion

If you accept the cosmic validity of the Second Rule of Envelope Copy—the only purpose of an outer envelope is to get the recipient to open it—you automatically shove the egomaniacal component of your creativity into a corner because you force yourself into the <u>recipient's</u> position.

This means you'll subordinate all those clever ideas that revolve around overproduction, in-the-office "How clever you are" reactions, thunderbolts hurled from Mount Olympus, overproduction for no purpose, and any other decision as to what should be on the envelope <u>other than one directly related to getting that envelope opened</u>.

Please think that way. Why? Because then the person who gets your piece of mail might actually open it and see the letter inside.

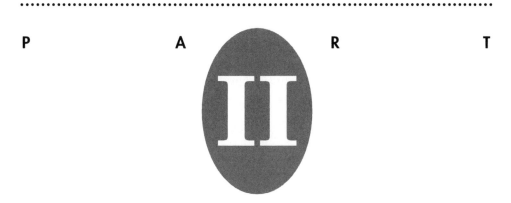

P   A   R   T

Your Library of Letter-Openings

Part II of this book isn't about letter-<u>writing</u>; it's about letter <u>openings</u>. After a brief chapter outlining the basic rules for opening letters, you have an extensive four-chapter library of 100—yes, 100—letter openings designed to grab attention for <u>any</u> circumstance, and start the sizzle.

Every writer knows the one great truth of direct response letter-writing:

> At the moment reading begins, you're a point-blank range. You'll never again have that big an advantage over the reader. So: FIRE!

This is why the choice of openings—the first one, two, or three paragraphs—has such a profound effect on response. And the power of the opening applies not only to mass mailings of two million pieces but also (often more crucially) to a single letter aimed at a key business prospect.

The advantage of having a full library of letter openings parallels having a full wardrobe. You choose this outfit for this event, that outfit for another event. Your attire always matches who you are, who you're supposed to be, and what your hosts are wearing.

Will you use every one of the 100 letters listed in this part of the book? Probably not. But as you use some of them, you'll begin to experiment and revise and tweak. You'll develop your own "masterpieces" tailored to the individual position and image you project.

Two ultimate benefits of this library of 100 openings:

1. Sorting through these openings forces you to analyze the three-way relationship—you, what you're writing about, and your target.
2. The very process of analyzing who and what prevents you from the tired sameness typical of so many other writers.

And let's hope for a third benefit: those other writers are your competitors.

6

The Importance of the Opening

"Do They Really Read Beyond the Opening?"

That question justifies this book.

Too often, your brilliant quips on page 3 go unread because your not-so-brilliant overline or Johnson Box or printed imperative at the top of page 1 or your first two paragraphs of text weren't all that brilliant.

People skip-read.

They'll read the overline, if one exists. They'll read the p.s., if one exists. They'll look at the first couple of paragraphs. <u>Then</u> they'll decide whether to read the letter or not.

Many times, curious observers outside our industry ask, "Do you really think people read all the way through a four-page letter?" My own standard answer, in three little words: "I don't care."

And I don't. I care about response, not analysis. Anyone who sees the results of competitive mailings has had too many instances of conflicting results to make a flat statement about letter length, except with unconvincing bravado.

Six-page letters have far outpulled four-page letters; two-page letters have far outpulled four-page letters. Two-paragraph letters can demolish an eight-page epic.

Which proves what?

Nothing much. One useful result is recognition that testing letter length for each individual offer pays off.

More to the point: Changing the opening—the first few paragraphs—has the capacity of generating a huge increase (or decrease) in response, often far more profound than letter length. Don't believe it? Test a couple of these openings against each other, without having a preconceived prejudice as to which one will pull better.

Changing the opening will surely change your mind.

The Three-Way Matchup: Message . . . Target . . . Motivator

If a single rule can apply to the total concept of letter openings, that rule is . . .

Match the opening to both the target and your chosen motivator, and the reader will positively read on beyond the opening.

How many "pet" openings do you have? All of us tend to run on tracks, especially when we find an opening that works for us or reflects our opinion of what our personality is.

From a virtually limitless storehouse of openings, I've chosen 100 that I regard as (1) easy to construct and (2) not yet clichés. In the next four chapters we'll take a look at each and examine the benefits and detriments of each.

Why? Because a three-way matchup—(1) what you're saying (message), (2) who your reader (target) is, and (3) the reason for responding now (motivator), when done with any professionalism—which means your persona matches these—will result in a more powerful response than any haphazard choice of openings might be. And it's the opening that either performs or ignores the matchup.

In Favor of Provocative Openings

In any list of rules for letter-writing, one applies 100 percent to the remainder of this book:

 Fire your biggest gun first.

But modify that rule with the governor on the throttle, an equally valid caution:

 Credibility is the key, opening the door to persuasion.

So: "Should the opening always be provocative?"

This is the type of question the professional letter-writer faces, internally or externally. It's the result of saturation—overawareness of apparent sameness in message-creating philosophy.

The routine answer to that question, in the late-1990s, would be <u>yes</u> for two reasons:

First, the writer (and whoever supervises or produces his/her writings) requires extraordinary discipline to obliterate a writer-as-writer reaction to the words. We see each letter 50 to 100 times before it's printed; the recipient (with luck) sees it once.

So the reader doesn't share our feeling of sameness . . . unless the same day's mail has brought a similar letter. With 100 openings listed here, and hundreds more beyond these, the odds are in our favor.

Second, a nonprovocative opening implicitly is intellectual; and in any cerebral battle, emotion will whale the tar out of intellect. A provocative opening demands ongoing reaction. Why not go with the higher percentage?

When Does a Letter Actually "Begin"?

As I've mentioned earlier in this book, calling the examples of the next four chapters "100 of the Easiest Ways to begin an Effective Sales Letter" includes a word that isn't always valid.

No, the word is neither *"Easiest"* nor *"Effective"*; it's <u>begin</u>.

That's because the first words of about a third of today's sales letters aren't the traditional beginning—"Dear Friend" or one of its latter-day surrogates. The message begins with an overline or a Johnson Box or a hunk of type, sometimes occupying half a page or more.

Are these devices good or bad? Do they help or impede the selling power of the letter?

A broad late-'90s opinion: They help if they tease the reader into the letter; they hurt if they betray the letter's intent without first justifying why we want money or action.

Have you tested the same letter with and without an overline, Johnson Box, or chunk of type? If you have, you know what works for <u>this</u> letter to <u>this</u> target at <u>this</u> time. Fact always is better than speculation as a criterion of what to do in our brutal battle of wits with "Those people" out there.

"Are There Really a Hundred Ways to Begin a Sales Letter?"

100? Oh, no. The number is well above 200. Maybe 500. Maybe 1,000. *But the question isn't valid for professional communicators because <u>it</u> leaves out the key word—<u>effective</u>.*

Without that word, any of us has a thousand ways to begin a sales letter. But any professional recognizes the difference between a way to begin a sales letter and an <u>effective</u> way to begin a sales letter.

The library of 100 letter openings described in the next four chapters isn't supposed to be an encyclopedia; it's a reminder. If we recognize how fragmentary even 100 openings are, we also recognize how many choices we have.

"With so many choices, why limit yourself to 100?"

Why, indeed? This group of 100 should qualify itself as a <u>mini</u>-group, because anyone who has started his/her own list of ways to begin a letter will testify: 100 isn't even halfway home.

The caution I do want to superimpose: Don't led a mad desire to be "different" lead you to strange, bizarre letter openings which may be different . . . but stink.

"That which is different = that which is good"—what an ugly equation!

So every one of the ways to begin a sales letter described in this group of 100 is a logical component of the communications mix. Not one of them is supposed to startle the reader without also motivating the reader.

What if having a list of <u>specific</u> openings increases the possibility a competitor might use the same one you do?

Possibility? So what. Actual occurrence? Not likely.

My point: Sameness of letter-opening isn't likely to be anywhere near as probable a factor as sameness of offer. So worry about dullness and lack of dynamism based on a "running on tracks" mindless hammering at the keyboard instead of wringing your hands over what your competition might do.

Creativity isn't limited to lifting an entire document from a template, the way you might pick up a legal form from a computer disk of standardized forms. The creative process is alive and well . . . and those who either depend on incessant repeats of the same theme, or pick up someone else's letter and change only the names, are doomed to the eternal damnation of coming in second.

This may not reassure you, if you're afraid another mailer may use the same opening you do. More reassuring: Every one of these openings—and the hundreds of others not included in this series—has been used before any of us was born.

Your advantage: No previous mailer has used them as effectively as you will.

Subtle Differences Can Be BIG Differences

A suggestion: Don't test two similar openings against each other. For example, I wouldn't test no. 8, "I have a free gift for you," against no. 10, "I have something good for you." I wouldn't test no. 2, "Ask a Provocative Question," against no. 3, "What if. . ." Why not? Because I won't learn as much as I would testing no. 8 against no. 2. Broader strokes yield broader information. Let the refinements come later.

The Benefit of Multiple Options

Having multiple options is a benefit in almost every endeavor—buying goods and services . . . evaluating job opportunities . . . choosing a permanent mate . . . running or passing . . . seats at the opera . . . and, yes, beginning a sales letter.

Which to use? The choice of openers is crucial because if you're wrong, the reader may never reach the core of your selling argument. It's parallel to an amusement park ride—a spectacular, thrilling ride—but the entrance is shabby, or the carnival barker hasn't shaved, or a casual passerby whom you don't even know says the ride isn't so hot, or the ride is enclosed in a tent and no sign gives you a clue about its capacity for exhilaration. You pass.

That's what readers do. They pass. BUT—readers aren't bugs in a bottle, a homogenized mass of ectoplasm. Some respond to one stimulus and others to another. Matching the message to the target is the peculiar edge the alert letter-writer has over the journeyman letter-writer.

The very act of selection goads us into nonautomatic decision making. We have to evaluate. So a major benefit of being able to choose from a number of possible letter openings is the enhanced possibility that we'll match the message to the recipient.

Another benefit is more subtle: Selection interferes with our natural tendency to run on tracks, to use a "standard" opening. Placing personal comfort above a commitment to communicate at maximum thrust inevitably reduces response. Even a one percent loss of response we might have had if we'd shifted our concern away from "I like to do it this way" (or worse, "We've always done it this way") is a minor disaster.

Minor? Sorry. "Disaster" parallels uniqueness and pregnancy: It exists or it doesn't, without shades of gray.

So having two options means having a greater possibility of matching the message to the target. Having 100 means an almost absolute probability of matching the message to the target.

As you note and evaluate letter openings, you'll undoubtedly see some similar to others.

Similar but not identical. . . .as no. 16, "Because you did that, we're going to do this" is similar but not identical to no. 17, "Because you are who you are, you may get special attention" or no. 36, "Because you're

'A' you're also 'B'". . .or as no. 14, The Cry of "Fire!" is similar but not identical to no. 64, the cry of "Wolf!": Someone yells (or prints) "Fire!" and those who hear (or read) may or may not feel threatened by <u>that</u> fire; someone yells (or prints) "Wolf!" and it means the wolf is stalking <u>you</u>.

Are the differences subtle and unnoticeable? Sometimes they may be subtle and unnoticeable to us as we write them; but the results <u>will</u> differ. We all know the letter is the ideal component for a test. Letters hold the motivators; and other than price, motivators are as logical a test as we can mount.

25 Key Psychological Approaches

If you limit yourself to just these 25 ways—to these old and not-so-old dependables—you'll still have a lifetime of variety because these cover the key psychological approaches—happy, sad . . . aggressive, pleading . . . sophisticated, straightforward. This is a tight grab-bag of guaranteed-useful openings.

We'll start with my personal favorite, one which can't miss if you're determined to proclaim affinity with the reader and have that reader accept your relationship.

1. "If you're like me . . ."

My high regard for this opening stems from two bases. First, it strides across all barriers of consumer/business, highbrow/lowbrow. Second, it establishes immediate rapport. This works as a receptivity softener for messages from an anonymous signatory; better yet, it adds arm-across-the-shoulder "buddy-binder" to a communication signed by a recognizable power name.

I sometimes use "If you're like I am" instead of "If you're like me." Why? "If you're like I am" seems just a tad less presumptuous than "If you're like me" because it's a tad less all-inclusive.

Usually, the word following "If you're like me" is an automatic "you" or, to complete a parallel, "you're." You can see why this opening is implicity reader-involving.

I take a parental view toward this opening, and I'm torn between statesmanship—directing me to share it with those who haven't yet sampled its joys—and proprietorship—predicting application of the deadly rule:

> Overuse = abuse.

Statesmanship wins out because I suspect, from my own incoming mail, word is already out.

A letter from a scuba diving organization begins:

> Dear Diving Enthusiast:
> You and I are part of a remarkable group.
> Someone who's never been on a scuba dive could never understand it.

The National Center for DATABASE MARKETING, inc.

Administrative Offices: Suite 888 • 14618 Tyler Foote • Nevada City, CA 95959-8599 • USA • (916) 292-3000 • FAX (916) 292-3504
Research Institute: Suite 11G • 435 E. 65th Street • New York, NY 10021 • (212) 465-1801

ADVISORY COUNCIL

CHAIRMAN
Howard E. Flood
General Manager
McGraw-Hill Inc.

John A. Adams, President
DialAmerica Marketing, Inc.
Ed Burnett, President
Ed Burnett Consultants, Inc.
R. Bruce Carroll
President
Compusearch
Richard J. Courtheoux
President
Precision Marketing Corp.
Charles A. Eby
Director, Technical Services
Fidelity Investments
Bruce Gache, President
Prudential Mail Marketing, Inc.
Jerry A. Goldstone, Publisher
Business Communications Review
Ashleigh P. Groce
VP/Account Director
Leo Burnett, U.S.A.
John E. Groman, Senior VP
Epsilon
C. Rose Harper
Chairman & CEO
The Kleid Company Inc.
Victor Hunter, President
Hunter Business Direct, Inc.
John H. Jones, Executive VP
Webcraft Technologies, Inc.
Philip Kotler
Professor of Marketing
Northwestern University
Charles D. Morgan, Jr.
Chairman of the Board & CEO
Acxiom Corporation
Andrea R. Nierenberg
Publisher
Target Marketing Magazine
Robert Perlstein
Information Advisor
Lifestyle Change Marketing
Stan Rapp, Co-founder
Rapp & Collins, USA
John Stevenson
Executive Vice President
Krupp/Taylor USA
Anver S. Suleiman, President
The Marketing Federation
Henry O. Westendarp, President
Strategic Marketing Systems, Inc.
Jack D. Wolf
Corporate Senior VP
M/A/R/C Inc.

EXECUTIVE DIRECTOR
F.E. (Skip) Andrew

~~January 21, 1992~~
(Update Sent at Request)

TO: Marketing Management

FROM: Skip Andrew

SUBJECT: Smart Marketing for Uncertain Times

If you're like I am, you're searching for every way possible to leverage each marketing penny -- and probably having to live with budget cuts, even as you're held accountable for profits in tight, competitive markets.

The enclosed reply card provides just one example of what I'm doing to cut costs without losing important prospects. I send you lots of mail because you, or someone in your organization, said you wanted it. But I never mail more than a one-time inquiry generator to mass mailing lists. The resulting database regularly yields almost 20% in sales -- at a 75% cost savings over tested controls! And, of course, database marketers use a whole host of other tricks, tips, and techniques to beat their competitor's ho-hum, habitual programs.

Maybe that explains why so many savvy marketers have already registered for the encore of the 4th Annual Conference, "Database Marketing -- The Newest Breakthroughs in Profit Strategies and Tactics," at the fabulous all-new Chicago Sheraton Hotel and Towers, July 8-10, 1992. I hope you, too, will join us!

Sincerely,

Skip Andrew

Francis E. (Skip) Andrew
Executive Director

P.S. Only this Conference gives you a feast of new ways to cut costs and increase profits -- and many of the latest insider methodologies don't require huge outlays of capital, computer expertise, or even new software. Over 70+ in-depth concurrent expert briefings, cream-of-the-crop exhibitor vendors, a 900+ page Conference Workbook, and networking opportunities galore! If your company wants to make it big during these uncertain times, you will want to invest in this unprecedented event! See page 45 of the enclosed for making your tentative, no obligation reservation now!

FIG. 7-1 Letter-opening type 1: "If you're like I am . . ." is a bonding letter opening. Opinion: What follows this opening should have heads nodding in agreement, quickly. A ponderous 35-word first sentence requires "breathing stops," slowing down comprehension—and acceptance of the bonded relationship.

See the exclusivity building here? See how much stronger this opening is than "You're part of a remarkable group"?

A variation on the you-and-I theme is "The source from which I got your name tells me. . . ." This opening isn't as convivial nor as personal because it separates writer and reader instead of welding them together, and the writer runs the risk of antagonizing the reader instead of drawing him/her into the net. The value of this variation is its side-stepping of circumstances in which the reader thinks, "Who the hell is he to think I'm like him?"

A recent letter within the communications community begins:

> Dear Direct Marketing Colleague:
>
> The source of your name given to Bob Stone and me indicates to us that you're obviously deeply involved in direct marketing and want to continue learning about it.

I don't like that word *learn* because, sent to professionals, this approach suggests the writer thinks they aren't quite professional; nevertheless, the concept is arresting.

2. Ask a provocative question.

This one isn't as automatic as the first suggested letter opening because it doesn't indicate what the question is. Nor does it help to point out that the question depends on what we're selling.

I'm guessing that thousands of sales letter writers sense the value of an interrogative opening. . .but don't recognize the qualifier, *provocative*. Some uses of this opening are ludicrous; others are preposterous. What destroys their value is their disregard for the reader's own experiential background.

Lack of understanding leads to reader rejection because the writer opens the letter with a question whose relevance the reader dismisses without analysis.

For example: If I open a letter with, "Do you know the name of the ninth incarnation of Vishnu?" your response has to be,

a. "Are you nuts?"
b. "Who cares?" or

The Bloch School
Center for Direct Marketing

University of Missouri-Kansas City
5100 Rockhill Road
Kansas City, Missouri 64110-2499

816 235-2208
FAX 816 235-2312

**Marketing/Direct
Marketing Advisory Board**

Bob White, Chairman
Marketing Communications, Inc.

Martin Baier
Center for Direct Marketing

Bill Berkley
Tension Envelope Corporation

Chuck Curtis
Valentine-Radford Advertising

Bernard P. Erdman
Path Management Industries, Inc.

Pat Friesen
J. Schmid & Associates

Earl Hogan
Hogan & Associates

Janine Hron
Crittenton Center

Annie Hurlbut
The Peruvian Connection

Bob Johnson
Marion Merrell Dow, Inc.

James McQuaid
Metromail Corporation

Dr. Richard Montesi
Direct Marketing Educational
Foundation, Inc.

Leo Reichert
UARCO, Inc.

Bob Stone
Stone & Adler

Bob Walsh
Directories America

Bernie Webster
Center for Direct Marketing

John Wurst
Henry Wurst, Inc.

Ex Officio Members

Greg Bruner
Old American Insurance

Debbie Hagen
Fleishman-Hilliard, Inc.

Ron Juergensen
Juergensen Advertising

Raj Arora
Bill Eddy
Jerry Hamilton
Richard Hamilton
Bloch School, UMKC

Dear Direct Marketing Colleague:

The source of your name given to Bob Stone and me indicates to us that you're obviously deeply involved in direct marketing and want to continue learning about it.

You may be uncertain as to how this program can give you an even greater understanding of direct marketing than you already have. If so, take into consideration that the average level of experience of those who have been professionally certified under this new program is many years.

One graduate, with more than 22 years experience in direct marketing, had this to say when asked to critique the PDM certification program:

> "Other advanced programs I've attended over the years have not been as <u>intensive</u> as this one, particularly with respect to strategic decision-making. The breadth of experience which presenters and classmates alike brought to the program will prove invaluable to me in the years ahead."

Please realize that there are many comments that I could share with you if space permitted, but rather than taking my word for it, I invite you to call <u>any or all</u> of the people who have successfully completed the professional certification requirements. I have compiled a complete listing of our participants. It is available for your review by request.

The list of participating companies includes several Fortune 500 companies already heavily involved in direct marketing -- such as Anheuser-Busch, Apple Computers, Kraft General Foods, GTE, National Liberty Insurance, Meredith Publishing and others. There are many small, lesser known companies as well.

If you're still undecided and have other specific questions you want answered, please don't hesitate to call me now at (816) 235-2208. If I'm not in when you call, ask for Bernie Webster, my associate director.

Please don't delay, as the class that will begin on October 15 is <u>limited</u> to the first 35 qualified enrollees. It will not be offered again for one full year.

Phone, fax (816) 235-2312, or mail your registration as soon as possible.

Sincerely,

Martin Baier

Martin Baier
Director

an equal opportunity institution

FIG. 7-2 Letter-opening type 1: Envision a direct marketing problem: No list can segment direct marketer names according to number of years' experience. So this approach straddles the problem of reaching those whose experiential background might cause rejection of this letter's assumptions. Suppose segmentation were possible. This letter, hitting a veteran direct marketer whose years of experience parallel those of the writer, would be considerably less likely to provoke a positive response than an "If you're like me" opening.

c. "Something is wrong with you, and if I did know the name of the ninth incarnation of Vishnu, there'd be something wrong with me."

Now, suppose I open that same letter with, "Why do I think you might know the name of the ninth incarnation of Vishnu?" I've added the element of provocation. You're involved even though you haven't the foggiest notion of where I'm heading. (Neither of us has the foggiest notion of what the name of the ninth incarnation of Vishnu is.)

Would "Why should you know the name of the ninth incarnation of Vishnu?" be as on-target? Certainly not. You at once penetrate my veil: I'm taking a superior position and I'm selling something, both positions perilous in establishing rapport.

Questions are easy, and that may be why they rank number one as misused openers. A letter from a trade magazine opens with a double question:

HAVE YOU NOTICED?

Dear Business Marketing Reader:
    Have you noticed the major commitment that Business Marketing has made to help you do your job better?

The lack of a question mark is the letter-writer's, not mine. But that isn't the major flaw here. What's wrong is the thrust of the questions: They're totally, baldy self-serving. The all-caps first question grabs the reader; the second question takes off the mask too soon. This opening parallels the windbag dinner-partner who says, "I've talked about myself long enough. Now let's talk about you. What do _you_ think of me?"

3. "What if . . ."

"What if" openings are often the instruments of choice for a touchstone opening:

- What if you had bought Miami Beach property in the 1920s?
- What if you could go back to the day you graduated from college?

Business Marketing

HAVE YOU NOTICED IT?

Dear Business Marketing Reader:

Have you noticed the major commitment that Business Marketing has made to helping you do your job better. How it has greatly expanded its coverage of:

* advertising and marketing activity at the nation's leading business marketers--from giants like IBM to fast-growing pacesetters such as Conner Peripherals, a fast-track manufacturer of disk drives who cracked the Japanese market.

* hot, new trends such as our advance word on partnering, outsourcing and target selling that help you to stay ahead of your competitors.

* "action plans" you can put to work immediately. From how to make more sales at trade shows, to how to harness the rapidly growing field of marketing automation.

It's our constant evolution, our commitment to never standing still, that keeps Business Marketing the leader in the field of business-to-business selling. It's why we number successful executives like Lee Iacocca, Chairman of Chrysler Corp.; Paul Allaire, Xerox's Chairman and John Sculley, Chairman of Apple Computer, Inc. among our avid readers. It's why we constantly receive comments like these:

> "The article on the CEO's knowledge of marketing was G-R-E-A-T."
> Brad Stribling, President
> The Marketing Group

> "Every time I get a new issue of Business Marketing, I keep saying I should write Cliff Mulcahy (publisher) and tell him how terrific the magazine looks."
> Betsy Lembeck, Vice President,
> Management Supervisor, Ogilvy & Mather

Comments like this tell us we're doing the job. That we're helping you use the many and varied tools in the marketing mix more effectively. Helping you improve sales force results by reporting on the many innovations in automation. Helping you to stay abreast of the most recent marketing and sales developments at the nation's leading corporations.

Which brings me to the important reason for writing to you.

(over, please)

Circulation Department • 965 E. Jefferson Avenue • Detroit, MI 48207

FIG. 7-3 Letter-opening type 2: This letter has a heavy boldface question as its overline . . . and opens with another question. Problem: The questions are self-serving, not reader-serving. Questions have power in any component of any medium, but relating the question to the target individual is the key to getting attention.

- What if you had been in the audience at Gettysburg in 1863 when Lincoln gave his speech?

"What if" also fits a "hurl down the gauntlet" approach:

- What if I could prove you can make a thousand dollars before sundown today?
- What if you could double your reading speed?

Obviously the word *you* is a significant factor in a "What if" opening. Without *you*, the reader has the option of translating "What if" as "So what?" "What if every member of Congress were to resign?" (Yeah, I know: Good idea.)

4. Suggest a cataclysmic decision.

This one bursts with power; but as the automobile commercials say, don't try this at home. It's the first one in this group requiring the professional laying on of hands.

At the fingertips of an amateur or dilettante writer, cataclysm can degenerate into comedy. "The decision you make today can. . ." is a grabber if the recipient of your message at once agrees with two precanned conclusions: first you're in a position to judge and guarantee; second, the decision is possible and logical.

A fund-raising organization has this cataclysm as its opening:

> Dear Friend,
> I've enclosed a Life or Death Seed Catalog for you.

Okay, what's wrong with that? Right! We just can't think of a seed catalog as a life or death determinant. We'll explore this example more fully in the next chapter in a discussion of no. 29 (I've enclosed . . .").

The same organization follows the formula more logically—if with a mildly contrived device—in this opening:

> In the ten seconds it took you to open and begin to read this letter,
> five children died from the effects of malnutrition or disease
> somewhere in the world.

United States Committee for

unicef

United Nations Children's Fund
333 East 38th St. New York, NY 10016

Hugh Downs
Chair

Dear Friend,

I've enclosed a Life or Death Seed Catalog for you.

I call this the Life or Death Seed Catalog because what you do after looking through this catalog could help save the life of a small child ... a child like Youssouf.

Youssouf is a little boy who lives in Mali, a landlocked nation of the African Sahara. Mali was once called the "granary of Africa" because its farms were so productive.

But the horrible droughts of the 1980s destroyed Mali's agriculture. In some areas 80 percent of all livestock perished during those years. People were so hungry that many farmers like Youssouf's father were forced to eat their seed stocks -- the very seeds they need to plant new crops. They destroyed their futures -- in a desperate attempt to keep their families alive!

Now Mali's farmers face the nearly impossible task of trying to rebuild their harvests and livestock herds while trying to feed millions of hungry people ... without good seeds.

They may lose the battle ... and as always, the children will suffer most.

Youssouf's memories of the worst years of the drought are surprisingly vivid for a child who was only a toddler at the time. But I suppose that's understandable since he nearly died of starvation, and two of his sisters did die during the drought.

Even now, though the rains have returned, three out of ten children in Mali are still malnourished.

Youssouf is now old enough to help his parents in the fields ... and old enough to know that without good seeds there will be no harvest ... and his family will again go hungry.

That's why UNICEF needs our help to provide seeds. We must help the farmers of Mali rebuild their crops of millet, sorghum, maize, rice, groundnuts, and bourgou.

Bourgou is a perfect example of the help that's needed. It's a plant that once grew in most of the rivers and streams of

over, please

FIG. 7-4 Letter-opening type 4: Even after the explanation in the second paragraph, the reader has difficulty relating a seed catalog to a life or death situation. Rewording would help this letter—whose thrust is more intellectualized than a desperate situation warrants—penetrate the reader's apathy.

I'd have left off "somewhere in the world" because it shifts the reader somewhat out of the arena. And, yes, the opening is a mite trite. But it grabs.

Cataclysmic declarations should have two mechanical components: a cut-off date and a suggestion of exclusivity. If the reader concludes the entire world has the opportunity to profit from the identical decision, the argument doesn't work because the cataclysm is too universal to generate a head of steam.

5. "I [We] need help."

At one time a generic fund-raising opening, this one suffers from overuse and from sociological evolution (devolution?). Among fund raisers it's just as popular as ever, even though the impact isn't as formidable as it once was. Its use is actually growing because it no longer is the exclusive property of fund raising.

"We need help" flourished during the 1950–80 period—a kinder, gentler time, when guilt was a more automatic motivator than if has become in the self-centered 1990s. Many of today's old-line donors are holdovers from "We need help" recruitment campaigns of 15 to 30 years ago.

Oh, sure, fund raisers still use "We need help," and it still pulls well enough, for some, to maintain position. That's one reason it's on the list. But another reason is the spillover from fund raising to commerce. A paradox! Business mailers have discovered <u>need for dominance</u> as a burgeoning motivator. By appealing to this need for dominance . . . by putting their target in a position of make-or-break supremacy . . . shrewd mailers have picked up the slack.

Few commercial mailings use the words "We need help" because 1990s consumers don't buy from weaklings. Instead, the mailers use a form of primitive psychology we all recognize when it's used on somebody else and seldom recognize when it's used on us:

- You're the one person in a thousand who can. . .
- I want your opinion on something. Will you tell me what you really think?
- I admit: I need a favor from you.

6. "Congratulations!"

In for a penny, in for a pound: If you're using that single word, I suggest following with an exclamation point, not a period. A calm congratulation has its uses, but calm doesn't match the single word. Mogul-to-mogul might be, "I congratulate you." That's not exclamatory. The single word *is*, which means you use it only if what follows justifies the exclamation.

A letter to one of my decoy names begins:

> DEAR H. GORDON,
>   Congratulations! It's my great pleasure to welcome you to all the benefits and privileges of a Columbia House Club membership.
>
>   Your Pre-Approved MusiCard means you can receive our best offer to first-time members—not available through newspaper or magazine ads—but reserved for a select group of music lovers like you.

Opinion: Although I'd never use the indefinite article to describe the membership—I'd say "your Columbia House Club membership" or plain "Columbia House membership," not "*a* Columbia House Club membership"—this letter does maintain its congratulatory character. It adds automatic impact by capitalizing Pre-Approved MusiCard. Capitalization adds validation.

But "first-time members"? If they have any kind of database, they've suppressed lapsed members, goniff members, and users of stolen credit cards; so if they want to build rapport with me, why not maintain the tone of invitation?

Anyway, the point isn't merciless dissection of a cold list letter. It's recognition of "Congratulations!" as a dynamic opener, with the caution that you can't hit and run with it.

A properly-used "Congratulations!" letter, from a credit card company, came to my wife:

> Dear Margo E. Lewis:
> Congratulations! Because of the exemplary way you have handled your account you qualify for our new low variable rate on your Norwest credit card account. It's our way of saying "Thank you" and to show you how much we value your business.

WELCOME TO

COLUMBIA HOUSE

6/92-L

MusiCard
Priority Member Status*

H. GORDON

◄ Your name on the enclosed MusiCard
entitles you to choose immediately
8 CDs Or
12 Cassettes FREE!
with membership

DEAR H. GORDON,

Congratulations! It's my great pleasure to welcome you
to all the benefits and privileges of a Columbia House
Club membership.

Your Pre-Approved MusiCard means you can receive our
best offer to first-time members--not available through
newspaper or magazine ads--but reserved for a select group
of music lovers like you.

> **Choose 8 compact discs or 12 cassettes FREE,**
> **plus have the chance to get bonus selections**
> **when you join our exciting Club.**

It's a fabulous deal either way. You can choose from any
of the hundreds of top selections in the listing enclosed
including artists like:

> GARTH BROOKS...BRUCE SPRINGSTEEN...
> BONNIE RAITT...U2...

All your personal favorites are here for the picking.

> **PICK 8 CDs OR**
> **12 CASSETTES--FREE--NOW.**

When your free shipment arrives, be sure to jot the
membership number onto the back of your MusiCard. And you're
set! About every 4 weeks (13 times a year) you'll get our
Magazine, with hundreds of choices. And, up to 6 times a year,
you'll receive offers of Special Selections (usually at
discounts off regular Club prices). That's up to 19
opportunities a year to build your music library.

> **CHOOSE ONLY SELECTIONS YOU WANT.**

If you want the "Feature Selection" of the month, chosen
by our expert panel in the music category that interests you

(over please)

FIG. 7-5 Letter-opening type 6: Can you envision any opening for this letter that
can match the effectiveness of "Congratulations!"? The word sets a receptive mood for whatever the offer may be. And it has another advantage:
Any text that follows can pound away at urgency and reader obligation.

The pitch is the standard credit card "Transfer other balances to this account" sales argument, but couching it in a congratulatory message makes it both more readable and more palatable.

7. "I invite you. . ."

This is the sibling of "Congratulations."

A point we all know (anticipating Opening No. 9): The invitation has to follow through <u>as an invitation</u>. No, this doesn't mean locking into an invitation-size format and including an engraved enclosure . . . although some of the more thoughtful invitations do this. It does mean keeping the <u>tone</u> invitational throughout the letter, never lapsing into hard-sell or going out of character.

I have a letter from a publication which begins:

> Dear Nominee Elect:
> It is my pleasure, to inform you that you have been elected as an Associate Member of the American Museum of Natural History.
>
> We would request that you return the enclosed invitation as soon as possible, indicating whether or not you will be accepting this election. Your temporary Associate identification card is enclosed. You may sign it and begin using it immediately.

Except for the comma in the first sentence and the factory-like phrase "identification card" instead of "membership card" and the "mother, may I?" tone of "You may sign it," this is a model of its type. One clever touch: Moving into the subjunctive to avoid the appearance of pressure—"We would request . . ." instead of the more imperative "We request . . ."

The text of the letter does point out benefits other than the opportunity to get the magazine, such as free admission to the Museum and various discounts; and it closes with a reaffirmation of its point: "We put a great deal of care and thought into the election process. . . ."

Even knowing the ploy, who can resist an invitation that stays in character?

**United States
Golf Association®**

P.O. Box 746
Far Hills, NJ 07931-0746
1-800-223-0041

Dear Fellow Golfer:

I'm writing to invite you to become a USGA Member. I'd like you to join golfers all across the country who are choosing to help us better serve golf -- and ensure that it remains the great game we enjoy today.

Our goal is aggressive. We want to add 100,000 new Members to our roster by March 31st. But the rewards of membership will be great. Contributions from golfers, like you, will help the USGA, a non-profit organization, continue its vital programs and services.

Some of the challenges we face this year include conducting research to develop improved turfgrasses, and examining the impact golf courses have on our environment. Our equipment testing programs will ensure that skill remains the major determinant of success. And the USGA's junior golf programs will continue to give kids of all ages and backgrounds the chance to discover this wonderful game.

When you become a USGA Member, you'll gain something immeasurable: the personal satisfaction of making a difference for golf. Plus, you'll receive many tangible membership benefits, including a year's subscription to the USGA's *Golf Journal* and the *Rules of Golf.*

USGA membership is an investment in our game. I've made that investment, and I hope you will too. Our Membership Drive celebrates that commitment, so help us reach our goal by March 31st. Please join me as a USGA Member today.

Sincerely,

Arnold Palmer

Arnold Palmer
National Chairman
USGA Members Program

P.S. Take part in our 1994 Membership Drive today, and save $10 off your first year of USGA membership, and on a gift membership as well!

FIG. 7–6   Letter-opening type 7: When you get an invitation, one question comes to mind at once: What are the benefits of membership? "I'd like you to join golfers all across the country who are choosing to help us better serve golf—and ensure that it remains the great game we enjoy today" is just so many words. The USGA wants "to add 100,000 members." This is just about as exclusive as being invited to have your name in the phone book.

8. "I have a free gift for you."

Over a long period of years, advertisers and marketers have agreed that "free gift" is a redundancy, and all have agreed it works. So free gift it is.

Okay, what is a free gift?

Two schools of thought on this. One is the voice of utter integrity: It's free only if it's free. The other is the voice of sales logic: It's free if you don't pay extra for it.

Neither of these addresses the matter from the proper point of view—reader reaction. We have another mini-rule:

 A free gift as a letter opening has impact in direct ratio to the reader's recognition of the value of that gift.

I bring this up because we all damage future impact of the much-scarred phrase "free gift" by calling a sample issue of a magazine a free gift. It isn't. It's a free issue, or a free sample or a free look. A token outside the arena of what we're selling is a gift.

A magazine renewal letter states in an 18-point overline:

Here's a free gift for you.

The letter is well-written, except for a mechanical decision with which I don't agree: Paragraphs aren't indented. And a curiosity: Except for the aristocratic putoff "We would now like to reward you for your loyalty," the gift is buried in the text. After the overline, it isn't mentioned until the fourth paragraph. Good or bad?

I'm not privy to the results, and I don't know whether this subscription renewal letter is a control that survived an onslaught by challengers. Yes, I do understand the nature of thanking the subscriber before banging away at the gift. Ah, but I don't understand using "Here's a free gift for you!" in 18-point Garamond, then holding back on what it is (a shoe bag set—nice!) until paragraph 4.

One compromise, using the combination of "free gift" to gain attention and then expostulating on the main issue before getting to the gift in the body of the letter: Circle that fourth paragraph.

2nd Reminder

Dear Subscriber:

The midnight Hour has arrived. As you know, last year, the Mailing Rates raised dramatically. We, at the Lotto Advisor decided to bite the bullet and hold off passing along this increased cost to you, but that is all about to end.

We are going to have to increase our subscription rates in July 1992 to make up for the added expense. Therefore, we are writing to GIVE YOU ANOTHER CHANCE TO JOIN THE LOTTO ADVISOR SOCIETY AND SUBCRIBE, OR TO RENEW YOUR CURRENT SUBSCRIPTION UP TO THREE YEARS AT THE OLD DISCOUNTED RATES.

ACT NOW... AND RECEIVE YOUR FREE GIFTS ABSOLUTELY FREE...

We extend a cordial invitation for you to join our LOTTO ADVISOR Society. Enjoy a year's FREE membership, including a one year subscription to the LOTTO ADVISOR magazine...

for dues of only $9.

We'd like you to know that the modest cost of membership (savings of $19) is only the first of many pleasant surprises in store for you. As a subscriber of LOTTO ADVISOR you'll be continuously receiving important information you can learn from... enjoy and... use to win.

And equally important, as a subscriber, you'll receive:

One year of the LOTTO ADVISOR magazine.
    In-depth background information on the best US and World lottery games. Winning methods and strategies that have won millions. How to play money-saving games, how to enter the one-billion dollar "El Gordo" game, and much more.

Superb "What's Hot" publication.
    In 1992 you'll discover six winning methods used by six Jackpot winners..plus two ways of playing you should avoid!

Odds Improvement Chart. Learn how to improve your odds to win second prizes or even Jackpot.

▲ *Don't pay postage! Tear along this perforation. Apply glue, fold over and seal.* ▲

Cash now, not over 20 years.
    There are dozens of cash games that pay up to millions in one lump-sum payment. Now, you can cash in without any delay and enjoy your winnings immediately.

Play for as low as 7¢ a game...every week.
    For the next 12 months we'll keep you informed about where and how to enter the best lottery games for as low as 7¢ per game (instead of spending $1 per game or more).

Of course, there's more to a subscription than just the magazine. You're also invited to share other LOTTO ADVISOR Society privileges. You'll enjoy *FREE* information on **Hot Numbers**, **20 Best Bets**, plus...*FREE* **Jackpot Traps** intended as an inexpensive way to build a home library of the most successful winning methods used by multi-million dollar Jackpot winners. Plus we'll enter you into:

Subscribe today and we'll enter you into a   This is your sweepstakes entry I.D. LLAS20 027

$520 Million Australian Sweepstakes

How does the world's largest "GIGANTIC $520 Million Aussie Sweepstakes" work? Each week you'll be entered in a draw to enter *52 WEEKS FREE PLAY* in Australia which pays out $10 Million weekly—that's a total prize pool of *$520 MILLION TO BE WON.* Wins (all free of Australian Tax) are paid in one *LUMP SUM*—what you win is what you get right *NOW*!

Can You win more? Yes! There are many other *Australian Tax FREE prizes** to be won! On receipt of your entry (you'll receive it directly from Australia) you'll be entered into the *$520M Sweepstakes* on an *ONGOING BASIS*! So when you win a prize in the sweepstakes you go *STRAIGHT BACK* into the draw to win the sweepstakes again —*EVERY WEEK!*

How can I learn about my entry and winnings? You'll receive *PERSONAL* computerized result sheets. And when you win millions, we'll notify YOU!

• Even though all the winnings are Tax Free in Australia you must pay your taxes within USA. Void where prohibited.

CUTLINE

I honestly believe you'll enjoy being a member of the LOTTO ADVISOR Society...and, because this may be the only invitation you'll receive this year, I urge you to mail the subscription renewal order form with your payment today. If you prefer, call toll free 1-800-229-2946 and use your credit card. Meanwhile, I look forward to welcoming you into the Lotto Advisor Society and sending your magazine and all the *FREE* gifts.

Sincerely,

Robert Serotic
Robert Serotic
Editor

FIG. 7–7 Letter-opening type 9: The overline is too long to produce much of a wallop. But the principal deficiency of this letter's opening is presenting an "As you know. . ." description the reader feels is trivial and unrelated to him/her. False heroics ("We . . . decided to bite the bullet and hold off passing along this increased cost to you") are a cliché. Follow "As you know. . ." with apparent benefit for maximum impact.

9. "As you know. . ."

A classic way of establishing rapport is telling the reader something he/she already knows. . .or thinks he/she should know.

"As you know" is one of the great argumentative ploys of our time. You can use it without fear to drive an imperative all the way to the insult border because those three little words say to the reader, "You and I are knowledge-confrères."

The psychological value of "As you know" goes beyond artificial comradeship. The reader is supposed to think, "I <u>do</u> know," and, depending on how professionally the message is transmitted, the reader's previously nonexistent position is (a) established and (b) polarized.

So "As you know" enables opinion to masquerade as fact. It can sell where a bald imperative can't.

And, in bumbling hands, it can turn off the reader before the real point of the message ever gets under way.

A letter from an Australian Lottery publication begins:

> Dear Subscriber:
> The midnight hour has arrived. As you know, last year, the Mailing Rates raised dramatically. We, at the Lotto Advisor decided to bite the bullet and hold off passing along this increased cost to you, but all that is about to end.

Punctuation problems aside, do you see what's wrong with this use of "As you know . . ."? The writer wastes it on a point the reader has to regard as trivial and without mutual import.

A credit card company drops "As" but uses the device:

> Dear H.G. Lewis: *(I hate that impersonal personalization)*
> You know that motivating your company's top performers can have a crucial impact on the bottom line, especially in today's competitive market.

Again the writer wastes the device, because "As you know" as an opener has to tie itself to the firing of a big gun. This generalization is at best a self-serving little gun.

10. "I have something good for you."

This one is dangerous if the opening makes the promise and the text becomes a letdown.

My friend Bob Dunhill of Dunhill International List Company sent me a fund-raising letter from a college. It begins:

> Dear Mr. Dunhill:
> Bill is a student here at Cumberland College.
>
> And, he is probably going to save you money on your federal income tax return.
>
> Incredible?
>
> But true. Please let me explain.

Well, the explanation, on page two, is that Bill is going to save Bob Dunhill money because if we help him go to college by making a contribution, Bill won't be a tax burden.

You know what this is like? It parallels the fellow who kept a bank from being robbed. He changed his mind.

Another example of this tenth opening is an eight-page document—printed, not typed—with the subtly condescending overline, "How to Get The Life You Want!" (I should say insulting, not condescending, because it was addressed to me, and I already have the life I want.) To list and database companies I repeat the old saw: Garbage in, garbage out.

The letter begins:

> Dear Friend,
> My name is Virginia Lloyd and I have something valuable to give you. This letter is very important to you because it details how you can dramatically improve your life, in every way that you want.
>
> First let me tell you that I am a successful author, businesswoman, and mother. If you wish, I can furnish you with my complete personal references and business credentials.

The letter goes on to tell me she transformed her life 22 years ago from bad debt and bad health to financial freedom and vitality.

Lady, you may be a successful author, but you aren't a successful sales letter writer. This technique is about 20 years out of fashion . . .

"The Sedona Release® Technique has always been a lifesaver for me."

Sally Jessy Raphael,
Emmy Award Winning Talk Show Host

Lester Levenson,
founder of the Sedona Institute, is a self-made multi-millionaire who has unselfishly devoted the last thirty-five years of his life and his entire personal fortune to helping others discover the way to the success, health, peace, and happiness he achieved over thirty-eight years ago.

How to Get The Life You Want!

Dear Friend,

My name is Virginia Lloyd and I have something valuable to give you. This letter is very important to you because it details how you can dramatically improve your life, in every way that you want.

First, let me tell you that I am a successful author, businesswoman and mother. If you wish, I can furnish you with my complete personal references and business credentials.

And second, I don't believe in wasting your time, so I want you to know that I have proven to myself that anyone can live a life of abundance. You can live a life filled with financial freedom, health and peace of mind, too. And, you should want to prove this to yourself.

You may not know this but you have actually been walking around with an ability that you've rarely, if ever, used. And, this ability is the key to improving your life beyond your greatest hopes and dreams. It is my sincerest wish that you become aware of it, and start using it, as soon as you can.

That's why this letter is so important to you. Please read it at least twice. Then contact me as soon as you can. Any delay can prolong needless suffering and cost you the abundant life you deserve.

By the way, please keep this letter because much of the importance and meaning within it may be overlooked by you the first time you read it. Losing it could be a mistake.

Twenty-two years ago, I transformed my life from one of constant money worries, health problems, guilt feelings, fears about going after what I wanted, inability to speak up for myself and marital problems into a life of financial freedom, vitality, contentment, fulfillment and peace.

Since then, I have also directly and indirectly helped over 7,000 other people, just like you and me, to remember and use this ability to improve their lives too. Some have become the biggest stars on TV and in Hollywood. And, others have risen to leadership roles in top Fortune 500 companies and in their own private enterprises. (They all weren't stars or financial or personal successes when I first met them.)

Later in this letter, you'll read what Sally Jessy Raphael, Shirley Jones, Barry Farber, Dr. David Hawkins (associate of Nobel Prize Laureate, Dr. Linus Pauling) and others have to say about how their lives have improved by using this ability.

As I've already said, I've become an author and have written extensively on this important subject. One of my books, CHOOSE FREEDOM, outlines my teacher's life and how he came to discover this remarkable ability at the age of 42...after being given only three months to live.

This book tells how this compassionate, giving man, Lester Levenson, so gently and effortlessly guided me to discovering it within myself. Lester is 81 now and he is the embodiment of unshakable peace and radiant health. Later, I'll tell you how you can get your free copy of this book.

In addition, I want you to know that Lester has given away a multi-million dollar fortune to establish the Sedona Institute - our NOT FOR PROFIT INSTITUTE - dedicated to one purpose...sharing Lester's discovery...which is the how to of remembering this ability.

(continue reading my letter on page 2)

FIG. 7–8 Letter-opening type 10: The setup of this letter is confusing. The first sentence begins, "My name is Virginia Lloyd," but the photograph is Lester Levenson. His segment should have been boxed or set off as a sidebar. The letter makes one of the most common miscalculations in force-communication: It misuses "important" by using the word to lecture. (If you were to read the entire letter, you'd find a multitude of buried nuggets.) A suggestion: if you use the "I have something good for you" opening, tell the reader fast and hard what that "something good" is. Another point, which applies to business deals as well as direct response: Don't offer references unless the other party asks for them. Presenting references without demand automatically makes you the lesser of the parties to a negotiation.

and even then, those who wrote classic "I transformed my life and so can you" letters didn't beg the issue and weaken their image by offering references—<u>references</u>, for God's sake—before even making a point.

11. A specific episode narrative

Fund raisers know three communication truths too many writers of conventional sales messages either ignore or don't discern:

1. Episodes outpull statistics.
2. Examples are more credible than exhortation.
3. Coupling examples <u>with</u> exhortation geometrically expands the emotional impact of a message.

Outside the fund-raising arena, even the giants stumble over that tricky third truth. They unearth esoteric or confusing examples the typical reader can't penetrate, or they become shrill, fearing any message short of screaming on paper won't penetrate the reader's apathy.

Difficulty of execution isn't germane to <u>this</u> list of openings. If we limit ourselves to the basic concept, a specific episode narrative, professionalism requires no more than finding an episode which makes your point for you.

A flawed example from—where else?—the world of fund raising:

> Dear Friend,
>   Unlike most kids, 12-year-old Patrick J.* rarely looks forward to the end of a school day.
>
>   That's because his journey home is often a terrifying one. Clutching his books tightly in his hands, Patrick runs at top speed through his South Bronx neighborhood, fearful of getting caught in the crossfire of a drug deal gone bad, or terrorized by a street gang. . . .

I warned you it was flawed. That asterisk is <u>deadly</u>. I'll interrupt my own narrative to repeat the easiest rule ever offered to a communicator, <u>The Asterisk Exception</u>:

When should you use asterisks in a direct response message? Never.

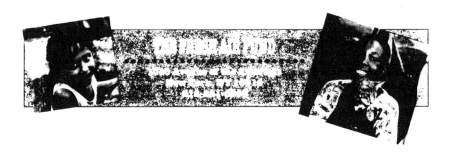

Dear Friend,

    Unlike most kids, 12-year-old Patrick J.* rarely looks forward to the end of a school day.

    That's because his journey home is often a terrifying one. Clutching his books tightly in his hands, Patrick runs at top speed through his South Bronx neighborhood, fearful of getting caught in the crossfire of a drug deal gone bad, or terrorized by a street gang.

    With danger swirling around him, Patrick feels as if he is literally running for his life.

    But last summer, Patrick had the chance to experience a different kind of running -- the type that takes you to first base on the swing of a bat ... or carries you in hot pursuit of a fly ball.

    During his two week FRESH AIR FUND vacation in upstate New York with the Collier family -- his "Friendly Town" hosts -- Patrick fell in love with baseball. And, along with his new friend, 10-year-old Neal Collier, Patrick went swimming, caught frogs and butterflies, and rode horses.

    For the first time in Patrick's life, the outdoors was a place to relish rather than a place to fear.

    Thanks to the help of generous people like you. THE FRESH AIR FUND gave more than 10,000 children like Patrick the same opportunity -- the chance to escape the difficulties of inner-city life, and discover all that nature has to offer.

    They spent two glorious weeks with loving Friendly Town families up and down the Eastern Seaboard, and at our four camps in upstate New York -- including Hidden Valley, where children with disabilities play alongside able-bodied boys and girls.

    Today, I'm writing to ask that you help us to give even more kids that same chance for a country vacation.

Printed On Recycled Paper   (over, please)

FIG. 7–9 Letter-opening type 11: The asterisk and emotion-draining words such as "clutching" and "fearful" and "crossfire" damage effectiveness, but the impact of any specific episode narrative is light years beyond a recital of statistics.

(This asterisk referral at the end of the letter is predictable: "Names have been changed to protect individual privacy." Ugh.)

Some of the terminology is arm's length, too. Each of these suppresses emotional impact: <u>clutching</u>; <u>fearful</u>; <u>crossfire</u>. An episode has to grab and shake. Any one of us might have humanized that opening. And since they've changed the name anyway, it doesn't have to be the formal "Patrick":

> Bobby is 12. Every day he's afraid to go home from school.
>
> One of his friends was shot dead crossing the street, when a drug deal went bad and a random bullet smashed through his neck. Bobby himself was lucky one day when he was able to get away with just a torn shirt, from a street gang that wanted his schoolbooks—to sell for drug money.
>
> So Bobby runs home . . . literally for his life. . . .

The concept works, even when execution is weak. When execution has some bite, the concept has great power because if you create an episode the reader can envision, you've drawn the reader into your emotional net.

Oh, another mini-rule:

 Present tense episodes have more wallop than past tense episodes.

12. Private invitation

How do you get somebody who never heard of you before to feel specially chosen for the signal honor of hearing from you?

Exclusivity is one of the four great motivators of the 1990s (the others, remember, are fear, greed, and guilt, with need for approval coming up fast on the outside). It's the easiest of the great motivators to construct; and "A Private Invitation" is one of the most logical manipulations of exclusivity because being "one of the chosen few" is a universal grabber.

A private invitation has significant differences from "You're a very special person," which emphasizes stroking beyond emphasis on the offer.

A classic "private invitation" opening is this letter:

> A Private Message to a Very Special Person
> Dear Friend,
>   This private invitation is going out to just a handful of people, your-self included. I hope you'll accept my invitation. And even if you decide not to, I want to send you a gift. . .ABSOLUTELY FREE. . . .

I don't know what "yourself included" is doing there, but you get the idea: "You're one of the chosen few." This letter stays in character, continuing the stroking with "I believe you're someone who travels well, eats in fine restaurants—and appreciates the difference between dinner at a four-star restaurant and a hamburger on the run."

The power of private invitation exclusivity, when well-handled, lies in its ability to cause the recipient to think he/she has to live up to your expectations.

13. "We don't know each other, but it's time we did."

This one is dangerous because you're at the mercy of both the recipient's background and the recipient's mood of the moment. "We don't know each other, but it's time we did" is just as likely to generate "Who the hell do you think you are?" as "Yeah, you're right."

This opening has value as a precursor to a follow-up phone call. It has the guts any assumptive opening commands. It also works when the writer can throw in a third name known to the recipient.

An example of "We don't know each other, but it's time we did":

> Dear Mr. Lewis:
>   YOU DON'T KNOW ME, BUT. . .
> I've been asked by Terry Winter, Vice President of Uniprop, Inc., to contact you regarding your investment in one of their Manufactured Home Community programs. I believe, the firm that set this up for you is not now handling Uniprop investments. There are, Mr. Lewis, some potentially very important developments shaping up that you should know about. Communication between us over the next few months will be very important. . . .

You guessed it. The writer is a financial planner. The major fault with this letter isn't its failure to indent paragraphs nor the strange comma after the word "believe"; no, this letter builds a reef and then

**Valentine
Investment Advisors**

704 S. Florida Avenue
Lakeland, FL 33801

Dick Valentine, CFP
Certified Financial Planner
Registered Investment Advisor

Lakeland	(813) 683-4991
Winter Haven	(813) 299-9289
FAX	(813) 683-4299

Herschell G. Lewis
340 N. Fig Tree Ln.
Plantation, FL 33317

Dear Mr. Lewis:

YOU DON'T KNOW ME, BUT . . .

I've been asked by Terry Winter, Vice President of Uniprop, Inc. to
contact you, concerning your investment in one of their Manufactured
Home Community programs. I believe, the firm that set this up for you
is not now handling Uniprop investments. There are, Mr. Lewis,
some potentially very important developments shaping up that you should
know about. Communication between us over the next few months will be
very important.

Since Uniprop asked me to contact you and we have not met, an
introduction is in order. I am a Certified Financial Planner with
considerable knowledge in Uniprop programs. The clients I usually work
with are probably a lot like you. Let's face it, Mr. Lewis,
everyone wants to enjoy their retirement years with some protection to
their principal. Before you retire, your primary goal is probably to
maintain consistent growth and factor out a high degree of risk. But once
you've achieved those goals, you still have to avoid paying too much in
taxes -- keep it out of Uncle Sam's hands and in yours!

That's why this type of an investment can provide you with benefits but
there are some risks. That's why I think YOU SHOULD work with someone
who works with investments that have as one of its objectives capital
preservation.

The more I know about you, Mr. Lewis, the better equipped I'll be to
help you make the right decisions. In order to make the "getting to know
each other" process easier, I'll be sending you a brief questionnaire
shortly. For you to get to know me better, I've enclosed a brief
outline of my background and what I do. Please do any checking or ask
any further questions you may have.

• Securities by Licensed Individuals Offered Through Investacorp, Inc. • A Registered Broker/Dealer • Member NASD, SIPC •

FIG. 7–10 Letter-opening type 13: This letter makes a crucial mistake in its use of a potentially commanding opening. Whoever Terry Winter is, if he told this man to contact me, I want to know why. Instead, the letter degenerates into an apologia for the writer and a pitch for business.

runs aground on it by ignoring the one rule a "We don't know each other, but it's time we did" letter has to follow:

 After claiming a need for relationship, <u>immediately</u> explain why.

Incidentally, I wouldn't know Terry Winter if I fell over him.

14. The cry of "Fire!"

"Fire!" differs from "Wolf!" (no. 64, chapter 9) in just one respect: The issue is broader. A wolf can eat you (yes, dear fellow-environmentalists, I know we've never had a recorded case of a wolf eating a human being), but a fire can wipe out a whole town.

The problem with the cry of "Fire!" isn't that it'll start a panic inside a crowded theatre; it's that the cry demands a statesmanlike attitude and we're wallowing in "Me"-ness. From greedy politicians to self-centered athletes, our society has turned away from issues affecting anybody but <u>me</u>.

Still, it's comforting to know that somebody cares. Dedication is so rare today we should honor it by responding—which I did to this cry of "Fire!" (strange overuse of hyphens and capitalizing "Schools" are the writer's doing, not mine):

> Dear Friend,
> **America's Schools are in crisis!**
> Twenty-two percent of all first, second, and third grade students fall-behind their age groups!
>
> Each year, more than five-hundred thousand children fall-behind, or fail <u>in first grade alone!</u>

The cause is a worthy one, so I hope the rapport-killing statistic "Twenty-two percent" didn't maim its impact.

15. "What I want you to do is. . ."

This one is delicate. Written with delicacy and finesse, it achieves that wonderful connection, <u>rapport</u>; written with a heavy-handed bludgeon, it alienates the reader.

ARTHUR G. HAGGIS, Ed. D.

Dear Friend:

<u>America's Schools are in crisis!</u>

Twenty-two percent of all first, second, and third grade students fall-behind their age groups!

Each year, more than five-hundred thousand children fall - behind, or fail, <u>in first grade alone!</u>

Thirty-three percent of all high school students are dropping-behind or out! (U.S. Census Bureau, 1992).

Clearly, the "laissez faire" school systems are ineffective in educating <u>all</u> of our nation's youth.

As a result, our schools no longer produce a workforce to meet the challenges of a modern world.

<u>A national disgrace? You bet it is!</u> And, it is going to get worse, much worse, unless you join me to save our nation from this education catastrophe.

I have <u>the plan</u> to insure that all children, upon entering first grade, have an <u>"equal opportunity to learn and to achieve"</u> as they begin their educational careers...

<u>... but, I really need your help to make this plan work!</u>

I want you to sign the enclosed title page of the "National Plan & Agenda" prepared by the Atlantis Research Institute (A R I) for the President of the United States, Members of Congress, and State Governors.

This is your personal opportunity to endorse A R I's dramatic effort to rescue our nation's education systems from certain disaster.

<u>... and, I need you to do it today!</u>

Hello. I'm Dr. Arthur G. Haggis. You know me through my pioneer research with preschool children at the Atlantis Private Schools and the Atlantis Research Institute in Florida.

I established A R I as a private nonprofit organization to conduct "in-depth" analysis of educational issues of national importance.

3325 Hollywood Boulevard, Suite 404
Hollywood, Florida 33021

FIG. 7-11 Letter-opening type 14: This writer does a lot of things right. Paragraphs are short and pointed, and the text is loaded with action words such as "crisis" and "national disgrace." But percentages don't motivate as strongly as examples, no matter how worthy the cause . . . and this cause <u>is</u> worthy. ("I need your help" doesn't have the strength it had before overuse in the late 1980s.)

GROUNDBREAKING NEW DOCUMENTARY — AS SEEN ON PBS!

Land of the Eagle

What did the eagle symbolize to many
Native Americans?

According to Cherokee legend,
what was the source of human illness and disease?

What was there about the European system of barter
that native fur traders found insulting?

You are eligible for a FREE museum-quality print!
(Read on, the answers are contained below...)

Dear Viewer,

Just for a minute, I want you to forget everything you've ever
learned about American history.

Because I want to take you back -- 400 years and more -- and make the
story of North America <u>come alive</u> for you and your family.

<u>How?...By showing you history the way you've never seen it before.</u>
For example...

Have you ever wondered how the "discovery" of North
America might have looked through the eyes of the <u>Native
Americans</u> who'd lived here for centuries?

...Or can you imagine seeing America in a time before
<u>cities and highways and shopping malls</u> -- a time when
eagles and snow geese dominated the eastern sky?

...How would <u>you</u> feel as a European settler -- <u>3,000 miles
from your family and friends</u> -- in a world filled with men
and creatures unlike any you'd ever seen before?

That's the way you'll see the natural history of America -- once you
preview LAND OF THE EAGLE, a groundbreaking 8-part video documentary
produced by Thirteen/WNET in association with BBC/Bristol and brought to
you by TIME-LIFE VIDEO.

(over, please)

FIG. 7–12 Letter-opening type 15: The Johnson Box at the top—as is too often true of Johnson Boxes—is wordy. That first question has a near-zero impact factor. But once one gets beyond the Johnson Box, into the letter itself, the polished text quickly grabs and holds the reader. That's what a professionally written letter opening is supposed to do. But why didn't the letter answer at least one of the Johnson Box questions, however weak the questions are, on page 1?

An excellent example of this approach is a letter which, following a too-lengthy Johnson Box, has this superior beginning:

> Dear Viewer,
> Just for a minute, I want you to forget everything you've ever learned about American history.
> Because I want to take you back—400 years and more—and make the story of North America <u>come</u> <u>alive</u> for you and your family. . . .

Visualize that letter with a more pedestrian opening. This writer makes the demand both soft and logical, an indication of a professional at work.

16. "Because you did that, we're going to do this."

This opening can be a powerhouse when you use it properly because, unlike "I have a free gift for you" or "I have something good for you," this offer ties itself into a positive action your target has accomplished. The tie-in adds both credibility and rapport.

A letter addressed to my son begins:

> Dear Robert Lewis:
> Because of your company's growing commitment to the Windows environment, I'd like to send, for your evaluation, a free copy of Correct Grammar for Windows.

Now, what if this letter had begun, "I have a free copy of Correct Grammar for Windows for you"? Neither rationale nor reader involvement would have been as powerful.

Often, levels of power stem from the amount of information we have about the target. So don't discard the "I have a free copy of Correct Grammar for Windows for you" opening; rather, make a substitution <u>when you have enough information to replace it with this opening</u>. "I have a free copy of Correct Grammar for Windows for you" has its uses . . . for example, a retail store wielding Correct Grammar as an incentive. In such a circumstance, "Because you did that, we're going to do this" would be presumptuous.

Only partly parallel to "Because you did that, we're going to do this" is. . . .

WRITING TOOLS
GROUP

```
Robert Lewis
Star Tribune Newspaper Twin Ci
425 Portland Avenue
Minneapolis MN 55488

Dear Robert Lewis:

Because of your company's growing commitment to the Windows
environment, I'd like to send, for your evaluation, a free copy of
Correct Grammar for Windows.

Correct Grammar for Windows identifies errors in grammar, style,
punctuation, usage and even spelling.  It improves all your
company's communications and helps you project a professional image
with precise, highly polished writing.

And Correct Grammar for Windows is the only sentence checker that
works within all Windows applications

        .... from word processing programs (including Word for
             Windows, WordPerfect for Windows and WordStar Legacy)

        .... to spreadsheet programs

        .... to page layout and presentation software

PC Computing singled out Correct Grammar as the best grammar
checker and urged readers in its June 1991 review of the Windows
version "get one of these applications and poor writing has nowhere
to hide."

To receive your free corporate evaluation copy of Correct Grammar
for Windows, simply mail or fax the enclosed request form.  Or call
1-800-523-3520.

This is a limited time offer and may be withdrawn at any time.  So
please don't delay in requesting your copy.

Cordially,

Camilo Wilson

Camilo Wilson
President

P.S. Correct Grammar for Windows installs automatically and feels
like it is built right into any Windows application.  You'll be
able to use and evaluate it quickly and easily.
```

One Harbor Drive, Suite 111 • Sausalito, California 94965 • 800-523-3520 • FAX 415-883-1629

FIG. 7–13 Letter-opening type 16: The word "because" is a wonderful marketing word <u>because</u> it forces the writer to specify a reason. This is the implicit strength of the "Because you did that, we're going to do this" opening. Another benefit is its automatic reader involvement.

17. Because you are who you are, you may get special attention.

Note that word <u>may</u>. It's the huge separator from no. 16.

This one is just as close to no. 12, Private Invitation, as it is to no. 16. In fact, an example in my file has an invitation above the overline:

> You are invited to apply for a free subscription.
> Please reply by [DATE].
> Dear Computer Professional,
> Your position suggests that you may qualify for a complimentary subscription to InfoWorld. . . .

You can see the difference: Conditions peek slyly through tiny holes in the invitation. I'm invited to <u>apply</u>. An applicant is implicitly on a lower plane than the person to whom he/she applies. So this isn't a genuine "invitation," any more than a note from a club or a business or a college agreeing to look over your application is an invitation.

See that word *may* lurking in the first sentence? It makes the offer equivocal . . . which is what we want to do if we aren't certain of the applicant's credentials. I'm sure this publication, like all controlled-circulation publications, analyzes the application and then sends one of two messages: either no. 16, which we just discussed, or a "We're sorry, but. . ." letter rejecting the applicant and "inviting" him/her to become a paid subscriber.

18. Stroke, stroke—"You're a rare bird."

If you think many sales letters begin with flattery, you're right. After all, every one of these samples is based on the hope of doing business, and flattery does outpull insults, doesn't it?

A stroke, stroke opening can become treacly and oleaginous. I don't recommend it on the executive level because if the recipient immediately pierces the phoniness you're better off sending a bald offer without a letter. "You're a rare bird" works best among the less sophisticated.

Who's Who
Among Rising Young Americans™

Chief Executive Officer
Communicomp
340 Fig Tree Ln.
P.O. Box 15725 (33317)
Plantation, FL 33318

Dear Executive:

You are a member of a company made up of high achievers. As such, you know how a little recognition goes a long way to encourage ever-greater levels of performance.

Citation Directories, Ltd. is offering your company yet another way to reward employees for outstanding accomplishments -- in the professional arena as well as within your community. **And, the only cost to you is 15 minutes of your time.**

We publish *Citation's Who's Who Registry of Rising Young Americans*, an annual directory dedicated to recognizing those individuals with superior potential for contributing to the future of American business. We are always searching for qualified people who deserve the recognition and prestige associated with this honor.

As we prepare the 1993 edition of the *Who's Who Registry of Rising Young Americans*, **we are requesting nominations of individuals within your company who meet our requirements for acceptance.** The qualities our successful candidates share include:

- 40 years of age or below
- Significant professional and community involvement
- Achievement of success in his or her chosen field
- Demonstration of potential for continued success

Please take 15 minutes and fill out the enclosed nomination form with the names and addresses of employees who may qualify for this honor. After you return it to us in the postage-paid envelope provided, we will then send applications to your nominees. Our selection committee will review the application for inclusion in the 1993 edition, which will be published early next year. Nominees will be notified of the status of their returned application within four to six weeks of receipt.

Citation's Who's Who Registry of Rising Young Americans provides a quick, easy way to credit some of your best and brightest. Please help us recognize America's **(and your)** greatest assets: Rising Young Americans!

Sincerely,

Marilyn A. Riley

Marilyn A. Riley, Publisher
Who's Who Registry of Rising Young Americans

Published by Citation Directories, Ltd.
P.O. Box 1036
1003 Central Avenue
Fort Dodge, IA 50501
800-848-9059

FIG. 7–14 Letter-opening type 18: When a letter begins with stroking, persuasion is in direct ratio to the credibility the reader attaches to the sender. Two immediate questions:
1. Does the stroking justify the directory?
2. Might a more straightforward exposition, emphasizing promotional benefits rather than unexplained "significance," generate greater response?

So this example, which combines stroking with an obvious lack of information about the recipient, is in my opinion the <u>wrong</u> way to begin this particular sales pitch:

> Chief Executive Officer
> Communicomp
>
> Dear Executive:
>
> You are a member of a company made up of high achievers. As such, you know how a little recognition goes a long way to encourage ever-greater levels of performance.
>
> Citation Directories, Ltd. is offering your company yet another way to reward employees for outstanding accomplishments—in the professional arena as well as within your community. *And, the cost to you is 15 minutes of your time.*
>
> We publish *Citation's Who's Who Registry of Rising Young Americans*, an annual directory dedicated to recognizing those individuals with superior potential for contributing to the future of American business. . .

What's wrong here isn't the vanity aspect of a directory that, if every recipient used all five nomination blanks, could fill a five-foot shelf. No problem with that, from a promotional point of view. No, the problem lies in using <u>this</u> approach to <u>this</u> recipient.

If you say, "But the sender couldn't know who the letter recipient would be," I reply, "Exactly." That's why a "Stroke, Stroke—"You're a Rare Bird" opening is dangerous when mailed at random. Save this one for those who either (a) will believe they're rare birds or (b) will believe you have a genuine reason to know they're rare birds.

19. "Here's what the experts say."

This is a no-nonsense opening, and that's why I like it for business-to-business mailings. Sometimes it appears cold-blooded because it gets directly to the point; this means the writer has to consider not only who gets this message but what the state of mind probably will be at the time of receipt.

One danger: "Here's what the experts say" too often is followed by self-applause without substance. If that's your approach, then <u>don't</u>

inflict it on business mail recipients. Dedicate applause without substance only to consumers—preferably downscale ones, at that. Heed this warning, relative to business targets: Unless what the experts say relates to the reader, don't waste your paper.

Here's a typical "Here's what the experts say" opening. Note that it jumps in without prelude; with a prelude, it <u>isn't</u> this type of opening.

> Dear Windows Resource Kit owner:
> *Windows User Magazine* voted it the *Best Windows Utility of 1992.*
> *PC Magazine* says it's". . .essential. . .hard to imagine running Windows without it.."
> *PC Computing* says it's ". . .a lean and mean program-launching machine that should be found on every windows user's computer. . . .

See that third encomium ". . .program-launching machine"? This is a specific, which gives the reader some meat to chew.

20. "Why are we doing this?"

"Why are we doing this?" belongs to a group of openings that hurl down the gauntlet in front of the reader. Rather than establishing conviviality with an opening such as "I have a question for you" or "As you know," this one <u>assumes</u> the recipient starts reading with an apathetic/adversarial attitude . . . and therein lies its strength.

A "Why are we doing this?" opening often is tied to a seemingly incredible admission, accusation, offer, or gift. And, I submit, it's one best left untouched by dilettantes. Like opening no. 4 (Suggest a cataclysmic decision), "Why are we doing this?" demands the professional laying on of hands.

An example of this type of opening, in which a shiny new penny was glued to the letter:

> Dear Mr. Johnson,
>
> Why have I enclosed this FREE penny?
>
> Because it represents the introduction of a NEW Medicare Supplement Insurance Policy that completely <u>eliminates</u> every penny of your out-of-pocket doctor expenses for all <u>Medicare covered services</u>. . . .

I'd have dropped the underlining as used and saved it for <u>every</u> penny to point up the parallel with the free coin.

21. "This is disgusting and you're the one to fix it."

As you evaluate this opening, you have to think of what's wrong, not what's right. Yes, yes, positives usually outsell negatives; but *guilt* is a potent motivator, and looking back at opening no. 5 ("We need help") or opening no. 14 ("Fire!), we've <u>approached</u> but not equalled this one— *guilt PLUS anger.* Wow!

Opening No. 21 is geared to the 1990s. Its strength comes from anger, not a plea. We don't have a kinder, gentler society; your dog has to eat their dog. What this opening has is <u>guts</u>, and we admire guts.

An example of this opening is a letter from an environmentally aimed fund-raising group. The letter begins (regrettably after a far too long typed 3-paragraph overline which diminishes its impact):

> Dear Friend,
>
> Our world is drowning in filth. Garbage covers the land, and toxins seep into our groundwater and our homes. Our cities sprawl beneath skies awash with a brown haze. . . .

This writer starts with guts and shifts to poetry. Uh-uh. You don't set a charge of dynamite and then pull out the wire. "Our cities sprawl beneath skies awash with a brown haze" isn't gritty enough to qualify for this opening.

Understand, please: The writer may not have wanted a full-scale "This is disgusting and you're the one to fix it" opening. If he/she had, the wording might have been. . . .

> Our world is drowning in filth. It's up to troubled citizens like you to do something about the garbage in the streets, the drinking water poisoned by chemicals, the smog that half-blinds you and deposits ugly black soot on your windows. . . .

If I had my druthers, I'd pick our opening over theirs because the key to making anger work for you is <u>staying in character</u>. (That's true

VAWTER "BUCK" PARKER
Executive Director

It is entirely possible that we may be the last generation of humans to know this wondrous earth as it was meant to be.

We have befouled our environment terribly -- and we continue to do so with relentless fury. It is an open question whether humanity will be able to survive the 21st century. **But it is virtually certain that millions of people will suffer and die because of environmental degradation,** and millions of others will be unable to experience lives of meaningful quality.

But there is some hope: we are NOT too late! **We do have the means to stop the destruction, and save this planet...**if we so choose. So today, the Sierra Club Legal Defense Fund asks you to commit yourself to stopping the destruction. Please help us force the "powers that be" to assure the next generation a real future.

Dear Friend,

Our world is drowning in filth. Garbage covers the land, and toxins seep into our groundwater and our homes. Our cities sprawl beneath skies awash with a brown haze.

The numbers are staggering: in the United States alone, we dump 2.7 billion pounds of toxics into our air every year, discharge over 500 million pounds of toxic waste into our rivers, and bury 160 million tons of trash. Worldwide, we annihilate 74,000 acres of rain forest a day... 17,500 plant and animal species a year. World population is 5.1 billion and, unchecked, will hit 10 billion by 2050.

Yet as frightening as these facts are, I profoundly believe that we possess the power to stop this reckless destruction. It is not yet too late to save our planet -- our home.

Make no mistake: the time has come when no one -- not one of us -- can remain complacent, waiting to be rescued. It is time for every citizen to stand and fight for our environment. For if we are to save ourselves, this new decade may be our last chance to do it.

And that's why I'm writing you today. I'm trusting that you feel much the same way I do...agreeing with me that by intelligently using what we've learned in the past two decades, we can stop humanity's reckless slide toward environmental suicide.

THE SIERRA CLUB LEGAL DEFENSE FUND is a unique organization that has developed, and knows how to use, a most powerful weapon for environmental sanity. But we can't use it alone: we must have committed partners like you supporting us with a common vision.

(over, please)

SIERRA CLUB LEGAL DEFENSE FUND
180 Montgomery Street, Suite 1400, San Francisco, CA 94104-4209

Unbleached, 100% Recycled Paper

FIG. 7-15 Letter-opening type 21: The logic behind a lengthy pre-greeting message escapes me. The longer the message, the greater the detraction from the opening <u>impact</u>. Imagine how much more powerful this opening would be <u>without</u> the long header and <u>with</u> an in-character followup to the textbook-perfect first sentence.

of every role we actors play. Stanley Kowalski doesn't say, "Oh, what a rogue and peasant slave am I.")

22. We've got bad news. . . and we've got good news.

I like this one because it's an irresistible "grabber." Every one of us has had this phone call: "I got good news for you and bad news for you. Which do you want first?"

In a letter opening, we usually go just one way: Bad news first. Why? Because stating a problem, then giving the solution, is far more potent that stating the solution, then explaining what the solution covers.

The exception: When the <u>bad</u> news brings relief.

A classic example of the "bad news first" opening is a letter from a paper company (compare it with the "good news first" counter-example in the analysis of Opening No. 23):

The bad news is. . .

I'm sure you've heard many bad news/good news stories over the years. Well, here's a bad news/good news story that can be quite beneficial for you.

The bad news is Weyerhaeuser no longer manufactures Cougar Laser Opaque. The good news is we've replaced it with not one, but two new *guaranteed* laser compatible papers. . . .

The disappearance of Cougar Laser Opaque is hardly life-threatening. That's why this opening works. It pulls pedestrian information out of the "So what" muck and tags it with a magic wand.

23. "Good News!"

This opening isn't at all related to the one we just explored. "Good News!" is a one-string fiddle, a straightforward pitch. The reader recognizes it as a pitch from the first handful of words.

If "we've got bad news . . . and we've got good news" is a rocket among openers, "Good News" is a sturdy bicycle. Bad news/good news requires sophistication from both writer and reader; "Good news" operates on an uncomplicated plane.

The benefit of "Good News" is its universality. The danger of "Good news" is using it and then falling flat with self-serving information that may be good news for the message sender but not for the message recipient.

An easy rule to follow: As you write the first paragraph following your proclamation of Good News, ask yourself, dispassionately and cold-bloodedly: *If I were getting this instead of sending it, would I think it's good news?*

A laser-personalized letter from a university begins. . .

> Dear Mr. Lewis:
> Do you want to hear some <u>good</u> news?
>
> Twenty-three months ago we got a very special person, Dr. Denis Waitley, on the calendar. If you know of him, you probably will want to skip the rest of this letter and simply call in for your tickets for the November 20 Florida International University "Lessons in Leadership" program. . . .

See what I mean? Yes. I've heard of Denis Waitley. No, I can't "hear" some good news by reading a letter. And no, no, no, the "Good News" opening is a misfit for this communication. This letter should have tied the information to another opening. Even the one we just discussed, "We've got bad news . . . and we've got good news," would work better, using the "good first" exception:

> Dear Mr. Lewis, [I prefer commas]
> I've got good news . . . and I've got bad news.
>
> The good news is that we've been able to convince the renowned Dr. Denis Waitley to present his "Lesson in Leadership" program here, November 20. The bad news is that seats are <u>very</u> limited.

The example points up the difference between Opening No. 22 and Opening 23.

The bad news is . . .

I'm sure you've heard many bad news/good news stories over the years. Well, here's a bad news/good news story that can be quite beneficial for you.

The bad news is Weyerhaeuser no longer manufactures Cougar Laser Opaque. The good news is we've replaced it with not one, but two new *guaranteed* laser compatible papers.

They are: **Cougar Opaque – Laser Guaranteed** and **Lynx Opaque – Laser Guaranteed**, and both offer you the versatility you need for any electronic imaging application.

Both papers feature:

- built-in moisture and curl control for dimensional stability
- unsurpassed opacity to minimize show-through in duplexing applications
- enhanced resolution due to stringent smoothness specifications
- a choice of three basis weights – 50/20, 60/24 and 70/28 lb – for versatility
- excellent brightness for high contrast reproduction and high quality image
- guaranteed laser compatibility for your peace of mind
- acid-free manufacturing for archival quality

The enclosed brochure will tell you more about these two new electronic imaging papers. Please take a few minutes to read it and, after you have, call a leading Weyerhaeuser paper merchant in your area to see why Cougar Opaque - Laser Guaranteed and Lynx Opaque - Laser Guaranteed will be good news for you.

Thank you.

Sincerely,

Jeff Brundage
National Market Manager
Business & Reprographic Papers

P.S. We need your help! At Weyerhaeuser we are constantly striving to meet our customers' needs for electronic imaging papers. You can help us meet your needs by filling out and returning the enclosed postage-free card. Thank you.

**Weyerhaeuser
Paper Company**

▲
Weyerhaeuser

P.O. Box 829, Valley Forge, PA 19482   Printed on 60/24 lb Cougar Opaque – Laser Guaranteed

FIG. 7–16 Letter-opening type 22: The "bad news/good news" opening is perfect for this message. Most recipients have no immediate interest in a manufacturer's decision to switch paper stocks, but this approach makes trivia palatable.

Florida International University

Mr. Herschell G. Lewis
President
Communicomp
340 North Fig Tree Lane
Fort Lauderdale, FL 33317

Dear Mr. Lewis:

Do you want to hear some _good_ news?

Twenty-three months ago we got a very special person, Dr. Denis Waitley, on the
calendar. If you know of him, you will probably want to skip the rest of this
letter and simply call in for your tickets for the November 20 Florida
International University "Lessons in Leadership" program.

If you don't yet know of Denis Waitley, look at what others have said:

> "Denis Waitley's teaching transforms employees into entrepreneurs,
> coaches and managers into leaders, and individuals into champions. His
> newest program wins the gold medal as his best ever."--Harvey Mackay,
> author of How to Swim with the Sharks

> "Denis Waitley is not only a top quality speaker, he is a top quality
> person. His message is both practical and truly inspirational."--
> Stephen R. Covey, author of The 7 Habits of Highly Effective People
> and Principle-Centered Leadership

Dr. Denis Waitley is a man with credentials that simply do not stop. A
graduate of the Naval Academy, former Navy pilot, and holder of a Ph.D. in
human behavior from American University, he is best known as the author and
narrator of "The Psychology of Winning," the all-time best selling audio
cassette album on personal and professional development. Waitley has studied
and counseled organizations and individuals in every walk of life, from
"Fortune 500" companies, NASA's astronauts, returning POWs and foreign
hostages, to Super Bowl and Olympic athletes.

"Breakthrough research," "piercing truth," "in-depth insights," "marvelous word
pictures," "cutting edge relevancy," "real life examples and humor," "a common
sense approach to uncommon success"... these are some of the words that
describe why Denis Waitley--as heard on his "The Psychology of Winning"
audiotapes--is known as the man with "the most listened to voice in the world"
(outside of entertainment and media broadcasts.) You will see what we're

Division of Continuing Education
University Park, Miami, Florida 33199

Equal Opportunity/Equal Access Employer and Institution

FIG. 7–17 Letter-opening type 23: "Good news" has one edict: the reader has to
think, "Yes, that _is_ good news." By that standard of judgment, this letter
hits and runs. Nothing following the first sentence continues the "good
news" theme. A parenthetical admonition: Don't use "hear" when referring to the eye.

24. "Are you paying too much?"

This opening is loaded with power because it combines absolute one-to-one personalization, an immediate reader-involving question, and an appeal to greed.

This recognition should lead to a second recognition—whatever follows is a <u>comparative</u> pitch. If you want to be gentlemanly or ladylike, this opening is not for you.

Here's an example of the "Are you paying too much?" opening. It's an execrable example. Can you tell why?

> Dear Mr. Sax:
> Are you paying too much for life insurance?
>
> The Multifunding Agency has made arrangements to offer term*
> life insurance at a substantially reduced rate. This outstanding
> opportunity is available to non-smoking clients** who also qualify
> as select health risks. . . .

The first line is a grabber, a classic use of this opening. But ugh! Asterisks all over the place. Immediate lapsing into obvious puffery ("outstanding opportunity"). Referring to the targets as "select health risks."

For heaven's sake, with this or <u>any</u> opening, STAY IN CHARACTER. If you or I had written the letter, we'd have maintained the tone and pace of the gauntlet-hurling opening:

> Dear Mr. Sax:
> Are you paying too much for your life insurance?
> You bet you are, if you're paying more than the rates you'll see on
> this page. You wouldn't knowingly overpay for a car or a maga-
> zine or a computer. Why overpay for insurance?. . .

The opening is a supercharged Harley-Davidson. You wouldn't use a Harley as an exercycle. Open up that throttle and barrel down the highway.

25. "Did you know..." or "Do you know..."

"Did you know . . ." is another question-opening, implicity reader-involving. It's one of the easiest openings to construct . . . and that means it's one of the most misused.

**CHUBB
LifeAmerica**

multifunding agency, inc.
5340 north federal highway, suite 106, lighthouse point, florida 33064
broward (305) 421-7300   palm beach (407) 732-6111
fax (305) 421-7688

Mr. Lewis Sax
340 N Fig Tree Lane
Plantation, FL 33317-2561

Dear Mr. Sax:

Are you paying too much for your life insurance?

The Multifunding Agency has made arrangements to offer term* life insurance at a substantially reduced rate. This outstanding opportunity is available to non-smoking clients** who also qualify as select health risks.

The table below shows you how inexpensive $1,000,000 of term life insurance can be. Just compare these annual costs against other term policies or any employer-sponsored group term life plan...and stop wasting your hard-earned money.

Age	TrackOne One Year Term	TrackFive Five Year Term	TrackTen Ten Year Term	TrackFifteen Fifteen Year MPWL
30	$ 510	$ 850	$ 800	$ 940
40	$ 730	1,200	1,300	1,590
50	1,510	2,350	2,750	3,430
60	4,160	5,970	7,000	8,740

   *   TrackFifteen is a Modified Premium Whole Life (MPWL) policy
  **   Policies available for smokers at higher rates

To receive a quick phone quote just call our office at the above numbers, or return the enclosed <u>postage-paid</u> reply card. Personal consultations are available by appointment.

<u>Mr. Sax, in addition, you may qualify to have this insurance coverage, but invest "all premiums" in a mutual fund of your choice.</u>

Sincerely,
Multifunding Inc.

Donald N. Deutsch, C.L.U.
President

DND:jb
enc

FIG. 7–18 Letter-opening type 24: If you ask the question, "Are you paying too much?" for heaven's sake <u>answer</u> the question. This letter slops off into loose puffery and, worse, a bunch of asterisks. Both those mistakes diminish reader involvement.

Investor's Business Daily

Dear Business Reader...

Did you know that Investor's Business Daily is now the "Hottest Business Newspaper in America"?

It's all new with 68 features added in just the last 12 months (we've even changed the name)...subscriptions and advertising are up, while older Wall Street publications are down.

Did you make big money in last year's market recovery? Did you own either Home Depot, Costco, Merck or U.S. Surgical?

If you had taken Investor's Business Daily regularly you would have known exactly how to select and own those types of companies.

I sincerely believe if you were reading Investor's Business Daily, you would have owned at least one of those stocks, because they were all repeatedly spot-lighted in stories, charts and our "exclusive, intelligent stock tables" showing the highest rankings.

Isn't it time you got rid of some of those out-moded papers that don't really help you make money and find out about Investor's Business Daily?

Here's my special "FREE" offer to you...send us the enclosed postage-paid order card now, and we'll send you Investor's Business Daily for 2 weeks-FREE! You will not receive a bill. There is nothing to cancel.

PLUS...we'll also send you 2 FREE audio tapes..."Investing to Win" recorded by David Ryan, Three-Time Winner of the U.S. Investing Championships, and a brand new audio cassette..."Your Guide to Investor's Business Daily" plus a booklet that can help you learn how to spot the next hot, new market leaders and avoid the ice cold laggards.

Don't delay. Do it now--before you forget.

Sincerely,

William J. O'Neil
William J. O'Neil
Chairman

P.S. For faster service, call toll-free 800-451-1223.

"The Business Newspaper for People Who Want to Make Money"
1941 Armacost Ave., Los Angeles, CA 90025

NO792

FIG. 7-19 Letter-opening type 25: Follow a "Did you know. . ." statement with solid backup. This letter follows with "It's all new with 68 features added. . ."—<u>not</u> a verifier for the claim. The writer should ask himself/herself, "What makes this the hottest business newspaper?"—then answer the question.

The writer who starts a letter with "Did you know" or "Do you know" has to be sure to key whatever follows to the <u>reader</u> as <u>fact</u>, not <u>puffery</u>. And even though present tense ordinarily outpulls past tense, for this opening "Did you know" is usually more appropriate, for two reasons: (1) Logic says this is information the reader didn't have before and now will have; (2) "Do you know" is more quiz-like, giving the writer an olympian position the reader may dislike.

An example of this opening:

> Dear Business Reader. . .
> Did you know that Investor's Daily is now the "Hottest Business Newspaper in America"?
> It's all new with 68 features added in just the last 12 months (we've even changed the name). . .subscriptions and advertising are up, while older Wall Street publications are down. . . .

In my opinion this letter would be stronger if it had observed the rule of "Did you know" openings and followed those three words with fact, not puffery. Example:

> Did you know Investor's Business Daily subscriptions and advertising are <u>up</u>. . .and the older Wall Street publications are <u>down</u>?

25 Steady Starters

Properly used, these 25 workmanlike ways to start a sales letter are all reader-involving, and—another benefit—most are relatively easy to create.

26. "Have you ever wished. . ."

This lyrical opening can penetrate defenses which leap into position against more hard-boiled attacks.

In use, too often even the most professional practitioners shoot a coat of dulling spray over "Have you ever wished . . ." by having an introduction so long, tedious, or dynamic the opening itself becomes ancillary instead of primary—a harsh switching of gears.

Don't do that. Harshness destroys wistfulness.

I'm looking at a letter selling computer software. The actual letter begins:

> Dear Friend,
> Have you ever wished that you could produce incredible looking documents, construct bigger than life posters, build dazzling looking slide presentations—or even touch-up photographs and drawings, just like a world class graphic artist might do?

A workmanlike job—although I'd have hyphenated "bigger-than-life," taken the hyphen out of "touch up," and dumped the weak "looking" after "dazzling." These are tweakings, not objections. The opening does stand up.

But this opening <u>starts</u> two-thirds of the way down the page. A batch of rock-em, sock-em display type above the greeting shouts:

> Now Two PC Magazine's Editors' Choice
> Award-Winning Software Programs
> can be yours . . .
> Get three of the world's easiest to use desktop
> publishing packages, bundled together
> **for only $49.95!**
> You save $527 off the price [and on it goes. . .]

A legend above a "Have you ever wished . . . " greeting isn't damaging per se; it's damaging when it's exclamatory. When you're writing a letter, pretend you're in a play. Who are you? Stay in character.

MEDIA CYBERNETICS ®

Phone: 1-800-772-3250

* *

Now Two PC Magazine's Editors' Choice Award-Winning Software Programs can be yours...

Get three of the world's easiest to use desktop publishing packages, bundled together

for only $49.95!

You save $527 off the price you'd pay if you bought these must-have programs separately!

With these amazing programs, even beginners can use their PCs to do all this and more...

> Make wall sized posters -- EASY!
> Retouch photos -- EASY!
> Perfect image printing -- EASY!
> Build professional slide shows -- EASY!
> Develop your own fonts -- EASY!
> Design top-grade logos -- EASY!
> Capture screen images -- EASY!
> Draw like Chagall -- EASY!

* *

```
Dear Friend,

    Have you ever wished that you could produce incredible looking
documents, construct bigger than life posters, build dazzling
looking slide presentations -- or even touch-up photographs and
drawings, just like a world class graphic artist might do?

    Even if you failed high school art you can do all this and more
right now with your PC and the easy-to-use software I'm going to
describe in this letter.  And you can do it faster and easier than
you'd ever imagine!  Listen hard to me!  You've already got all the

                                    (Please continue reading...)
```

FIG. 8-1 Letter-opening type 26: Opinions, please: Would the "Have you ever wished. . ." opening have been more of a grabber if the superstructure at the top of the page hadn't stolen the thunder? Don't misunderstand: A powerful lead-in jump-starts a message; in this instance "Believe it or not—Save $527 off the regular price—Yours for only $49.95!" would have been enough and wouldn't have made the "Have you ever wished . . ." opening anticlimactic.

"Have you ever wished . . ." is a natural for travel, investments, fund raising, and self-improvement. Its most attractive virtue is that it's easy to write.

27. You're in trouble (or you and I are in trouble), and this is what you'd better do.

This opening differs from no. 21, "This is disgusting and you're the one to fix it," because "You're in trouble" is a direct accusation of existing involvement instead of a command for post-trouble involvement.

"You're in trouble" or "You and I are in trouble" is loaded with dynamite, and that should be a caution as well as a challenge. The driver of a dynamite truck usually gets a bonus for safe delivery . . . and a funeral for steering into an accident.

As you undoubtedly have already concluded, this opening explodes with force when used for fund raising and politics. The first sentence should include the word "you" or "our."

A fund raising letter begins:

> Right now, our oceans are in serious trouble. Coral reefs, the marine equivalent of tropical rain forests, are dying. Beaches are fouled by oil spills and wastes. Fisheries are in decline. Many species of sea mammals are in danger of extinction.

Is this an example of Opening no. 27? Partly. In my opinion, the writer decided to soften the opening; in my opinion, softening also softens personal impact; in my opinion, softening personal impact reduces response, and that's the way we keep score. You or I might have opened the letter this way:

> We're in trouble, you and I. Our oceans are dying. Yes, dying. Look at any beach. Chances are it's fouled by oil spills and wastes. Fish can't even breed. Sea mammals? Take a good look while you can, because a few years from now they might be added to the melancholy list of extinct species.

Please understand: I'm not criticizing the letter because whoever wrote it didn't write it the way I would have; I'm just explaining how this <u>semi-</u> "You're in trouble" opening can be shifted to a full-scale "You're in trouble" opening.

28. "Why do they..." or "Why don't they..."

<u>Don't</u> regard "Why don't they . . ." as a parallel for "Why don't <u>you</u>. . . ." The difference is immediate and potent: "Why do they" or "Why don't they" places you arm in arm with the message-sender as either (1) coach or (2) critic.

"Why don't you" is a cousin of an opening we've already discussed, no. 15 ("What I want you to do is. . ."). It's more imperative, which can make it more rejectable.

But "Why do/don't they" has the wonderful capacity to place the target reader, together with the writer, above "those people." Rapport is implicit, ergo instant.

An example of a "Why do/don't they" opening:

> Dear Marketing Professional:
> Exasperating, aren't they?
> I'm talking about human beings. Americans. Consumers. The public. The markets. The crazy-making jury out there you're paid to understand—and whose whims and flights of fancy you're rewarded for predicting.
> Just what <u>do</u> they want? And what will they want tomorrow?

You can see the immediate advantage of this opening. The reader knows an imperative is on the way, but it's padded and softened and covered with downy feathers.

(As used in this example, the opening loses impact because too much claptrap precedes the greeting. <u>Before</u> "Exasperating, aren't they?" we have this text: "Why do people buy what they buy? Two reasons, according to one marketing guru: 'To get what they don't have—and to keep what they've got.'" Marketing guru? Marketing cliché expert is a better title.)

Consider the "Why do/don't they" opening when you want the reader to superimpose an attitude the reader won't reject, or to ridicule a competitor mildly instead of fiercely.

**AMERICAN
DEMOGRAPHICS**
A Dow Jones Publication
P.O. Box 58184 • Boulder, CO. 80322-8184

Why do people buy what they buy?

Two reasons, according to one marketing guru:
"To get what they don't have -- and to keep
what they've got."

There you have it.

But if that's not quite enough; if you still
have a few questions about who, what, where,
when and at what price; you should get to
know the lively, authoritative magazine that
fills in these details. It's called

                    American Demographics

... and this is your chance to get the next
issue FREE!

Dear Marketing Professional:

    Exasperating, aren't they?

    I'm talking about human beings. Americans. Consumers. The public.
The markets. The crazy-making jury out there you're paid to understand --
and whose whims and flights of fancy you're rewarded for predicting.

    Just what do they want? And what will they want tomorrow?

    My guess is that like most of us in this line of work, you could use all
the reliable help you can get -- not only in digging out the facts about what
really is going on, but what's likely to go on in the future.

        Fortunately, there's a bright, incisive magazine that
        specializes in this kind of help. A magazine that cuts
        through hype, fantasy, and wishful thinking -- and that
        gives you the figures and analyses you need to distin-
        guish received wisdom from reality.

        A magazine, what's more, devoted to helping you see
        around corners.

    It's American Demographics, the magazine of Consumer Trends for Business
Leaders, and if you've been looking for a publication that can breathe life,

                                            (Over, please)

FIG. 8–2 Letter-opening type 28: Does the typed material before this letter begins
enhance or diminish the reader's interest in the message that follows?
Opinion: It diminshes interest, _not_ because pre-greeting devices don't
work but because _this_ pre-greeting device is too primitive to stimulate
interest. Suggestion: If you're putting text before the greeting, be sure it
brings the reader into the store.

29. "I've enclosed. . ."

"I've enclosed" is a straightforward, businesslike opening. This makes it a logical opening for a letter accompanying samples, evidence, or validation.

The opening isn't parallel to "I have a free gift for you" (no. 8) or "I have something good for you" (no. 10), each of which specifies benefit before naming what's enclosed (or, more frequently, promised).

"I've enclosed" gets to the point immediately, so it's more straightforward and less emotional than an opening that states a problem, then offers a solution to that problem. Frankly, I'm puzzled to see fund raisers using "I've enclosed."

I'm guessing this opening (also used as an example of no. 4 ("Suggest a cataclysmic decision) from a major nonprofit organization was supposed to have an emotional wallop:

> Dear Friend,
> I've enclosed a Life or Death Seed Catalog for you.
> I call this the Life or Death Seed Catalog because what you do after looking through the catalog could help save the life of a small child . . . a child like Youssouf.
> Youssouf is a little boy who. . . .

Had they asked me, I'd have tied an acknowledgment of the mismatch into the mix:

> Dear Friend of [NAME OF ORGANIZATION],
> I know it's hard to believe. But what you do with the little seed catalog I've enclosed should literally make the difference between life and death for a helpless child.

Within the "enclosed" framework, adding "Why" immediately establishes a more emotional, more motivational opener. "Why have I enclosed . . . ?" is a variation of no. 20, "Why are we doing this?"

Compare the potency if the writer had started the appeal with a "Why" opening:

> Why am I sending you a seed catalog. . .and why do we call it the Life or Death Seed Catalog?
> Because a few seeds literally might mean the difference between

life and death for a little boy. The seeds you buy for him might
mean he'll still be alive next year.

But suppose we ignore altogether that unfortunate appellation, "Life or Death Seed Catalog," which before we even get into the letter makes us uncomfortable (not guilty) with an unpleasant challenge—Dracula Plants sprouting and blooming only at the stroke of midnight. We're discussing letter openings, not product psychology.

An "If . . ." opening would be completely safe as a substitute:

If you'll buy a few packets of seeds, a little boy in Mali might
live another year.
Those seeds are for <u>him</u> to plant. If they sprout, he won't starve.
It's as simple as that.

Can you see the difference in both impact and rapport the choice of letter openings can make? With such a huge menu, why choose an appetizer the reader finds distasteful?

30. Here's the sermon for today.

What a dangerous instrument this opening is!

In my opinion, sermons are best left to the clergy. They can get a reaction no outsider could ever induce because they address the Captive Willing Guilty. Anyone who shows up for a religious service expects a sermon and is schooled to respect the person delivering the sermon, if not the content.

But how about sermonizing in a nonsecretarian ambience? Will the reader think you're making assumptions, <u>even though they may be true</u>? Worse, will the reader doze off during your sermon because he/she is preconditioned to regard sermons as dull?

Those are the dangers. As an example:

Dear Herschell Lewis:
Making the right decisions on y our business travel policies
requires a thorough grasp of what's happening in the marketplace.

Widely considered the definitive source for information from T&E
experts, _The American Express Survey of Business Travel_

> *Management, 1993 Edition, can be invaluable in optimizing your travel investment.* Published only once every two years, the *Survey* gives you an inside look at the travel policies of America's corporations thanks to interviews with over 1300 top travel executives.

Snor-r-r-e.

Look at that stultifying opening sentence: "Making the right decisions on your business travel policies requires a thorough grasp of what's happening in the marketplace." Aside from the "Huh?"-inducing rhetoric, the sentence uses the word "policies," which invites multiple interpretations.

The sermon-like aspect of this opening, unbacked by specifics, turns the reader away. If we <u>had</u> any specifics, we might suggest replacing the sermon with a "Here's what the experts say" opening (no. 19) or the yet-to-come "Here's the deal" (no. 65) or "You want it. We have it" (no. 79) or even "Why do you need this?" (no. 94). But we don't have any specifics; so what if, instead of a sermon, the letter opened with a gauntlet-casting question:

> Are you making the right management decisions about your company's travel practices? Are you <u>sure</u>?
> Now you can have an <u>inside</u> look at what 1300 other top travel executives are doing. . . .

Sermons do work when the sermonizer and sermonizee are in sync. For mailings, I suggest saving this approach for continuation or resuscitation of an existing relationship. Example:

> Trouble. It's just around the corner.
> Trouble comes from having to "fly by the seat of your pants" in a tough, competitive business climate. That's what faces you, unless. . .

31. We've missed you.

A cliché? You bet. Effective? Usually in two separate directions, geared to the sophistication of the reader.

"We've missed you" as a mass appeal to dormant customers works best within the lower echelons of buyers. An appeal which is recogniz-

**RESERVED FOR H. GORDON,
VALUED FRIEND &
FORMER VIDEO CLUB MEMBER
YOU HAVE BEEN SPECIALLY SELECTED
FOR "WELCOME BACK" V.I.P. VIDEO CLUB SAVINGS
NOT AVAILABLE TO THE "GENERAL PUBLIC."**

Take Any 6 Movies FOR 39¢ EACH

Dear H. Gordon:

You're the kind of individual any company would be proud to have as a customer. And we've missed you since you left us.

And because of the responsible way you handled your Columbia House membership privileges, you have been selected to receive this special V.I.P. "welcome back" savings offer reserved <u>exclusively</u> for special friends of Columbia House.

  Come back now to the Columbia House Video Club and take
  any 6 hit movies from the enclosed stamp sheet for just
  39¢ each plus shipping and handling. This is a V.I.P.
  offer made only to special friends of the Club.

    <u>YOU'RE PRE-APPROVED TO RECEIVE THIS V.I.P. OFFER,</u>
      <u>H. GORDON</u>

Special friends like you deserve super savings. And to get yours, simply select the 6 hit movies you want for 39¢ each from the enclosed giant stamp sheet of over 270 selections. We'll rush your hit movies factory fresh, factory sealed. You'll enjoy tremendous savings right away.

And what a selection to choose from! Our library is bursting with stacks and stacks of the latest hit movies. Pick your 39¢ selections from today's biggest box office smashes such as Dances With Wolves ... Ghost ... Home Alone ... Sleeping With The Enemy ... The Silence Of The Lambs ... City Slickers ... plus others. Or select from all-time classics such as The Wizard Of Oz ... The Ten Commandments ... Ben-Hur ... The Sound Of Music, and more. Take any 6, yours for 39¢ each.

        - over, please -

COLUMBIA HOUSE   Entertaining America... One Person at a Time.

VIDEO CLUB

FIG. 8-3   Letter-opening type 31: This is a classic "We've missed you" opening, complete with the necessary followup—"and here's what we're going to do to get you back." Even though the letter is computer-personalized, it's obviously bulk-mailed. So what? The offer validates the sentiment, even if the sentiment is artificial.

ably "bulk" in creative approach isn't state-of-the-art, but to lower-levels, or greedy former buyers it's an old dependable, working like a Heimlich maneuver.

On a business-to-business or executive level, don't you dare let the look of a mass mailing peek through. To these targets, "We've missed you" has to be one on one, with a hand-finished look. If you can't do this, don't waste the postage.

A second qualifier: If you can't tie "We've missed you" to a special resuscitation offer, don't waste the postage.

A Video Club uses—quite properly—the "mass" approach, complete with Johnson Box. (As mentioned in Chapter 3, I've come to regard Johnson Boxes as de-personalizers.) A truly personal "We've missed you" to somebody who dropped a negative option video would seem gushy and phony.

Under the Johnson Box is another "bulk" line, printed in Goudy hand-tooled:

> Take Any 6 Movies FOR 39¢ EACH

Okay, we know this isn't going to be a personal "We've missed you." Here's the opening:

> Dear H. Gordon:
> You're the kind of individual any company would be proud to have as a customer. And we've missed you since left us.
>
> And because of the responsible way you handled your Columbia House membership privileges, you have been selected to receive this special V.I.P. "welcome back" savings offer reserved exclusively for special friends of Columbia House. . . .

This is the way to do it, all right. "We've missed you" doesn't generate any commiseration unless it's tied to the opportunity to get "Dances with Wolves" for 39¢.

32. We're solving your tough problem.

This opening is tricky, because problem-solvers tend to emit a self-serving aura. Result: The person with the problem becomes resentful rather than grateful.

Dear Struggling Holiday Gift Shopper,

Finding just the right gift for those special people on your holiday gift list can be tough. Especially if they live out of town, certainly if they "have everything," and most assuredly if they're people of discriminating taste.

This year, why not give a truly unique gift ... one they're not likely to find in any store ... a gift that will stimulate, challenge and delight the mind ... one that is <u>guaranteed</u> to please every puzzle enthusiast on your list!

<u>Give the gift of membership in the Crossword Puzzles of the Month Club -- a gift that keeps on giving all year long!</u>

Members receive five challenging new puzzles (and their solutions) in the mail each month for a full year! These are not reprints, but <u>original,</u> full-size puzzles edited exclusively for the Club by the noted crossword puzzle expert Henry Hook. They are intriguing, <u>challenging</u> puzzles with the same degree of difficulty as those in the Sunday New York Times.

Even the most discriminating puzzle solver will enjoy hours and hours of stimulating fun, month after month, all year long!

<u>Membership in the Club comes with a 100% money-back guarantee.</u>

Unlike many store-bought gifts, here's one you can "return" anytime ... no matter where you live! If, for any reason, you or the gift recipient is not completely satisfied, simply let us know and we'll promptly refund your membership <u>in full.</u> What store can make a "risk-free" offer like that?

<u>The world's best puzzles for less than $2.50 a month!</u>

A full year's membership is just $29.95. We pay all the postage. In a world where the price for comparable intellectual stimulation is constantly rising (i.e., movies, books, and theater), it's nice to know that something as high in quality as the

Over, please ...

THE CROSSWORD PUZZLES OF THE MONTH CLUB · 5311 FLEMING CT · AUSTIN, TX 78744 · 800-433-4386

FIG. 8–4 Letter-opening type 32: Does the letter actually solve the reader's tough problem? Partly. The handwritten overline says, "Your search for 'the perfect gift' is <u>over</u>!" then the second paragraph admits the gift is guaranteed to please "every puzzle enthusiast on your list!" Why not word this so everybody, pre-enthusiast or not, <u>can be</u> an enthusiast?

Here's where the writer has to hope either the database is accurate or the message-recipient isn't sensitive. Here, too, is an opportunity for light-hearted, non-preachy solutions to non-threatening problems.

The handwritten overline on a letter:

Your search for "the perfect gift" is <u>over</u>!

Not the stuff awards are made of, but the overline does serve a purpose: It tips off the reader that what follows won't raise hackles. Reading the greeting—"Dear Struggling Holiday Gift Shopper"—we can see how the handwritten overline <u>tempers</u> our reaction to the greeting itself. Proof? Visualize "Dear Struggling Holiday Gift Shopper" without that overline. Presumptuous, isn't it? The overline douses the negative fire.

The letter then begins:

Finding just the right gift for those special people on your holiday gift list can be tough. Especially if they live out of town, certainly if they "have everything," and most assuredly if they're people of discriminating taste.

This year, why not give a truly unique gift . . . one they're not likely to find in any store . . . a gift that will stimulate, challenge and delight the mind . . . one that is <u>guaranteed</u> to please every puzzle enthusiast on your list!

<u>Give the gift of membership in the Crossword Puzzles of the Month Club—a gift that keeps on giving all year long!</u>

Oh, yeah, it's mushy and generalized and never quite gets into gear. That reflects on the execution, not the concept. If you or I had written that letter, we'd have remembered the purpose of Letter Opening No. 32 and come out swinging: <u>We're solving your tough problem</u> (something like this) . . .

Dear Struggling Holiday Gift Shopper,

All right, quit struggling. Quit worrying about neckties he may never wear and candies her diet says are a no-no.

Instead, look how easy it is to get <u>just the right gift</u>—a gift that tells those special persons on your list you respect their intellect: One entire year's membership in the Crossword Puzzles of the Month Club.

My point: The looser the rhetoric, the harder it is to knock over your target. A tight argument, even for a nonsensical notion, demands consideration.

33. This is short and sweet.

Overall, in consumer mass mailings most writers I know have had better luck with long letters than with short letters. But I certainly wouldn't quit testing, especially since the heartless 1990s give us results which seem to point in both directions.

So "This is short and sweet" is the perfect test vehicle. Just three cautions:

1. Tell the reader, flat out, your message will be short and sweet.
2. <u>Keep it</u> short and sweet.
3. Keep sentences and paragraphs in character—short. Terse. Quick.

I treasure a letter that came to me a couple of years age. On page 2, the writer said, "To make a long story short. . ." The letter ran six pages.

You be the judge: Does this opening qualify as a classic "short and sweet" approach?

> This letter is going to be short and to the point. We don't want to make a big thing out of it. Not yet, anyway.
>
> We'd like to invite you to take advantage of what we call our "no-strings" membership.
>
> This offer extends an unusually generous introduction to you: choose any 4 books for only $1.

How did you vote? I vote <u>no</u>, and I'll tell you why: Even though the sentences are short and the paragraphs are just a couple of lines each, the letter is injected with fat.

Compare the approach with what you or I would have written—a true, genuine, authentic short and sweet opening, something like this:

This letter is going to be short and to the point.
Choose any 4 books for only $1. That's it. No strings.

See the difference? Our opening actually is short and sweet.

34. Believe it or not.

The value of "Believe it or not" is its recognition of The Age of Skepticism—in which we're wallowing, up to our armpits. The very admission builds rapport. The writer says to the reader, "Yes, I know this is hard to believe, but it's true."

For product introductions, especially on a pseudo-"breakthrough" level, this opening can bring a response when the usual puffery and bombast won't.

What cautions should we observe when we're using "Believe it or not"? Two major ones:

1. Don't misuse this as a phony justification for bending credibility beyond the level of acceptance a skeptic will allow—wild claims . . . an obviously preposterous discount . . . an unvalidated declaration of superiority.
2. Don't hit and run. Back up your argument so the reader begins to nod—"Yes, this might be true after all."

A computer software company starts with a Johnson Box that discloses the deal: "Announcing a once in a lifetime special sale" and "Save 80% for a limited time only" and "Get $2,195 worth of the PC world's top rated typefaces for just $49.95," so the "Believe it or not" aspect is drowned in a sea of puffery. For analytical purposes let's ignore that (and also ignore the peculiar arithmetic—$49.95 is about 2% of $2195, not 20%) and look at the letter itself:

Dear PC User:
This is no hype! It's hard to believe, but absolutely true. I want to give you over $2,000 worth of fonts for the amazing low price of only $49.95.

This top rated collection of typefaces is MoreFonts. And, for sure, it is the most important printing bargain of the century.

MicroLogic Software

3261 Ash Street · Palo Alto, CA 94306

✦ ✦

Announcing a once in a lifetime special sale!
Save 80% for a limited time only!
Get $2,195 worth of the PC world's top rated typefaces
For just $49.95!

✦ ✦

Dear PC User:

This is no hype! It's hard to believe, but absolutely true. I want to give you over $2,000 worth of fonts for the amazing low price of only $49.95.

This top rated collection of typefaces is MoreFonts. And, for sure, it is the most important printing bargain of the century.

With MoreFonts you'll be able to pick from an endless variety of typefaces, point sizes, and special effects (like outlines, shadows and backgrounds) from within WordPerfect, Works, Word and all Windows applications. And you'll be able to print like the world's best typesetter.

Gigantic Font Collection

I'm talking about a gigantic, all inclusive collection of fonts. This would cost more than $2,195 if purchased from BitStream, Adobe or Agfa/CompuGraphic -- and they are available to you for a limited time only for just a fraction of their original cost. These fonts are more than just bargain priced, they have set the quality standard in the industry.

Sounds too good to be true, right? But bear with me here! Go ahead, first, before you shake your head, and see for yourself what you get in this killer $49.95 package:

First you get the MoreFonts Basic Business Collection. It contains 14 typefaces including Geneva (including regular, italic, bold and bold italic), Tiempo (regular, italic, bold and bold italic), Financial, Showtime, Burlesque, Pageant, Opera, and Poster.

In retail stores, this entire package is worth $249.95 -- or $39.95 for each basic type style. Even at this price, the Business Collection is a mind blowing bargain -- especially when you consider that Adobe

---

FIG. 8–5 Letter-opening type 34: Be careful with "Believe it or not!" openings. Too often, a writer selects this opening without having the right ammunition to implement it. The result? Stridency, unbelievable claims, and use of adjectives such as "amazing" and "important" as band-aids over a thin selling proposition.

Nope. This letter doesn't qualify because it violates both cautions. It doesn't justify credibility, and it hits and runs.

Hey, don't write slop such as "And, for sure, it is the most important printing bargain of the century." Don't use "amazing" and expect it to stick without rhetorical glue. That isn't copywriting, it's just word-grabbing. And as long as we're picky, why not indent the paragraphs?

You or I would have opened the letter this way:

> Dear PC User:
> If I told you I'm going to give you more than $2,000 worth of fonts for $49.95, you'd probably think, "This guy is lying."
> I'm not lying, and I'm about to prove it.

Actually, the offer is more credible if the company is offering $700 worth of fonts. And as it turns out, on page 2 the writer admits, "This award-winning program sells for the extremely low price of $149.95 in most computer stores." Huh?

The logic of this argument is neither our problem nor our subject. We just want the pieces of a sales argument to be in sync. If you tell the reader what you're about to say is incredible, don't make "This is incredible" your only credible statement.

35. I know who you are.

Danger! This isn't parallel to opening no. 1, "If you're like me," or no. 17, "Because you are who you are, you may get special attention." This is Zeus hurling thunderbolts from Mount Olympus.

The key to an Olympian position is the reader's acceptance of you as Zeus. "I know who you are" is a terrific guilt-generator when the reader either is preconditioned to accept apparent judgment, or the writer is adept enough to create that acceptance.

Two examples. The first:

> I know all about you. Yes, I do.
>
> I know you'd like to be a world traveler. I know you'd like to enjoy the good life. I know you sometimes aren't quite able to enjoy all the good things of life you deserve. That's about to change.

The second example:

> You're someone who really appreciates fine dining.
>
> Like you, our customers are also discriminating fine food lovers. But since we couldn't find your name on our lists, I'm sending you the enclosed certificate to introduce you to the unique pleasures of Vermont's cuisines.

Both examples are flawed. The first, by using "you'd" instead of "you," nails the recipient as a loser. Even losers resent being called a loser by somebody who's trying to sell them something.

The second is non-threatening and convivial, but why make the flat statement, "You're someone who really appreciates fine dining" and then say, ". . . we couldn't find your name on our lists." The reader may reinterpret the first statement as speculation. An easy way to avoid the paradox: "The source from which your name came to us suggests you're someone who really appreciates fine dining."

36. Because you're "A" you're also "B."

This one isn't easy and isn't often interchangeable with other openings, even no. 17 ("Because you are who you are, you'll get special attention"). It's best used when adopting a patriarchal position because implicitly "Because you're 'A' you're also 'B'"places the writer on a judgmental plane.

Quick question: Which of the previous 35 openings is closest to this one?

If your choice is no. 9, "As you know," we're in sync. "As you know" is an assumptive opener, more convivial (and therefore more peer-positioned) than this one. The relationship suggests a choice: If after writing an "As you know" opening you think it's too weak, switch to this one; if after writing a "Because you're 'A' you're also 'B'" opening you think it's too condescending, switch to "As you know."

An example of this opening is a letter from a nonprofit organization pitching an internal motor club:

> Dear Member,
> As a driver, you know all about the problems that can arise when you're on the road. Your Association membership includes eligi-

From the Office of
the Executive Director

Horace B. Deets

Dear Member,

As a driver, you know about all the problems that can arise when you're on the road. Your Association membership includes eligibility for the AARP Motoring Plan among its member benefits to offer you peace of mind while driving and dependable help when you need it.

The Plan, provided by the Amoco Motor Club, has an excellent record of service. And its low cost makes it particularly attractive. The AARP Motoring Plan is available for member and spouse (or one other AARP member living in your household) at a price lower than most motoring plans with similar benefits.

One significant benefit the Plan offers you is the 1-800-START-UP service. When you need emergency road service throughout the U.S., in most instances, all you have to do is call this toll-free number.

AARP is proud of the plan – of the service and value it provides our members – and I encourage you to consider taking advantage of the protection it affords.

Sincerely,

Horace B. Deets

Horace B. Deets

National Headquarters: 601 E Street, N.W., Washington, DC 20049

FIG. 8–6 Letter-opening type 36: The organization mailing this letter is held *in loco parentis* by its senior citizen members. Does that justify the simplistic first sentence? Probably yes, because of the relationship. For a more commercial supplier, the opening would be far too low-key.

bility for the AARP Motoring Plan among its member benefits to offer you peace of mind while driving and dependable help when you need it.

A good match. Members give their Association a Big Daddy image, and the letter carries the image of this paternal benevolence. A more commercial group might have begun the message more promotionally: "As you know, when you're on the road you can run into a sudden problem at any moment."

37. Historical buildup

I like narrative openings, but by golly they'd better be bright. Many letters, especially those four or more pages long, get into a historical buildup—but not at the outset. Beginning with history requires both talent and guts because without an exquisite mixture of both, your reader is long gone before you've reached the year 1962.

The classic historical buildup embarks with something like "It all began with . . . " and includes at least one detail the reader already knows. Starting out that way <u>demands</u> a payoff before the reader asks, "So what?" Crucial to a historical buildup is the transition to <u>sell</u>. History per se doesn't sell; it opens the curtains.

Take a look at this historical buildup opening, plus the following paragraph:

> Dear Colleague:
>
> It started quietly with a simple affinity card. Then came the frequent flier cards, corporate cards, and now tiered pricing and a host of powerful enhancements offered by the big non-bank card players—from discounts on long distance phone service to rebates on cars.
>
> Like top executives in network television coping with the market fragmentation created by cable, astute executives in the credit card industry know they are witnessing a fundamental market change that affects everyone in the business—CEOs, product managers, marketers, finance and operations executives, even collections specialists.

CREDIT CARD FORUM

If you'd like to learn the "secrets" of competing successfully in the <u>new</u> credit card market, join <u>the</u> experts in Miami Beach.

Credit Card Management and Faulkner & Gray present
CREDIT CARD FORUM V:
The Death of Mass Marketing -- Segmentation Comes of Age

Dear Colleague:

It started quietly with the simple affinity card. Then came the frequent flier cards, corporate cards, and now tiered pricing and a host of powerful enhancements offered by the big non-bank card players -- from discounts on long distance phone service to rebates on cars.

Like top executives in network television coping with the market fragmentation created by cable, astute executives in the credit card industry know they are witnessing a fundamental market change that affects <u>everyone</u> in the business -- CEOs, product managers, marketers, finance and operations executives, even collections specialists.

Because thanks to market saturation, heightened competition and increasingly sophisticated consumers, the days of the monolithic "mass" card market are gone. The age of the segmented market is here. <u>Today!</u>

That is why I urge you to take this <u>advance</u> opportunity to secure your spot at CREDIT CARD FORUM V -- the fifth session of the credit card industry's most well-attended and highly-respected convocation -- sponsored by <u>Credit Card Management</u> and Faulkner & Gray.

Scheduled for March 30-April 2 at the Fontainebleau Hilton Resort and Spa in Miami Beach, CREDIT CARD FORUM V will feature your most astute and innovative colleagues -- and give you an opportunity to learn how they're capitalizing on the new segmented market to sign new cardholders and merchants, retain current members, improve customer service and increase revenues on every account. As an attendee:

* You'll share the cutting-edge insights of <u>Keynote Speaker James Bailey</u>, Executive Vice President, North American Consumer Bank, Citicorp, and <u>Conference Chairwoman Joanne Black</u>, Partner, Business Dynamics.

* You'll learn which <u>segmentation</u> strategies and techniques are favored by industry pacesetters such as Citicorp, American Express' Optima Card, and First Omni Bank.

* You'll have a unique opportunity to "compare notes" with senior executives and strategists from today's top bank and non-bank issuers, third party processors, retailers, credit bureaus and <u>more</u>.

(over, please)

Faulkner & Gray, Inc.   118 South Clinton Street   Suite 700   Chicago, Illinois 60661

FIG. 8-7 Letter-opening type 37: Mechanically, this letter suffers from an unrelenting sameness of paragraph length. Creatively, it suffers from an overline that begins with an impotent "If you'd like to learn," puts quotation marks around "secrets" and underlining beneath "the," and overlooks a buried dynamic overline candidate—"The death of mass marketing." Did a different writer create the provocative first sentence, "It started quietly with the simple affinity card". . .and then quietly expire?

Successful? In my opinion, anything but. This is a snore-maker because after the enticing first four words, the message starts to leak impact out its sides. The second paragraph is a naked laundry-list of everybody the writer wants to snare.

Match this same opening—"It started quietly with. . ."—to a genuine <u>buildup</u> and you'll have a readable, response-producing letter.

38. You just might be (and probably are). . .

This opening is a favorite of sweepstakes promoters. Because sweepstakes have such power, more and more marketers (and fund raisers too) are hooking their tails onto this high-flying promotional kite.

The difference between "will be" and "might be" is profound but often concealed. At the fingertips of an expert wordsmith, a properly structured "You just might be" opening <u>implies</u> the second half—"and probably are"—without running afoul of the spiderweb of legal restrictions.

Typical of this beginning is a letter with a provocative overline and ongoing amplification:

> **You may already have won a brand new 1993 Lincoln Mark VIII, An exotic 7-day Caribbean vacation, A convenient pocket-sized cellular phone, or A relaxing florida getaway.**
> Dear Florida Business Leader,
>   As part of an unprecedented promotion exclusively for Florida executives, you may have already won any one of these prizes—or more!
>   Imagine if you will. . .
> Watching the countryside roll effortlessly by as the exhilarating power and elegance of a brand new 1993 Lincoln Mark VIII heeds your beck and call.

The letter avoids the pitfall into which so many pretenders tumble—leaving Shangri-La too soon. Whatever you're selling, restrain the urge to pitch until you've painted a winning scene.

(Phrases such as "unprecedented promotion" and a dangling "or more" are touches of weakness, marching in place.)

Second Annual
FLORIDA TREND
Invitational
Sweepstakes
FOR FLORIDA EXECUTIVES

**You may have already won a brand new 1993 Lincoln Mark VIII,
An exotic 7-day Caribbean vacation,
A convenient pocket-sized cellular phone, or
A relaxing Florida getaway.**

Dear Florida Business Leader,

As part of an unprecedented promotion exclusively for Florida executives, you may have already won any one of these prizes -- or more!

Imagine if you will...

... Watching the countryside roll effortlessly by as the exhilarating power and elegance of a brand new Lincoln Mark VIII heeds your beck and call.

... Leaving your worries behind as you explore exotic ports like San Salvador, St. Thomas, San Juan and more on a 7-day Crown Cruise Line adventure.

... Basking in the Florida sunshine on a fabulous vacation getaway.

**PRIZE-WINNING NUMBERS HAVE ALREADY BEEN SELECTED --
AND YOU MAY BE HOLDING ONE OF THEM!**

In fact, more than 250 prizes will be awarded in the Second Annual FLORIDA TREND Invitational Sweepstakes for Florida Executives. And since this offer is being made exclusively to a select group of recognized Florida business leaders, the chances you're holding one of the winning numbers are extraordinary! But, to claim any prize, you must

**SEND YOUR OFFICIAL ENTRY TO BEAT THE ENTRY DEADLINE
OR ANY PRIZE YOU MAY HAVE WON WILL BE AWARDED TO SOMEONE ELSE.**

Don't let this happen! There's nothing more disappointing than to hold a winning number and forfeit your prize because your entry was not returned in time. To guarantee you receive the prize you justly deserve, mail your official sweepstakes entry right away. And, as a special bonus, if you return the grand prize winning entry in time to beat the January 30, 1993 "Early Bird" deadline,

YOU'LL GET AN ADDITIONAL $1,000 CASH!

But that's not all you'll get...

FIG. 8–8 Letter-opening type 38: This is the way to maximize the impact of the "You just might be (and probably are). . ." opening. Nowhere on the entire first page of this letter does the writer succumb to the bait always crouching temptingly at the elbow—to take off the seventh veil and pitch a subscription before the reader's skepticism has oozed away under a stream of happy promises.

39. I'll get right to the point.

"I'll get right to the point" parallels No. 3, "This is short and sweet," only in its promise of directness. The two differ in emotional thrust because "This is short and sweet" smiles and "I'll get right to the point" doesn't. The difference underscores the value of each. (The yet-to-come "I won't waste your time" [no. 92] makes a different promise altogether.)

A letter from a publication begins, "My message is short"; but it's all business, which shifts it into "I'll get right to the point" category:

> My message is short. . .
> . . .because it's simple. Here are three important reasons why
> you should get your own subscription to Advertising Age now.
> 1. To get ahead in business. Ad Age is read regularly by more
> executives than. . .

I sense some confusion hovering about the first few words—"my message is short because it's simple." That word "simple" is dangerous when used to influence professionals. Mightn't this letter have generated greater rapport by staying with a "This is short and sweet" attitude?

40. These are critical times.

Here's one that in less-than-expert hands can appear ludicrous. The writer has to be able to convince the reader that these <u>are</u> critical times, <u>relative to the reader's own experiential background.</u> Otherwise we've just cried, "Fire!" (no. 14) or "Wolf!" (no. 64) less competently than a professional cry of "Fire!" or "Wolf!"

Don't assume this opening is reserved for politics or religion or loathsome diseases. It has surprising universality. But recognize, too, the necessity for being able to read and bore into the reader's background.

A letter has this typed overline and opening:

> At no other time in recent history has it been more important for
> you and your family to understand the world around you.

> Dear Member,
>   In recent times, the world has witnessed extraordinary changes:
>
> • the dramatic dissolution of the Soviet Union—and emergence of the Commonwealth of Independent States. . . .

Weak? Yes. The overline exemplifies what's wrong with so, so many overlines. The writer just doesn't understand, care, or have the ability to cope with this fact of selling in print: The purpose of an overline is to initiate reader-salivating. Limp clichés such as "At no other time in recent history has it been more important for you and your family to understand the world around you" leave the reader with a dry emotional socket.

The purpose of this letter was to sell an atlas. Why couldn't the overline have had some guts, such as "Uh-oh. I'll bet your atlas still has a map of the Soviet Union and none of Belarus"?

The writer is in control . . . but only until the reader rises up in wrath, slumps down in apathy, or (joy!) lifts pen or phone.

41. Visualize this scenario. . .

I have a love/hate relationship with this sophisticated opening. When absolutely targeted, it's dynamite; when askew, it's stupid. When tightly structured, it's arresting; when larded with the fat of inconsequential details, it's tedious.

That's because an absolutely targeted opening harpoons the reader within his/her experiential background, and a mis-hit leaves the reader completely outside the message.

An example of "Visualize this scenario" is this opening of an eight-page letter:

> Dear Entrepreneur,
>   It's early morning, before your employees come in . . .
>   You unlock the door to your business, turn off the alarm and step inside. You pause for a moment to look around.
>   You take pride in the business you've created here. Every paper clip, desk, typewriter, machine, car and truck is yours (well, maybe the bank's too!)

Benjamin Ordover, President
The Hume Company, Inc.
835 Franklin Court
Box 105559
Atlanta, GA 30348-9756

HUME

```
          If you're running your own business (or plan to soon)

          I'll send you the SUCCESSFUL BUSINESS MANAGEMENT

          Starter Set -- free of charge.


Dear Entrepreneur,

     It's early morning, before your employees come in...

     ...you unlock the door to your business, turn off the alarm and step
inside.  You pause for a moment to look around.

     You take pride in the business you've created here.  Every paper clip,
desk, typewriter, machine, car and truck is yours (well, maybe the bank's too!)

     But it's your business.  Its success depends solely on your wits.
You call the shots, no one else.

     What's more, with hard work, you can probably make more money on your own than
you ever could with a lifetime of faithful service to a large company.

     You slide behind your desk and settle back in your chair.  You're looking
forward to the day!

YOUR DAY BEGINS...

     Just then the phone rings.  It's a key supplier telling you he can't meet your
deadlines.  Worse still, he can't make promises for future deliveries.

     Your brow furrows.  Hmmmm.  Soon after, your bookkeeper tells you stock is
missing from the shelves.

     Then it's your bank on the phone.  Because of a big order you're working on, you
need a quick loan to buy more raw materials.  But the bank is dragging its feet.

     On top of that, your employees are demanding an immediate 15% raise.

     Worse still.  You glance at today's paper and there, on page 1, is news that
your major competitor has developed something new.  It looks like a major

                                        (over, please)
```

SUPER GROWTH MARKET #1:

Cellular Telephones: The growing appeal and convenience of "take anywhere, use anywhere" telephones will
expand this market from 1 million phones in 1988 to 10 million by 1995.

FIG. 8-9 Letter-opening type 41: If you want to use a "Visualize this scenario" type of opening, two cautions: first, don't dally on inconsequential details; second, get to the point. This letter takes too long to get to the point, which is lost anyway because the typed three lines above the greeting give away the play.

But it's <u>your</u> business. Its success depends solely on your wits. You call the shots, no one else.

You slide behind your desk and settle back in your chair. You're looking forward to the day!

Ugh!

Re-read just the first two short paragraphs. Don't you get the feeling we're selling security devices? We aren't.

Reading the entire opening, do you yet have any idea what we're selling? I don't. Actually, the opening persists for more than a page.

A total misfit: What entrepreneur has the time to wade through treacle?

The last paragraph on page 2 tells the reader what's for sale—a book. By that time any entrepreneur worth a nickel is exasperated.

Now, in mitigation: <u>Above</u> the greeting is this legend:

> If you're running your own business (or plan to soon) I'll send you the SUCCESSFUL BUSINESS MANAGEMENT <u>Starter Set—free of charge</u>.

Does this save it? In my opinion it compounds the felony, because any wallop the opening might have had disappears in this betrayal of suspense. It's parallel to a mystery movie which opens with one of the characters telling the audience, "You'll be surprised when you find out I'm the murderer."

Tightened and oiled, this could have been a forceful, reader-grabbing opening.

42. If you like that, you'll love this.

What a reader-involver this one can be! Notice, please, I said "can be," not "is." In a major respect this beginning parallels no. 41, "Visualize this scenario . . ."—reader involvement depending squarely on relevance.

Suppose I say to you, not knowing what pleases your palate, "If you like squid, you'll love octopus." Not only are my parameters too narrow (and too squishy), but by selecting the wrong parallel I can destroy your latent positive response.

Smithsonian

*   *   *   *   *   *   *   *   *   *   *   *

WILL YOU PLEASE DO US A FAVOR?

SPECIAL HALF-PRICE OFFER!
A full-year's membership and subscription to Smithsonian
Magazine for just $11. It's like getting
SIX FREE ISSUES!

*   *   *   *   *   *   *   *   *   *   *   *

Dear Friend,

    If you're fascinated by the people and things that make
America so interesting and unique, then <u>you're going to love
SMITHSONIAN Magazine</u>!

    I'm sure you're familiar with our National Museums in
Washington, D.C. — and I hope you'll enjoy your HALF-PRICE
Membership to the fullest! — but you may not have discovered
the <u>interesting and informative publication that brings the
Smithsonian right into your living room</u>!

        <u>That's why we're making this limited time
HALF-PRICE offer. A FULL-YEAR'S Membership
and 12 full issues of SMITHSONIAN Magazine
at HALF PRICE</u>!

    You see, there are many fabulous benefits to Membership
in the Smithsonian National Associates, but by far the
greatest benefit is a subscription to SMITHSONIAN Magazine.
And the moment you read your first issue, you'll understand
what I mean!

    SMITHSONIAN Magazine is a treasure-trove of fascinating
articles on Americana from A to Z — such as these, from
recent issues:

    <u>A NEW LIFE BEGINS FOR THE ISLAND OF HOPE AND TEARS</u> —
Ellis Island in New York Harbor has reopened its

(please turn page)

FIG. 8–10 Letter-opening type 42: By generalizing ("If you're fascinated by the people and things that make America so interesting and unique") instead of naming a few "things" that make America interesting and unique, the writer loses impact. A question: Why start a Johnson box with "WILL YOU PLEASE DO US A FAVOR? and then not explain what the favor is?

Too, often, users of this opening water it down by <u>generalizing</u> the first half of the parallel. It still works, but the strength doesn't come within light-years of the same opening which brings up specifics.

An example:

> Dear Friend,
> If you're fascinated by the people and things that make America so interesting and unique, then <u>you're going to love SMITHSONIAN Magazine!</u>

See what happened? How can anybody be fascinated by "people and things"? What people? What things? Later on in the letter, the writer does begin to specify. Why not fire when at point-blank range? A suggested rewrite, based on examples <u>from within this same letter</u>:

> If you're fascinated by the Pennsylvania archaeological digs that show humans may have reached our continent well before the traditionally accepted date of 115,000 years ago . . . if you chuckle over teen-age scientists creating acid rain and showing how headache remedies affect radishes . . . you're going to love <u>SMITHSONIAN Magazine</u>, where every month brings hundreds of engrossing, riveting stories and articles.

Now, I grant you these aren't blockbusters, but they're what I found buried in the letter. A half-dozen issues of the magazine probably would have yielded more savory grist for the word-mill.

43. Whether you do this . . . or do that . . .

The best way to describe this boiler-plate opening is "serviceable." It's a workmanlike old dependable you'll call on when you're writing an umbrella-letter to a polyglot group of readers.

"Whether you do this . . . or do that . . ." says whatever you're selling covers a multitude of circumstances, a broad spectrum of situations that surely include the reader.

A typical example of this opening:

> Dear Reader,
> Whether you administer the business travel of 10 employees or 1,000 you can benefit from the most complete information source on corporate business travel: CORPORATE TRAVEL magazine.

Obviously this semi-targeted opening has less energy than a totally targeted opening. But two compensations: (1) This one works where the target can't be pinpointed; (2) this opening doesn't require changing the message as you change lists.

44. The classic quotation.

For heaven's sake be careful with this one. You're okay, if dull, with "A penny saved is a penny earned," but you're out of the reader's depth (and acceptance-range) with "Poetry fettered, fetters the human race."

We've all transgressed, but let's take the vow: No more rushing to *Bartlett's Familiar Quotations* to find a quotation we can use as our opening shot. Why not? Because if we have to lean on *Bartlett's* we risk alienating the reader who feels—correctly, as it turns out—we're trying to lord it over him/her.

I like quotations dipped in acid because the reader feels comfortable joining us in satire or disdain. Can't you see the reader staying with you when you open with something like these?

> Was Alexandre Dumas right when he said, "I prefer the wicked to the foolish, because the wicked sometimes rest."

Or . . .

> You probably feel the way Mary Buckley does: "Husbands are awkward things to deal with; even keeping them in hot water doesn't make them tender.

Lots of these around. They're grabbers. So why did the writer of this letter start by showing off?

> Dear Friends:
> *"Great things are done when men and mountains meet."*
> William Blake wrote these words, words that resonate today. I'd like to invite you to join me in proving this concept, in exploring the high landscapes, and in being a part of a chronicle of special places and times.

MOUNTAIN TRAVEL·SOBEK
THE ADVENTURE COMPANY ®

Dear Friends:

"Great things are done when men and mountains meet."

William Blake wrote these words, words that resonate today.

I'd like to invite you to join me in proving this concept, in exploring the high landscapes, and in being a part of a chronicle of special places and times.

You may know that last year I authored a coffee-table book, **ISLANDGODS**, celebrating the world's most exotic isles; and that prior to that I co-authored **RIVERGODS**, extolling the world's wildest rivers.

Now I've been asked to complete the nature-gods trilogy with **MOUNTAINGODS**, a large-format photo and prose work that will honor the finest mountain travel experiences in the world, many of them classic treks offered by Mountain Travel*Sobek.

I'd like to do something unusual, and personally invite you to join me on some of the mountain adventures that will be featured in **MOUNTAINGODS**. I'd love to share with you the process of creating a chapter for a book, of being part of a trip memorialized in words and pictures.

I've listed below some of the trips I will be taking over the next year for this project. If you might be keen to travel with me, to turn over the stones that pave these paths, then please give us a call. I'd love to shape some of these extraordinary journeys with you!

February 6-February 21, **Hiker's Patagonia, featuring moderate hikes in Chile's Paine and Argentina's Glacier National Park, remote wildernesses at the end of the earth. $2295.

March 18-April 5, **The Annapurna Sanctuary, into the heart of the Annapurna Himal. $2490.

October 2-October 17, **The Japan Alps and Mt. Fuji, challenging hiking with the rising sun. $3025.

November 20-December 4, **Angel Falls & Mt. Auyantepui in Venezuela, featuring a trek in "The Lost World" and a canoe trip to the base of the world's highest waterfall. $2495.

And there may be other **Mountaingods** available for guest participation as well. Just give us a call, and join me in making magical and great things happen as we meet the mountains...

Yours in adventure,

Richard Bangs

6420 Fairmount Avenue, El Cerrito, California 94530-3606
Phone: (510) 527-8100 Toll-Free:1-800-227-2384   FAX: (510) 525-7710 Telex: 335-429

FIG. 8–11 Letter-opening type 44: Okay, we're selling trips to the mountains. If this opening pulled a lot of response, it proves another quotation, one by Browning—"Faith moves mountains."

Don't you get the feeling that joining this guy will result not in special times but in torpid times? Aside from the plural greeting ("Dear Friends:") and the unindented paragraphs, quoting William Blake to start a letter symbolizes another Blake quotation: "Every night and every morn/Some to misery are born."

45. I have to tell you the truth.

Name somebody who isn't fascinated with soul-baring and you've named somebody who probably is a poor prospect for direct marketing.

"I have to tell you the truth" suggests we're going to read something private or slightly naughty or wayward, a self-immolating tale told out of school. Usually this doesn't materialize, but meanwhile we're temporarily hooked.

An excellent and persuasive example of this opening:

> Dear Herschell & Margo:
> I'd be lying to you if I suggested that the reason for my letter today is wholly selfless. But to some extent it is.
> That extent is a charitable trust I have set up for Meals-on-Wheels. . . .

My first move, reading the greeting, was to look for the signature to see who's calling us by our first names. By gum, it <u>was</u> a friend, as spokesperson for a non-profit organization.

I'd have put that second sentence in parentheses, but the letter has to succeed because it combines genuine personalization with self-revelation.

46. You're important to us.

Can you "over-stroke" (opening no. 18) a customer or a client or even a prospect? Only if your stroking is so blatant that it becomes obviously disingenuous.

Stroking isn't the same as claiming importance. You <u>can</u> destroy budding rapport by misuse of that word. And therein lies the danger of substituting "You're important to us" for "We love you."

The standard recommendation applies: After making a declarative statement, then quickly, quickly explain why. You've avoided the hit-

and-run syndrome that leaves the reader sitting as reader, not partic-ipant; and you've forced yourself to shovel some rapport-fertilizer into the mix.

An example of "You're important to us" is a subscription renewal letter from a controlled circulation magazine whose subscribers are computer dealers.

The letter begins:

> Dear Executive,
> Your business is important to us and that's why we're extending this limited time FREE offer especially to you.
> A full year's subscription to COMPUTER RESELLER NEWS—the Newspaper for Value Added Reselling—is being offered to you absolutely FREE.
> Chances are you've already heard of CRN. For over a decade, CRN has been the leading publication for resellers—bringing you late-breaking industry news, as well as in-depth analyses on emerging technologies and hot, new products.

Suppose you're a VAR. Would you accept this offer?

Probably . . . but not because "Your business is important to us"; no, you'd go for it only because it's free.

What happened here is a standard dereliction in letter writing, the whole point behind this listing of openings: The writer <u>begins</u> with a concept and then forgets or ignores that concept. Why do that? You chose an opening for a reason.

Not one word after the first six justifies the claim, "Your business is important to us." Instead, we sense a growing frenzy. What's going on here, since the magazine is free?

The publication could handle this in either of two ways: (1) Any one of 10 or 12 other openings already described might have been a better lead-in—such as numbers 17, 19, 20, 25, 32, 36, 38, or 39; (2) Justify the first six words.

47. Now you can. . .or At last!

"Now you can" and "At last!" are close enough to warrant a single entry, although they aren't identica. "Now you can. . ." is narrative; "At last!" is exclamatory.

THE NEXT
DECADE
1982-1993

Computer
ResellerNews

Dear Executive,

Your business is important to us and that's why we're extending this limited time FREE offer especially to you.

A full year's subscription to COMPUTER RESELLER NEWS— the Newspaper for Value Added Reselling— is being offered to you absolutely FREE!

Chances are you've already heard of CRN. For over a decade, CRN has been the leading publication for resellers—bringing you late-breaking industry news, as well as in-depth analyses on emerging technologies and hot, new products.

EACH WEEK YOUR SUBSCRIPTION TO CRN
WILL BRING YOU INFORMATION ON:

- News
- Networks
- Hardware
- Software
- VAR News
- Dealers
- Distribution
- The User Market

SO WHAT ARE YOU WAITING FOR?

Start your subscription now! There's nothing to lose and absolutely everything to gain. To qualify for a FREE subscription, simply complete the enclosed card, or fax it to (516) 562-5468.

Thank you—we look forward to hearing from you!

Sincerely,

Susan Eliasoph
Senior Circulation Manager

P.S. Please pass along the additional subscription card to a colleague who might benefit from CRN.

CMP PUBLICATIONS, INC. • 600 COMMUNITY DRIVE • MANHASSET, NY 11030

FIG. 8–12 Letter-opening type 46: This letter begins, "Your business is important to us." Does <u>any</u> statement in the rest of the letter carry through with this thought? Switching out of the theme established by the opening not only loses impact but sweeps away the writer's seventh veil.

"At last!" is an old dependable in many a space ad because it's an automatic statement of superiority. "At last" says both "This didn't exist before" and "You need it." For most business letters "Now you can . . ." is probably safer because this <u>seems to be</u> more the result of thought and/or investigation.

A letter for a "religious epics" video library, after a three-color Johnson box, begins:

> Dear Friend,
> Now you can own the best of Hollywood's grand and glorious spectaculars—inspired by the most powerful stories of all time.
> Academy Award®-winning actors and directors . . . stunning costumes and casts of thousands. . .striking locations and panoramic photography. . .scenes of passion, greed, terror, and salvation.

For me, that "®" mark maims the poetry; but can you see the mismatch? "Now you can . . ." demands a payoff. What's strange is that this letter is loaded with payoff lines, but they're buried. For example, the letter could have borrowed some text from a few paragraphs down:

> Now you can see internationally-renowned actor Max Von Sydow as Jesus, Charlton Heston as John the Baptist, José Ferrer as King Herod, Telly Savalas as Pontius Pilate . . . all right in your own living room.
> Take a look at just a few of the spectacular adventures that await you. . . .

"You're important to us" and "Now you can . . ." share a challenge: They demand a payoff. Hit-and-run will damage response.

48. They think I'm nuts!

"They think I'm nuts" or "I must be nuts" has two advantages over many types of letter openings: First, it's 100 percent informal, which means the seeds of rapport have already half-germinated. Second, it's disarming because it's self-denigrating, and it doesn't demand a specific follow-up.

**Now on home video
in one thrilling collection!**

**Hollywood's biggest stars and finest films,
the world's most dramatic and timeless stories!**

**Preview the first double-cassette movie
– *THE GREATEST STORY EVER TOLD*–
for 10 days FREE!**

Dear Friend,

Now you can own the best of Hollywood's grand and glorious spectaculars -- inspired by the most powerful stories of all time.

Academy Award®-winning actors and directors...stunning costumes and casts of thousands...striking locations and panoramic photography...scenes of passion, greed, terror, and salvation.

Columbia House Video Library brings you a blockbuster movie collection that ranges across the spectrum of human emotion and experience.

THE GREAT RELIGIOUS EPICS VIDEO SERIES

You're invited to preview the first thrilling double-cassette movie, THE GREATEST STORY EVER TOLD, for 10 days -- ABSOLUTELY FREE!

Internationally-renowned actor Max Von Sydow as Jesus heads a dazzling cast of Hollywood luminaries: Charlton Heston as John the Baptist, Jose Ferrer as King Herod, Telly Savalas as Pontius Pilate, along with Martin Landau, John Wayne, Angela Lansbury, Sidney Poitier, Pat Boone, Claude Rains, Sal Mineo, Shelley Winters, and so many more!

Hailed as a classic for generations, THE GREATEST STORY EVER TOLD presents the life of Christ with epic majesty, sweeping drama, and rich emotional power.

This is a film the whole family will enjoy -- one that belongs in the permanent collection of every Hollywood movie lover. And now it's yours to preview for 10 days FREE!

<u>Classics of the silver screen --
yours to view whenever you want!</u>

THE GREATEST STORY EVER TOLD is your thrilling introduction to THE GREAT RELIGIOUS EPICS VIDEO SERIES, a treasure-trove of some of the most lavishly-produced entertainment-packed epics ever brought to the screen.

These are genuine Hollywood classics -- inspired by some of the most thrilling and terrifying stories in the Bible. Stories so timeless and universally appealing that they challenged the finest directors and actors of the day.

You'll be transported to remote times and exotic places...mesmerized by glamorous costumes and gigantic casts...thrilled to the bone by the larger-than-life experience of these powerful, dramatic stories.

Here are the best of the movies that defined the Hollywood epic -- gathered together in one splendid home video collection from Columbia House Video Library

over, please...

1400 NORTH FRUITRIDGE AVENUE, TERRE HAUTE, IN 47811   293-L-R

FIG. 8–13 Letter-opening type 47: "Now you can . . ." implicitly says whatever this is wasn't available before. Following the "Now you can . . ." opening with a "For the first time . . ." follow-up might have been stronger grist for the writer's word-mill than dependence on too-familiar generalities.

A fund-raising letter begins:

> Dear Ms. Nelson,
> When we began sending out these free calendars, people said we were crazy!
> We mailed these beautiful calendars absolutely free to good, caring people like yourself.
> "You can't do it—the Veterans of Foreign Wars will go broke!" many doubters said. "People will use their calendars, but <u>you'll</u> never hear from them again."
> But, it didn't turn out that way at all. In fact, thousands of people like you . . .

Except for the unnecessary underlining of "you" and the comma after "But," I admire this letter, especially since it came from an organization usually regarded as stuffy and humorless.

Suppose the letter had begun, "We owe our veterans something. They fought for our freedom." Would this approach, even accompanied by a free calendar, have generated the immediate bond the "They think we're nuts!" approach accomplishes?

49. Before you do that, do this.

This opening makes sense for many business-to-business communications. The writer pre-establishes a favorable-to-vendor relationship between parties. "Before you do that, do this" suggests writer-superiority and reader inferiority without saying so, by imprinting an <u>acceptable</u> direction without being imperative.

An example, from a list company:

> Dear Business to Business Marketer. . . .
> **Before you look at your new Penton Lists Catalog, there's a few things you might want to know about your customers . . .**
>
> **Research shows:** More than $11 trillion in goods and services are sold each year in the U.S. *It is business and government, NOT individual consumers that account for two thirds of this spending.*
>
> **What does it mean to you?** Business and government markets offer far greater sales potential for many companies than consumer markets.

For this analysis let's ignore the grammar of "there's a few things" and the looseness of "It is business and government that account" and focus on the use of "Before you do that, do this." Does this opening maximize the function of this opening?

My opinion: No. The opening is provocative and pulls the reader into the letter; it then takes a strange turn, suggesting the reader doesn't really know his/her customers . . . which isn't the intention. What if the opening had been more letter-like, without boldface and with indented paragraphs, and had begun:

> Before you look at your new Penton Lists Catalog, take just one moment to consider:
> Does it mean anything to you that two-thirds of all spending in the U.S. is by business and government, not by consumer?

I cheerfully admit I'm not a fan of research <u>as a selling tool</u>. In my Book of Doom, researchers join lawyers and accountants as people so strangled by self-importance they're unable to sell. But that's a prejudice, not a researched fact.

50. Wouldn't it be lovely if. . .

I like this one for three reasons: First, it suggests hope in a troubled world. The psychology of this opening is unassailable: It suggests with gracious mildness that the world is imperfect but not impossible. Second, it has the reader pondering the better life around the corner, if only we'll look.

The third reason delights the copywriter's own troubled world. This is one of those magical openings that always seems to work. Somehow, those first few words steer the message on an inoffensive but impressive course.

A letter for computer software begins:

> Dear Word Processor User:
>
> Wouldn't it be great if your word processor had built-in macros to help you work faster . . .
>
> . . . if you could control the way your screen looked—without leaving your document . . .

RBF

WORDSTAR.

P.O. Box 2030   Cameron Park, CA 95682

LAN VERSION NOW AVAILABLE

INTRODUCING WORDSTAR 7.0

**The high-end word processor
with the features you've been waiting for.**

**Order yours now for
the special Upgrade Price of only $89
and get a FREE GIFT.**

Dear Word Processor User:

Wouldn't it be great if your word processor had built-in macros to help you work faster...

...if you could control the way your screen looked — without leaving your document...

...if you could work <u>exactly</u> the way you liked best — keyboard, mouse, pull-down menus, buttons or dialog boxes...

...if you could use it to send <u>laser-quality</u> faxes with your fax/modem...

...if you could quickly convert documents to and from dozens of popular word processors — including Macintosh...

...if you could use it with virtually every type and brand of printer available?

You don't have to wait a moment longer, because your word processor "wish list" just came true! Today, I'm proud to introduce <u>Version 7.0 of WordStar for DOS</u> — the upgrade with the "most-wanted" features our users have been asking for.

The suggested retail price for this important new version is $495. But I'm delighted to offer it to you for the special Upgrade Price of <u>only $89</u> — a savings of more than $400. Plus, if you respond by April 30, 1993, you'll receive a FREE GIFT worth $49.
(But more about that later...)

We created <u>WordStar 7.0</u> after listening to what our users loved — and didn't love — about the program. It's our biggest upgrade in <u>four years</u>.

FIG. 8–14 Letter-opening type 50: One huge benefit of a "Wouldn't it be lovely" opening is its quick acceptance by the reader. Another is its universality. This letter begins, "Wouldn't it be great if . . ." and has heads nodding in agreement at once.

. . .if you could work <u>exactly</u> the way you liked best—keyboard,
mouse, pull-down menus, buttons or dialog boxes . . .

See how effortlessly the text influences the reader? The writer isn't preaching, isn't selling, isn't demanding. The "if" factor disarms skepticism and antagonism. (I don't know why this wording moved into the less-motivational past tense.)

9

25 Startling Comparisons

The 25 examples that follow include "grabber" and competitive/comparative openings, some of which can startle as well as challenge. They direct the reader, which means you're faced with a logical challenge if you're going to use them for maximum impact. Intelligent targeting becomes a major ingredient of the marketing mix.

51. The best just got better.

This solid, serviceable boiler-plate opening incorporates a major advantage: It's comparative without stating a specific comparison because it's an implicit statement of superiority.

Where this old dependable can fall flat isn't in the statement itself; rather, it's in failure to follow up the statement with specific, ostensible proof: The best just got better <u>in this way</u>. . . .

What if you can't generate such a follow-up? No problem. You've just proved "The best just got better" is the wrong opening for the message at hand. Try a different start.

An example of "The best just got better" is a letter that <u>does</u> follow up the claim, but the example is flawed by presenting a generality as a specific:

> The best value in the computer industry has just gotten even better. Every new Swan 486 system you buy (V line and above) includes a complete package of free hardware, software, and service designed to insure more than your machine . . . it insures your productivity!

A couple of questions here. First—and I offer this as opinion, not fact—"has just gotten even better" is considerably more ponderous than "just got even better." Second, the parentheses make the statement before them a weasel rather than a fact. Using commas in this instance would have solved that problem.

If you're asking why this letter opens with generalities instead of specifics, this replication of the text cheats. Specifics do appear in a typed Johnson Box effect before the greeting.

Regardless, I'd have chosen a more inspirational overline and saved the meat for the first paragraph. You decide: Is that opening better than this suggested revision?

Swan
TECHNOLOGIES

CORPORATE OFFICES • PHONE 814-238-1820 • FAX 814-237-5416
SALES & SUPPORT • PHONE 800-468-9044 • FAX 814-237-4450

**Introducing Swan's New LifeLine Service! Every New 486 V and Above Comes With
<u>A Free Modem, Free Lifetime Remote Diagnostics, Free Software HelpLine Support
and Our Legendary 2-Year On-site Warranty -- STANDARD!</u>
Because "What's In The Box" Is Only The Beginning!**

Dear Swan Customer:

The best value in the computer industry has just gotten even better. Every new Swan 486 system you buy (V Line and above), includes a complete package of free hardware, software and service designed to insure more than your machine... it insures your productivity!

Swan's new **LifeLine Service** provides you with the solution to virtually any hardware or software problem you encounter. It's the single most complete hardware and software support system in the industry... and it comes standard with every V Line, Direct Bus or EISA system we sell. Here's how it works:

- **Free Internal Modem --** You're automatically connected to the world, but just as importantly, you're always directly connected to our expert technicians for instant service -- no matter how far you go.

- **Free Remote Diagnostics Software and Lifetime Service --** Remote Diagnostics is like having a technician on call right there in your home or office -- 24-hours a day. This unique software and service allows our technicians to see inside your PC and perform tests directly from our service center. Hardware problems can be diagnosed... even solved on the spot. You get the answers you need from a qualified technician in the fastest way possible... no waiting, no scheduling, no problem!

- **Free 1-year Software HelpLine --** OK, let's say you find yourself frustrated by a software problem. You could call the software manufacturer... if you have a few hours to burn waiting on the phone... and, if your software I.D. number is handy. Or, you can call your free HelpLine 800 number. Get instant answers on over 1,000 titles without searching for your I.D. number. And that means you're back to work within a minute or two... instead of an hour or two!

- **Free Two-year On-site Warranty --** If there is a problem with your Swan hardware you're still covered by the absolute best standard warranty in the industry. A highly skilled technician will arrive at your site, usually within 24-hours to make the necessary repairs, and keep you running!

The fact is, Swan LifeLine Service is more than a great warranty on our systems -- it's truly is a warranty on your productivity. It's the best protection you can get anywhere...and it's yours Free!

LifeLine Service is just one more way Swan is doing more to earn your business. Our lifetime technical support is another... it begins even before you purchase your first system. We also offer you free support materials like the 486 Configuration Planner, to help you make a more informed decision, before you ever talk to a sales representative.

3075 RESEARCH DRIVE•STATE COLLEGE•PENNSYLVANIA 16801 U.S.A

FIG. 9–1 Letter-opening type 51: The construction of this opening has many readers actually overlooking the typeset preliminaries at the top. Many readers look up above the greeting only when jostled. The first paragraph says, "The best just got better," then recapitulates some of the wording at the top of the page. Better: Expand on the theme be seeming to justify the claim the first sentence makes.

> The best value in the computer industry just got even better. Every Swan 486 system you buy, V line and above, <u>includes</u> an internal modem, two-year on-site service, one-year toll-free software helpline, and a whole bunch of other goodies—all free.

If your next question is "What about the software the original letter mentioned? <u>What</u> software?" Beats me. The letter never does tell us.

But none of this detracts from the dependability of this venerable opening.

52. If I can show you how to . . . will you . . . ?

Here's another "If" opening, joining all-time favorite no. 1, "If you're like me," no. 3, "What if . . . ," and no. 42, "If you like that, you'll love this." It's the distant relative of one yet to come, no. 98, "If you're worried, here's the solution."

I'm a fan of "If" openings because they're a <u>non-threatening provocative</u>. The assumptive attitude attached to "When . . . " doesn't apply to "If . . . " and the reader becomes involved in the "If" just as he/she would become involved in a question.

The one huge caution about this opening is the relevance requirement. Suppose I say to you, "If I can show you how to poach an Albanian squid, will you agree to try my exclusive Albanian Squid Poacher?" Chances are I'm aiming at a nonexistent target. <u>Any</u> "if . . . then" statement needs relevance to survive.

Does this example survive?

> Dear Mr. Lewis,
> If we could show you a way to increase your sales potential, generate higher income, and reduce your overall Marketing costs . . . would you be interested?

Opinion: Borderline. The thought is a mild cliché, and eliminating any one element would make it stronger: "If I could show you a way to generate higher income while reducing your marketing costs . . . would you be interested?"

I eliminated "increase your sales potential" because it's the most generalized of the three components; as long as we were in the oper-

March 8, 1993

H. G. Lewis
Communicomp
PO Box 15725
Fort Lauderdale FL 33318-5725

Dear Mr. Lewis,

If we could show you a way to increase your sales potential, generate higher income, and reduce your overall Marketing costs...would you be interested?

Enclosed are 2 _FREE_ offers to help you do just that!

First...we would like to send you a _FREE_ ticket to our upcoming Seminar, **_"The Next Dimension in Marketing"_** on Wednesday, May 19, 1993 from 9:00 am to 1:00 pm at the Holiday Inn, St. Petersburg-Clearwater Airport, St. Petersburg, Florida.

During this informative Seminar, Nationally known Marketing Experts will demonstrate how Database Marketing can improve your business and how companies will rely on these Marketing techniques to become more competitive..._now and in the future._

Just some of the topics we will cover include:

- **Developing a <u>quality</u> Marketing Database**
- **Improving the integrity of your Database using Enhancements**
- **Building a valid Statistical Model**
- **Mapping by Region or Penetration of Customers**
- **Tracking Leads and Sales**
- **Understanding Postage costs and Regulations**
- **_And Much More!_**

Next...we would like to offer you a _FREE_ one-year subscription to **_"Q-News"_**, our quarterly newsletter covering important Database Marketing News.

To receive your _FREE_ Seminar ticket and your _FREE_ subscription to **_"Q-News"_**, simply complete the enclosed questionnaire and return it to us in the postage paid envelope provided.

Don't let your competition beat you to it!

Sincerely,

Paul Wray
President

The Next Dimension In Marketing
28051 US Hwy 19 N. Suite E. Clearwater, FL 34621
Telephone: 813/725-9727 Fax: 813/725-2771

FIG. 9–2 Letter-opening type 52: The problem here is similar to that in Fig. 9–2. Many readers look up above the greeting only when jostled, and the construction of this opening has many readers actually overlooking the typeset preliminaries at the top. The first paragraph says, "The best just got better," then recapitulates some of the wording at the top of the page. Better: Expand on the theme by seeming to justify the claim the first sentence makes.

ating room, I also de-capitalized "marketing." And I changed first person plural to first person singular because, although you can't see it, the letter is signed by the company president.

Keep up the silent three-word scream as you write a letter opening: "Relevance and specificity!" Your response doesn't have any choice—it has to go up.

53. Let's face it.

I admit, I don't like this opening. It always strikes me as being too smug to establish reader rapport. But some writers I respect use "Let's face it," so it deserves inclusion among the Hallowed Hundred.

I offer a single caution for "Let's face it": Whatever follows has to be a problem-solver, an approach differing from Opening 32 ("We're solving your tough problem"). The difference between no. 32 and no. 53 is the potential of this one to establish immediate rapport and the ugly uncoupling if it doesn't. Here are two recent openings that exemplify how this opening can connect or disconnect. The first example:

> Dear Herschell Lewis,
> Let's face it: if you want <u>real</u> tax reform, you'll just have to do it yourself. Now you can—simply by using TurboTax®, America's #1 tax preparation software.

This one does qualify under our empirical set of standards. I wouldn't have used the weakener-word "simply," and I'm not sold on that "®" symbol in mid-text when other solutions to the legal requirement exist; but these are picky objections.

Now let's look at the second example:

> Dear Creator:
> Let's face it.
> Your job is unique.
> Unlike your friend, the accountant, you have to do more than put numbers in little squares all day long.

Any opening that has me asking, "Huh?" isn't a barn-burner. I enjoy being called The Creator (Oh, all right—Let there be light), but what does the assumed uniqueness of my job have to do with "Let's face it"? Does this use establish rapport or damage it?

54. It's late and I'm tired, but I have to tell you this.

This one is a favorite of fund raisers, and you can see why: The touch of martyrdom reaches out to the best prospects. A sidebar: No. 54 and the forthcoming no. 58 are the only openings in this group of 100 beginning with "It's . . . " because under most circumstances the word "It" doesn't hack it as an opening; the word works here because of its quick tie to emotion.

This opening is underused by commercial mailers, many of whom feel they're taking off their pants in public. In that objection is the nucleus of why no. 54 can work when no other opening can grab and shake your target. If you seem to be firing blanks, that's the time to strip for action.

A fund-raising letter is an archetype of "It's late and I'm tired, but I have to tell you this":

> It's 11:30 P.M. on a Tuesday night and I'm tired, I need a shower, and I want to go to bed.
> But I can't sleep . . . not until I finish this letter and pray that God will fill your heart with compassion for the poor of Appalachia—as he did mine in 1957.

See how the writer's agony coats the reader's attitude? Try it the next time you're mounting a commercial letter test.

55. We've chosen you . . . or . . . You have been chosen.

This is the cousin of two other openings, no. 17 ("Because you are who you are, you'll get special attention") and no. 18 ("Stroke, stroke— 'You're a rare bird'"). The difference between this one and the other two is that no. 55 puts the writer, or the organization the writer represents, in a parental position.

The obvious determinant of whether to use no. 55 in place of nos. 17 or 18 is who is sending the letter. If the recipient accepts the sender as a superior, then this is the preferred opening: If God walks among

We recently received a letter
from a new member who wrote:

"I wanted to subscribe long
ago but thought it would be
too expensive....

"Had I only known...."

Dear Friend,

Each year we invite selected candidates to join the
largest private nonprofit scientific and educational
organization in the world.

Your name has been selected as a
candidate for membership in the
National Geographic Society.

We extend a cordial invitation to you to join the
Society and enjoy a whole year of membership, including
12 monthly issues of NATIONAL GEOGRAPHIC magazine...

for dues of only $21!

We'd like you to know that the modest cost of membership is only the first of many pleasant surprises in
store for you.

By accepting this invitation, you become part of a
special group of people all over the globe whose enthusiasm and curiosity about their world are enriched by
belonging to the Society. Membership is an open invitation to investigate the world...to see the infinite variety, color, and richness of the universe.

And equally important, as a member of the National
Geographic Society, you provide every member of your
family with information they can use...learn from...
enjoy.

You may already be familiar with the Society's

FIG. 9-3 Letter-opening type 55: Only an organization with the stature of the National Geographic Society can position itself as this letter does. A less distinguished mailer might antagonize by such assumption of superiority. That suggests a novel use of this ploy: If you want the reader to equate your stature with the National Geographic Society, test the Olympian pose. "Key club" exclusivity can bring memberships, subscriptions, orders, and donations where Uriah Heep humility fails.

mankind, He's less Godlike—which would be the impression nos. 17 or 18 would transmit in this circumstance.

A subscription letter begins:

> Each year we invite selected candidates to join the largest private nonprofit scientific and educational organization in the world.
>
> Your name has been selected as a candidate for membership in the National Geographic Society.

Notice the word <u>candidate</u>. It's in key with the posture the writer takes.

56. I'm surprised I haven't heard from you.

Danger signals explode in every direction from this supercharged opening. Because "I'm surprised I haven't heard from you" can make you a hero or a bum, think of it as dynamite with a short fuse. If you don't get out of the way, it'll demolish you instead of your reader's apathy.

A better simile: It's the old "Frankly, I'm puzzled," laced with strychnine. The question you have to answer <u>in the very next sentence</u>: "Who is this person and what right does he/she have to expect a response from me?"

The clarity and persuasiveness with which you answer that question determines who gets wiped out by the dynamite. And this adds another caution, a universal rule of force-communication—

   Don't use dynamite to kill a butterfly.

A letter to my wife from a company pitching a refrigerator service contract begins:

> Dear Margo E. Lewis:
> We are surprised we haven't heard from you about our recent offer of Extended Service coverage. Maybe one of the following applies:
>
> - You haven't received our previous letters
> - We did not sufficiently cover the benefits of our Asure™ program
> - You are not interested in the extended protection. . .

Amana

Amana Iowa 52204

May 4, 1993

|.ıll...ıll...ıll....ılll..ıl.lıl.ı.ıll.....ılll.ılll...lıl.l

PS045207-022602 233172561 -5
Margo E Lewis
340 N Fig Tree Ln
Fort Lauderdale, FL 33317-2561

Dear Margo E Lewis:

We are surprised we haven't heard from you about our recent offer of Extended Service coverage. Maybe one of the following applies:

- You haven't received our previous letters
- We did not sufficiently cover the benefits of our Asure™ program
- You are not interested in the extended protection
- You already have a plan other than Amana's Asure™
- Or...you were waiting until the expiration of your first year of warranty and will buy today

As you can buy low cost extended service protection from Amana, <u>only</u> until the end of your first year of ownership, we wanted to give you one more opportunity to review Amana's exclusive extended service plan. Asure™ provides for FREE parts, labor, travel and in-home service for product malfunctions. Remember, since you bought your SZD27MBL, Side By Side (I & W) on 06/24/92, that first year's warranty is soon to elapse.

We have held the cost of the Asure™ program constant during the first year but we can't make promises that it won't rise due to inflationary factors in the future. You not only get a price break by purchasing multiple years, but you are also protecting yourself from possible higher renewal rates.

This will be the last time we can offer you the Asure™ Extended Service Plan at these rates:

1 year	2 years	3 years	4 years
$59.36	$113.42	$165.36	$210.94

(Tax is included if required by your state)

↓   Please detach and mail application today   ↓   (over please)

Amana
Extended Service Plan

Service Contract Application

Product: Side By Side (I & W)
Model: SZD27MBL
Serial Number: 9204247197
Date Purchased: 06/24/92

☐ Yes! I want to sign up for the Amana Asure Extended Service Plan.

MAKE ANY NAME AND ADDRESS CHANGES BELOW

Margo E Lewis
340 N Fig Tree Ln
Fort Lauderdale, FL 33317-2561

Follow these steps to purchase your Asure Extended Service Contract:

Step 1:	Step 2: How do you want to pay for it?
How many years do you wish to purchase?	☐ Full Payment Enclosed (Check or Money Order payable to Asure Extended Service Plan.) ☐ Charge TOTAL amount to: ☐ MasterCard® ☐ VISA®

		Be sure to complete the credit card information below and sign in the space provided
☐ 1 Year	$ 59.36	Sales tax is
☐ 2 Years	$ 113.42	included if required by
☐ 3 Years	$ 165.36	your state
☐ 4 Years	$ 210.94	

|_____|_____|
Credit Card Number   Expiration Date

Signature _____   Date _____   Home Phone Number _____

I understand that by returning this form with payment, my Amana Side By Side (I & W) will be fully protected by your Asure Extended Service Plan

This is only an application to purchase an extended service plan. The sale of the plan is complete only when the extended service plan agreement is issued by Asure, at Amana, Iowa. Please allow 4-6 weeks for delivery of your plan certificate.

6B3   04/25/93

FIG. 9-4 Letter-opening type 56: Careful with openings the reader may regard as adversarial! If the reader feels guilt, the "I'm (we're) surprised I (we) haven't heard from you" opening can get a quick and embarrassed response; if the reader thinks, "Who do they think they are?" the message is a disaster. Suggestion: Save this opening for circumstances in which you're absolutely positive you have "clout" with your target reader.

. . .and some more bullets, followed by a warning that the first year's warranty is about to expire.

See the hole here? Who the devil is the woman who signed this letter to try to nail us with the nasty mantle of causing an unpleasant surprise? Who is she to draw any supposition?

That's the key: We've never had <u>any</u> relationship. In this nonrelationship, the writer had a plethora of alternative openings that wouldn't have been abrasive—for example, no. 22, no. 9, no. 3, no. 32, no. 41, or others not yet covered; or on a lesser plane nos. 1, 10, or 23. If you can see the usefulness of each and the risk of this one or nos. 40, 45, 49, 15, or 6, you're well on your way to getting your "Dynamite Handler, First Class" designation.

57. How would you like to. . .

"How would you like to . . . " is a more personable cousin of no. 3, "What if . . . " The difference is that this one implicitly suggests you <u>can</u>; no "if" factor exists.

So the very natural follow-up to this opening is, "It's as easy as. . . ."

What the writer has to consider is whether the reader actually wants to accomplish or enjoy whatever the offer includes. This is a classic example of the benefit of demographic/psychographic/creative matchup.

An eight-page letter begins with a printed headline and a 10-line explanation of what the letter contains (a technique with which I don't agree), then launches into high gear:

> Dear Friend:
> How would you like to earn $1,000 a day—every day?
>
> Imagine! Making more money in one day than most people do in a week. You can do it! (You'll even earn big profits while you sleep!)
>
> Cash in on the most profitable field in the modern world.
>
> How? By publishing information.

To many, that last four-word paragraph is a letdown because it doesn't <u>seem</u> to validate the claim and doesn't seem easy to do. I would have used a comma, not a colon, after the greeting, and would have softened the apparent letdown with "How? Believe it or not, by being a respected publisher." Still, I understand this letter has been successful; and anyway, what matters is the choice of opening, not any particular use.

58. It gives me great pleasure to. . .

Unless it's tied to an emotional hook—"It's late and I'm tired, but . . . " —the word <u>It</u> is a weak opener because it's the most unspecific of all pronouns. But who has the guts (or the folly) of making this a blanket condemnation? "It gives me great pleasure to . . . " is a logical enough opening for a pleasant offering.

That's the key: What follows has to be pleasant for the message recipient. If you're writing, "It gives me great pleasure to tell you that your account has been assigned to me," not only are you losing stature by being recipient of the assignment instead of its instigator; you're announcing a nonevent that brings pleasure to you, not to your target.

So focus your pleasure on a tight beam aimed outward.

An example of this opening:

> Dear CorelDRAW Registered User:
> It's with great pleasure that I advise you of a brand new
> CorelDRAW User's Group that is forming in your region!

If this collection had a different theme, you and I might attack the double use of "that" in the same sentence, the standoffish "advise," and the overencompassing "region" instead of "area." Instead, let's reach agreement on the value of pleasure suggestion.

Suppose this letter opened, "A brand-new CorelDRAW User's Group is forming in your area. Don't you want to be part of it from the word go?" Would that be stronger or weaker? If you're undecided, don't use the "pleasure" approach. Save "pleasure" for more obvious pleasure.

59. I used to think that, but now I think this.

Once again we have a double-edged opening. If what you now think is immediately beneficial for the reader, you've established rapport on a level comparable to opening no. 1—"If you're like me." In fact, the rapport could be stronger because the ploy isn't as transparent.

But if your reference is abstruse or inconsequential—not to you but to your reader—ugh. It's too late for the caution flag because you've already wrecked your vehicle.

As you read this example of opening no. 59, ask yourself: What might I have done to use this same device, with parallel wording, more effectively . . . and what's the tipoff that the writer is unsure of the device?

> Dear Fellow Executive:
>
> I used to think that less was more when it came to managing people.
>
> I believed, in other words, that the less management interfered with the daily routine, the happier and more productive their people would be.
>
> Perhaps you once felt the same way. Perhaps, too. . .

The tipoff is the phrase "In other words." <u>Whenever</u> you see that string of words, feel free to conclude: The writer realizes he/she wasn't clear enough or emphatic enough or convincing enough the first time around.

So we knock off the obscuring first sentence and the message becomes clearer, more emphatic, and more convincing:

> Dear Fellow Executive:
> I used to think that the less management interfered with the daily routine, the happier and more productive their people would be.
>
> Perhaps you once felt the same way. Perhaps, too. . .

Okay, it's no barn-burner; but we've stifled the impulse to tamper with individual words, such as substituting "maybe" for "perhaps"; we're using the same basic words to drive closer to a point. And one of

CONCORD INDUSTRIAL PARK, CONCORDVILLE, PENNSYLVANIA 19331 • (800) 345-8101

Dear Fellow Executive:

I used to think that less was more when it came to managing people.

I believed, in other words, that the less management interfered with the daily routine, the happier and more productive their people would be.

Perhaps you once felt the same way. Perhaps, too, you eventually reached the same conclusion I did: That without guidance and direction --without leadership -- many people just drift aimlessly. They seem to live in an unhealthy vacuum, creating hopes and expectations that are often totally unrealistic.

Out of that realization, and our more than 60 years of bringing management and employees closer together, we've created a most innovative and exciting new program. One that will enable you to keep your values and ideals in front of your employees at all times, and help you provide the leadership most employees want and need.

It is called the Challenge-Poster Program, and it is designed to help instill and enrich the healthy attitudes that are so essential to high-level performance. Attitudes about teamwork, morale, quality, productivity, and all the other vital issues that concern you as a manager.

If I had to summarize the program, I'd put it this way: By skillfully combining attention-getting, full-color photographs with related and thought-provoking messages, Challenge-Posters will encourage your people to make the most of their ability and intelligence.

I think one executive (Jerry Smith, President and CEO of Dosco Manufacturing) phrased it perfectly when he told us, "Your posters think like I do. They say exactly what I try to communicate daily to my people."

Challenge-Posters always talk common sense to your people, in language they can easily understand, and without resorting to empty slogans and timeworn cliches.

Subtle and cumulative in their impact, these superb posters offer a succession of simple, straightforward messages that will gradually

(over, please)

FIG. 9–5 Letter-opening type 59: "I" as surrogate for "You" has been in favor since "They laughed when I sat down at the piano." It's a dependable rapport builder. Just one caution: When using "I used to think. . ." be sure whatever it is you used to think (1) is significant to the reader and (2) isn't obscure, complicated, or trivial.

the Great Rules of force-communication, applicable more to letters than to any other component, is:

 GET TO THE POINT.

If you can master this opening by being both relevant and pointed, you'll be well under way with a strong selling argument.

60. Does this sound (seem) familiar?

Properly used, this one can't miss.

What does "properly used" mean? Simple: It means matching whatever sounds familiar to an individual to whom it <u>should</u> sound familiar. This opening will find increasing favor as databases refine themselves and enable communicators to achieve near-perfect pinpointing.

(I'm using "sound familiar" instead of "seem familiar" because even though letters don't usually talk, "sound" is closer to actual conversation than the dreamier "seem").

A highly targeted letter selling a newsletter subscription begins, after the usual display type at the top of the page:

> Dear Network Administrator:
> C-R-A-S-H.
> Panic rages . . . Confusion reigns. Voices scream: "The network's down!"
> Sound familiar?
> Network Administrators like yourself face this nightmare every day. You're the one they turn to when. . . .

Yeah, whoever sent this might have handwritten the "C-R-A-S-H" and cleaned up that muddy "they" reference, but what terrific guts this opening has!

Now suppose I'm <u>not</u> a Network Administrator and I get this letter? Then the company should take issue with the list company or the database compiler, not the writer . . . who came up with a dynamic and readable opening.

Announcing...

Inside NetWare™
—the in-depth source of information on Novell® Networking Technology.

Try It Now!
Special Introductory Rate for Charter Subscribers...
Plus a Risk-Free Offer!
(details on the back)

Dear Network Administrator:

    C-R-A-S-H.

    Panic rages. Confusion reigns. Voices scream: "The network's down!"

    Sound familiar?

    Network Administrators like yourself face this nightmare every day. You're the one they turn to when work comes to a grinding halt. You're the hands-on person responsible for maintaining the network; the one everyone depends on to make things run smoothly.

    But it's not easy. In fact, it's often extremely difficult.

    That's why you need *Inside NetWare*, our monthly journal exclusively about Novell NetWare.

    Inside NetWare will explain--in plain English!--important networking topics such as:

* Managing server and workstation memory
* Using NetWare utilities
* Optimizing <u>Windows</u>™ for use on the network
* Optimizing <u>application</u> software for use on the network
* Choosing third-party products necessary for building a successful network

                           (over)

FIG. 9–6 Letter-opening type 60: A whole bunch of highly professional techniques here: Short sentences; a graphic example; and a tie to the reader's own experiential background. While this creative team was in the neighborhood, wielding the potent "Does this sound (seem) familiar" opening, why not handwrite "C-R-A-S-H"?

61. I'll tell you what pleases me:

This gentle opening has a benefit that doesn't exist in revelatory first-person openings such as No. 45 ("I have to tell you the truth"): The reader of no. 61 knows that whatever follows won't be abrasive or heavily challenging. It has a benefit that doesn't exist in first-person openings such as No. 54, which can carry the seeds of intrusion ("It's late and I'm tired, but I have to tell you this"). The reader of No. 61 knows that whatever follows will be upbeat.

Effective writers since the legendary John Caples ("They laughed when I sat down at the piano") and maybe before him have known how "I" as surrogate for "you" sidesteps hostility. Who can object to another person blabbing what he or she is doing?

By its nature, "I'll tell you what pleases me" has implicit limits on its use. This opening is a delicate tap on the shoulder, not an elephant gun. Consider it when your target <u>or</u> what you're hawking has over-tones of quiet, civilized pleasure.

A letter from a gardening publication begins:

> Dear Gardening Friend:
>   Beautiful gardens are inspiring to me. Whenever I see one, I immediately want to get in close to find out everything I can from the garden itself and from the gardeners who created it—how did they get that delphinium to grow so well in such terrible conditions . . . how did they come up with such an ingenious way of land-scaping that steep slope in the backyard . . . how did they. . . .

And on it goes. The opening paragraph is nine lines long, with some 88 words. As intolerable as I find a first paragraph of this length, the comfortable "I'll tell you what pleases me" opening is considerably better than it would have been if the writer had lapsed into the standard "you" opening:

> Dear Gardening Friend:
> Aren't beautiful gardens inspiring to you? Whenever you see one, don't you immediately want to get in close to find out everything you can from the garden itself and from the gardeners who created it—how did they get that delphinium to. . . .

Simplest suggestion for reader tranquility: Let the first sentence be the entire first paragraph.

Discover

FINE GARDENING

**Experienced gardeners share expert advice
and successful gardening practices,
with detailed instructions and dazzling
photography—all designed to
help you create your ideal garden.**

**RISK-FREE OFFER! RESERVE YOUR
FIRST ISSUE OF FINE GARDENING—TODAY.**

Dear Gardening Friend:

Beautiful gardens are inspiring to me. Whenever I see
one, I immediately want to get in close to find out
everything I can from the garden itself and from the gardeners who created it — how did they get that delphinium
to grow so well in such terrible conditions... how did
they come up with such an ingenious way of landscaping
that steep slope in the backyard...how did they get that
tender plant to grow outside of its range...what do they
do about Japanese beetles or blackspot?

The answers to questions like these are sometimes
complex, sometimes brilliantly simple. But they are
always sure to be the kind of practical ideas and
information you can't wait to bring back and try in your
own garden.

    Which is why I think you'll find FINE GARDENING
    magazine so uniquely exhilarating. <u>Its pages are</u>
    <u>filled with the ideas and discoveries of knowl-</u>
    <u>edgeable, successful gardeners</u> — professionals
    and amateurs — who take you into their gardens
    (and confidence) to show you exactly how they've
    worked their magic. I hope you'll join us (and
    contribute your own ideas) as a subscriber.

        We go where the information is.

Because FINE GARDENING is a national magazine, we go
everywhere there's something to be learned — we've
visited a California backyard with an ingenious

FIG. 9–7   Letter-opening type 61: Opinion, please: Does the printed pre-letter information improve this mailer's chances of having the recipient read the
letter? My opinion: No, because the type block gives away the letter's
intention without supplying a specific or a teaser. The first paragraph is
nine lines long. Had the first paragraph limited itself to the pleasant first
sentence, the opening would have appeared to be more digestible.

Incidentally, if you're a wordsmith you never would have written "How did they get that delphinium to grow so well in such terrible conditions." You'd replace <u>in</u> with <u>under</u>, wouldn't you?

62. This is what happens when they (you) do it wrong.

Talk about power! No. 62 couldn't be farther away from no. 61 in its demand for an immediate, red-hot, emotional response.

We all know The Inside-Out Power Rule:

 The more powerful the wording, the more dangerous the wording.

From the rule we quickly extrapolate the decision-making mechanism: "This is what happens when <u>they</u> do it wrong" has less power—ergo, less danger—than "This is what happens when <u>you</u> do it wrong." The reader can join the attack on <u>them</u>, but not so easily on himself/herself.

If you love comparative advertising (as I do), then this opening is dear to your heart. You recognize, going into the arena, a basic truth of both bull-fighting and bull-throwing: Your performance will bring some flowers and some brickbats.

But you won't be ignored.

A letter using this device begins:

> Dear Friend:
> The fastest indicator of a poorly designed vacuum cleaner is when somebody sneezes whenever you run it. You are most certainly recycling dirt and even molds from the floor right back into the air!

Clever: The writer has sneaked "you" into the mixture without your recognizing the inclusion. So <u>you</u> as victim are glued to <u>you</u> as observer.

In this use, an introductory sentence might have added a dimension of receptivity the immediate "vacuum cleaner" reference is too specific to permit. Example:

> Dear Friend,
> Here's what happens when they do it wrong:
> The fastest indicator of a poorly designed vacuum cleaner. . . .

Yeah, while I was at it I substituted a comma for the standoffish colon, and I indented the paragraphs. Mechanics aside, can you see how adding that opening brings universality to the sales argument?

63. Looking for . . . ?

Ever since Diogenes, we've all been looking for something or other. So this opening has two advantages: It touches an archetypical nerve and it asks a question.

Certainly you've spotted the obvious caution: Whatever follows shouldn't be stupid or irrelevant. If you open a letter with "Looking for a new type of wall-covering?" you'd better have the world's best data-base as your mailing list. (If you aren't sure, why not use no. 61, "I'll tell you what pleases me"? Self-examination is less intrusive and therefore less likely to seem stupid or irrelevant than the always exter-nally aimed "You.")

Here's a use of no. 63 that, because it includes an "If . . . " begin-ning, relates it to no. 52 ("If I can show you how to . . . will you. . . ?"). Ask yourself: Does the nature of "Looking for . . . " make this approach stronger without an "If . . . " filter?

> Dear Investor:
> If low CD and money market rates have you looking for higher
> yields, there is an important step you need to take before moving
> your money: decide how much you want to keep in <u>savings</u> and
> how much you want to <u>invest</u> for higher longer-term returns.

What's your decision? I vote for staying with the purified version of no. 63. It would read something like this:

> Dear Investor,
>   Looking for higher yields?
>   Who isn't?
>   Let's assume you <u>are</u> looking for higher yields, as any sane investor
> should during this period of low CD and money market rates. . . .

Understand, I'm not militating against expanding any of these openings. Every one of them can profit from experimentation and tweaking. But adding an "If . . . " clause to a positive question is dilu-tion, not expansion.

⚡ The Benham Group

Dear Investor:

If low CD and money market rates have you looking for higher yields, there is an important step you need to take before moving your money: decide how much you want to keep in *savings* and how much you want to *invest* for higher longer-term returns.

*For the savings you can't afford to risk...*Our Treasury bill-only money market fund can provide a safe place for your savings. The securities in which the Fund invests are backed by the U.S. Treasury as to the timely payment of principal and interest. The Fund is designed to provide yields that keep pace with the rate of inflation, and offers easy access to your money with free check writing.

*For higher yields...*The Benham Group offers three no-load U.S. Treasury and government funds designed for investors who want higher yields without high credit risk. These funds provide a conservative way to move into longer-term investments. But unlike money market funds and insured fixed-rate CDs, the value of your principal will go up and down as interest rates change.

*Total return -- the true test...*If you choose a higher yielding fund, you should understand that while yield is important, the true measure of fund performance is total return. It measures both the yield *and* changes in the value of your principal. Higher yielding funds have historically provided greater total returns over time, but it's important to have patience to ride out the market's ups and downs. Whenever you invest, you should be comfortable with the risk/reward characteristics of the funds you choose.

Our business is based on a "quality first" investment philosophy. Today, The Benham Group is the largest no-load mutual fund group specializing in U.S. Treasury and government securities. We manage over $9 billion for more than 400,000 investors.

To find out more, please review the enclosed brochure. Then return the enclosed card in the postage-paid envelope provided for a prospectus describing the funds. If you have any questions, you can call us toll free at 1-800-4-SAFETY (1-800-472-3389) for the information you need without sales pressure.

Sincerely,

James M. Benham

James M. Benham
Chairman of the Board

P.S.   Lower yields combined with annual IRA fees may mean your retirement nest egg is not growing as quickly as you would like -- so transferring assets to a free Benham IRA makes sense. Please call us for an IRA information packet.

Note: Fund shares are neither issued nor guaranteed by the U.S. government, and there can be no assurance that any money market fund will maintain a constant $1.00 share price.

B

1665 Charleston Road, Mountain View, CA 94043
1-800-4-SAFETY (1-800-472-3389)

FIG. 9-8   Letter-opening type 63: Looking for . . . ?" is an opening that suffers when the writer waters it down. "Looking for . . ." ostensibly is a shortened version of "If you're looking for. . . ." Adding a watering-down prelude, such as using the "If . . ." to activate a prior reference, weakens this opening.

64. The cry of "Wolf!"

In the last decade of the twentieth century the cry of "Wolf!" has come into its own. We use it as Post-It notes affixed to letters or printer-faked on envelopes. We use it as rubber stamps. We use it as hand-written overlines.

It works.

Prediction: Its form also has to mutate constantly, or it will have a short happy life because its message is both volatile and eventually recognizable. We all know the story of the boy who cried, "Wolf!" By the time a wolf actually appeared, the message had lost its impact.

While it lasts, let's use it . . . with one eye cocked open to watch for signs of flagging impact. Right now, as long as our targets think there's a wolf out there, let's bay at them.

A business letter begins:

> Dear Executive:
> Hiring workers as independent contractors instead of employees is getting much more risky.
> The revenue-hungry IRS is on a nationwide campaign to collect taxes and penalties from employers who pay workers as independent contractors when the IRS considers them employees.

A suggestion if you're crying "Wolf!": Stay in character. This letter says, "The revenue-hungry IRS is on a nationwide campaign to collect taxes and penalties from employers. . . ." A consummate wolf-cryer knows how to keep his victims ever-nervous. You or I would have written, "The IRS is hungry for more money. They're out to nail employers for more taxes and (slather) more penalties. . . ."

See the difference? You're supposed to <u>cry</u> "Wolf!", not whisper the word. But you can see, too, how reader-involving any opening of this type instantly becomes.

65. Here's the deal.

This approach is similar to no. 39, "I'll get right to the point," but it's more positive. It's not as close to no. 33, "This is short and sweet," because this one makes a hard promise.

Employer's Handbook:
Independent Contractor vs. Employee

Dear Executive:

    Hiring workers as independent contractors instead of employees is getting much more risky.

    The revenue-hungry IRS is on a nationwide campaign to collect taxes and penalties from employers who pay workers as independent contractors when the IRS considers them employees.

    IRS computers are analyzing each contractor's tax return. If you turn up as the major client -- ZAP, you could be stung with back taxes, interest and penalties.

    If withholding tax is involved, your owners or directors <u>could</u> <u>be</u> <u>held</u> <u>personally</u> <u>liable</u> <u>for</u> <u>the</u> <u>IRS</u> <u>claims</u>.

    What's more -- the former independent contractor may be entitled to retirement benefits and health insurance. If you fire him, he may go after you for workers comp and COBRA coverage!!

    Engaging independent contractors still can be done safely. You must do so in compliance with common-law principles of independence and current IRS policies. And, you must monitor your contractors to confirm their continuing independence.

    To help you avoid problems with the IRS and save time complying with the law, Thompson Publishing Group offers a new guide:

          <u>EMPLOYER'S HANDBOOK: INDEPENDENT CONTRACTOR vs. EMPLOYEE</u>

    The HANDBOOK is available on a <u>no-risk</u> 30 day trial review. And it has been specifically developed to help you:

    - classify workers properly, consistent with IRS criteria and
       rulings;
    - reclassify independent contractors as employees without implying
       admission of guilt;
    - file information returns in compliance with current tax policy;
       and
    - keep current with evolving IRS policy on independent contractors,
       court rulings and legislation.

    The HANDBOOK's authors are Washington, D.C. attorneys who are experts in taxation and IRS enforcement: Edward N. Delaney is a former trial attorney in the New York Region of the IRS. Russell A. Hollrah, formerly a senior tax consultant with Ernst & Whinney, has written extensively on independent contractor issues.

                                 (over, please ...)

Thompson Publishing Group • 1725 K Street, NW, Suite 200 • Washington, DC 20006 • 1-800-964-5815

FIG. 9–9 Letter-opening type 64: The cry of "Wolf!" is one of the most dynamic of all openings. To pump it up to maximum effectiveness, the writer has to start, continue, and finish in an excited tone. So "a nationwide campaign to collect taxes" doesn't cry "Wolf!" the way "They're out to nail employers for more taxes" would.

Need I point out that if you say, "Here's the deal," you then immediately offer a deal? No nonsense, no puffery, no "here's who we are." Offer a deal fast, or else choose another opening.

A communication from a printing company has "$500 for $19.95" in a sunburst at the right edge. The letter itself begins:

> Amsterdam's Special Introductory Envelope Offer is a great time to cash in on a real value. Naturally, our envelopes are constructed from the finest quality 24 lb. white wove stock, and are die cut to ensure easy insertion.

We ask ourselves, mightn't this have had considerably more wallop if the writer had actually used the words, "Here's the deal"? After all, it worked for Ross Perot. Compare this version with the original:

> Here's the deal:
> 500 envelopes for $19.95.
>   These aren't "schlock" envelopes. They're our finest-quality 24-lb. white wove stock, die-cut so you'll never have an insertion problem with them.

As is true of so many examples we've dissected, a principal barrier to effectiveness seems to be <u>staying in character</u>. If you make a deliberate choice of an opening, staying in character should be easy. In the words of no. 65: Here's the deal. Choose an approach and just stick with it. Okay?

66. We can do it where others can't.

This one suggests instant problem-solving, and the combination of absolute competence and absolute relevance has terrific impact. Consider it for two circumstances: business-to-business problem solving and consumer mailings in which a direct competitive comparison isn't feasible.

Improperly used, "We can do it where others can't" generates a negative impression rather than a positive one. And what's an improper use? Inability to make a good claim.

Does this opening make good on its claim?

Dear Reader,

The Literary Guild is the one book club that can change your mind about book clubs forever.

For over 65 years, *The Literary Guild* has worked to provide selective, discerning, demanding readers like you with the <u>best variety of all the best books</u> you could wish for, the cream of the crop from all publishers.

We're the club that makes this unrivaled array of books available to you in a way that's <u>convenient</u>, <u>uncomplicated</u> and <u>very affordable</u>.

We're the club that feels you're entitled to a great book every time you open the cover, so we put Guild editors to work picking and choosing only the best from the entire publishing world to present to you. That's right—<u>these 150 books are the best</u> fiction, mystery, adventure, fitness, health, nutrition, biography, how-to and reference books available <u>from all international publishers</u>.

We're the club that can spot the talents and the winners <u>before</u> they hit the best seller lists. For instance, in 1991, we took a chance on an unknown writer named John Grisham and his book <u>The Firm</u>. The rest is publishing history.

The 150 books you see in the brochure are an accurate representation of the <u>steady diet of top-drawer selections</u> you'll find month after month in our <u>free club magazine</u>. The book previews, author interviews and insider news help you decide if you're in the mood for today's best sellers, a favorite author's earlier hit or the new release by authors we just discovered.

We're the club that realizes you know your tastes and time schedule best. So *The Literary Guild* <u>puts you in charge</u> of choosing

FIG. 9–10 Letter-opening type 66: Does this letter follow through on its "We can do it where others can't" opening? By making its 65-year history the follow-up to a claim of being "the one book club that can change your mind about book clubs forever," the letter loses both pace and credibility. A rule that pertains to every aspect of direct response, not just letters: <u>Specifics outpull generalizations</u>.

> Dear Reader,
>   *The Literary Guild* is the one book club that can change your mind about book clubs forever.
>   For over 65 years, *The Literary Guild* has worked to provide selective, discerning, demanding readers like you with the <u>best variety of all the best books</u> you could wish for, the cream of the crop from all publishers.
>   We're the club that makes this unrivaled array of books available to you in a way that's <u>convenient, uncomplicated</u> and <u>very affordable</u>. . . .

Opinion? Nothing after the first sentence makes good on the claim. The writer should have asked himself/herself after writing the first sentence, "Okay, how does this club change their minds about book clubs forever?" That would have been the way to get the reader to think, "Yeah . . . they can do it where others can't." (Capitalizing "Club" would add stature.)

67. Remember when. . .

This is quiet nostalgia at work. Don't equate it with no. 37 (historical buildup), which recounts an action to which the reader wasn't privy. Don't equate it with the dangerous "If you'd done that then, you'd be in this position now," which is half-scolding.

"Remember when" has a huge benefit when used properly: It's an instantaneous rapport establisher because whatever it recounts cements a common experience shared by writer and reader.

Use this opening with two cautions. Caution 1: When you say "Remember when," be sure the episode is one the reader <u>will</u> remember, fondly. Caution 2: Follow up with "We're bringing it back for you," or you've wasted the opening.

A health magazine opens its letter with three bullets; but, indented, they're really a pre-opening. The message itself starts out in fine fettle:

> Remember when eating well was so simple?
> The days when we could savor a juicy shrimp without thinking twice about <u>cholesterol</u> . . . when we could tuck into a prime steak and not

worry about <u>growth hormones</u> . . . the times when an apple a day wasn't clouded with concerns about <u>pesticides</u> . . . the good old days when all the <u>salt</u> in chicken soup meant nothing to us. . . .

Altogether, a pretty good opening, isn't it? Heads nod, "Yes, that's how it was"; and the intention of this opening is fulfilled.

(This letter, in its move toward complying with Caution 2, for no good reason quickly turns cold and "pitchy"; but we're concerned only with the opening.)

68. Isn't it sad?

Peril lurks in this opening. I see two totally different uses for it—either a fund-raising letter basing its appeal on episode . . . or a tongue-in-cheek easygoing and humorous sales pitch.

Oh, does peril lurk! For fund raising, if you don't have the communicative power to convince the reader this is sad, you've struck a wrong chord; for tongue-in-cheek humor, if the reader isn't in sync with the satire, you've lost a possible sale.

Oh, but if you <u>do</u> connect, you can raise funds and make sales where no other approach cracks the barrier of apathy.

An example of "Isn't it sad?":

> Dear Friend,
>   A commercial whale hunt is a sad, bloody scene: Explosive-tipped harpoons shot from cannons on the "catcher" boats . . . the whales butchered right at sea in factory ships. . . .

Good, serviceable opening, isn't it? I think the writer could have gone even farther down the gory road, eliminating the nondescript "catcher" boats:

> A commercial whale hunt is a sad, bloody scene: Laughing, jeering "cannoneers" shoot explosive-tipped harpoons that tear great holes in the whale's flesh. Unbearable agony! The bleeding, tormented whale is hauled aboard, still alive . . . then butchered with no thought that a few minutes ago this was a majestic creature, one of the last of a vanishing species. . . .

My point: In for a penny, in for a pound. The benefit of choosing any opening—whether it's "Isn't it sad?" or "Congratulations!" —is lost in direct ratio to the amount of "water" in the rhetorical soup.

69. Ouch!

I've seen business-to-business mailings actually crack the impenetrable Secretarial Barrier with a one-word exclamation. I've seen astounding results in consumer mailings to people who seem to be impervious to more standard openings. Figures 3–3, and 3–4 in Chapter 3 reproduce letters that open with a handwritten "Wham!!" and "What!!" (My usual preference is for a single typed exclamation point, but single-word handwriting is exempt from this preference because it replicates cartoon lettering more closely than it does typing.)

To me, the biggest benefit of this type of opening is that it promises easy reading. An example:

> Dear Business Owner:
> Yeoww! Running a small business can mean a lot of aches and pains. But we don't need to remind you about the kind of unbearable pressure that pounds and throbs from the top of your overhead all the way down to your bottom line. You suffer from it everyday.

Well, the second sentence doesn't really grab us because it loses specificity and abandons the quickness of "Yeoww!" by lapsing into the non-specific "a lot of aches and pains"; and "every day" should be two words. But you certainly can see how a one-word grabber jump-starts a letter.

70. Chances are. . .

Here's an easy, low-key way to swing into a selling posture the reader implicitly accepts.

You aren't making a claim the reader can reject; you aren't establishing a position the reader can regard as adversarial; and you aren't being stiff-necked and distant. So this is a serviceable opening, a wel-

Southern Bell®
A *BELL*SOUTH Company

President
Margo Lewis
Communicomp Corp
PO Box 15725
Ft Lauderdale, FL 33318-5725

Dear Business Owner:

     Yeoww! Running a small business can mean a lot of aches and
pains. But we don't need to remind you about the kind of
unbearable pressure that pounds and throbs from the top of your
overhead all the way down to your bottom line. You suffer from
it everyday.

     What you need is strong medicine -- not just temporary relief
-- to cure the pains associated with running a small business...
like the constant threat of competition, the 25-hour demands on
your 24-hour day, the rise and fall of employee productivity.
And we've got it.

     EASY-TO-USE, EASY-TO-AFFORD services designed to help you
succeed, stay competitive AND turn a profit!

     You've already experienced the extra-strength relief CALL
FORWARDING gives you -- how it keeps you from missing important
calls while you're away from the office.

     But it's just one example of how you can get rid of small
business stress with communications technology -- the same
technology, on a smaller scale, that bigger corporations with
bigger budgets use. For lots more examples, take a look at the
Small Business Services Guide I've sent you.

FIG. 9-11 Letter-opening type 69: "Ouch!" and variations of the word bring a quick smile and quick interest. A nonthreatening, thoroughly convivial opening, "Ouch!"—or in this case, "Yeoww!"—demands an immediate validation. Opinion: This letter would have made better use of the single "grabber" word with text such as, "Yeoww! Missing a phone call is like hitting yourself in the head with a hammer. . . ."

come friend on those days when your imagination and apathy are engaged in a great Civil War inside your brain.

An example of this opening:

> Hi, there, and top of the morning to you. . .
>   Chances are you really aren't in the mood for a sales pitch
> this morning.
>   Okay, neither am I. . . .

Irritation, if any, stems from "Okay, neither am I," not from the opening sentence. As an opinion, a more-in-keeping second sentence would be, "Boy, do I understand that." Note the qualification—it's an opinion, not an edict.

Good thing, too. Chances are you'd resent an edict.

71. Take just two minutes.

See the difference between "Take just two minutes" and "It'll take you just two minutes"?

"Take two minutes" is an imperative. Letters are the imperative component of a mailing, and by lapsing into the declarative with the neutral "It" opening, your letter puts water on the flame instead of giving it a shot of gasoline.

A letter from Handgun Control, signed by Sarah Brady, begins:

> Dear Friend,
>   Please take two minutes to answer the National Public Safety Survey I've enclosed and return it to me today.
>   Your completed survey will help Handgun Control, Inc., the largest national organization devoted exclusively to <u>keeping guns out of the wrong hands</u>, convince the new Congress. . . .

Imperfect? Why in heaven's name did whoever wrote this put that "Inc." after "Handgun Control," immediately creating a corporate impression? And sure, many of the best potential donors have long since passed the point where they're surprised to find a request for donations hooked to the survey. What if, instead of the polite imperative "Please take two minutes," the letter had opened in neutral gear:

HANDGUN CONTROL

SARAH BRADY
CHAIR

Dear Friend,

Please take two minutes to answer the National Public Safety Survey I've enclosed and return it to me today.

Your completed survey will help Handgun Control, Inc., the largest national organization devoted exclusively to <u>keeping guns out of the wrong hands</u>, convince the new Congress and the new administration that Americans now want immediate action to end gun violence.

1993 could very well be the first year that Americans begin to win the protection we all deserve from the epidemic of gun violence that is sweeping the country. And that's because, for the first time since we started to fight for common-sense gun laws, we have <u>a President who has promised to enact gun control laws</u>. And we have <u>a Congress</u> in which the balance of power may have shifted enough to end the gridlock that, for years, has paralyzed our efforts to curb America's escalating gun violence.

That's why I hope you will help us seize this opportunity by completing the enclosed Survey. And when you do, I also hope you'll join hundreds of thousands of Americans as a member of Handgun Control, Inc. by sending a contribution to support our campaign to save lives.

Only by creating a powerful, united citizens' voice can we make sure our government enacts nationwide laws to stop the gun violence.

One national gun law in particular -- the Brady Bill -- might have saved the lives of Theresa Law and her three young children. After Mrs. Law requested separation from her husband, he entered a psychiatric hospital threatening suicide. But he was sent home. The very next day he bought a handgun and used it one hour later to kill his family and himself. Sadly, this sort of tragedy has become almost a daily occurrence in cities, suburbs and small towns all across America.

The Brady Bill mandates a <u>waiting period</u> and a background check before anyone can purchase a handgun to make sure that mentally incompetent people can't get their hands on guns. It also helps prevent gun sales to convicted criminals. And the waiting period gives hotheads who want a gun <u>time to cool down</u>.

We fought for years to enact the Brady Bill, against fierce opposition from the National Rifle Association, because without a national law to control handgun sales, in most states **it would be almost as easy to buy a handgun as it is to buy a carton of milk.**

And even in a state which has strict gun laws, a desperate person could merely cross a state line to buy a gun. That's why

 Recycled Paper   **1225 Eye Street, N.W. • Room 1100 • Washington, D.C. 20005 • 202-898-0792**

FIG. 9–12 Letter-opening type 71: The benefit of "Please take two minutes" is its definition of the time limitation. Everybody has two minutes. I'd have opened with "Take two minutes" and used "Please" differently, as a one-word <u>second</u> paragraph.

> Dear Friend,
>   It'll take you just two minutes to answer the National Public
> Safety Survey I've enclosed. . . .

See how much weaker "It" makes this opening? Opening no. 71 is an imperative. Use it when you aren't afraid your demand will prompt an "Oh, no, I won't" reaction.

72. Things were going great. . . Then all hell broke loose.

This type of confessional requires high professionalism or it comes off as stupidly self-serving. We see it in fund raising, but if you sell self-help courses or get-rich-quick concepts you might test "Things were going great" against a straightforward "Have I got a deal for you" approach or against nos. 1, 3, 6, 10, 47, and 52—which may be too transparent through overuse by competitors.

The power of "Things were going great" is the human desire to spy on somebody else's misfortune. No, not to share it; asking a reader to share misfortune is wastebasket-bait. We want to be voyeurs, not participants, when reading personal negatives.

A message headed "An Important Message from Annette Funicello" begins:

> Hello, Ms. Lewis. . .
>   I've always lived a kind of charmed life . . . starting with those
> years I had on the Mickey Mouse Club as a little girl . . . the great
> times I had making those "zany" beach movies in the 60's . . . and
> the wonderful years I've had with my family.
>   I guess I thought nothing bad would ever happen to me—but
> then multiple sclerosis struck.

Opinion: The concept is 100 percent sound. The heading, "An Important Message from Annette Funicello" (which many might regard as an outlandish concept), isn't as potent as opening <u>directly</u> with "I've always led a kind of charmed life."

73. I'm going to make your day.

This is the reverse spin of a Clint Eastwood homily. Because the reader might just as easily interpret its promise as arrogance-based instead of fact-based, handle with care.

"I'm going to make your day" properly reinforced within the next two or three sentences, has considerably more wallop than no. 10 ("I have something good for you") or no. 23 ("Good news!"). What's perplexing to me is a letter which chooses "I'm going to make your day" and then immediately loses its bravado.

An example is a letter which begins, curiously, with a backed-off approach:

> Good Morning!
> I want to make your day.
> You're one of a very special group of individuals we've chosen to get a <u>free desktop calculator</u> when you order a supply of the most elegant, most beautiful bank checks that ever graced anyone's checkbook.

Technically, no problem; it's clear, well-written, and to the point. But why take two sidesteps? (1) "I want to make your day" has only about 37 percent of the impact "I'm going to make your day" would have had; (2) Nothing in the following paragraph makes the reader's day.

Opening with no. 6 ("Congratulations!") or no. 23 ("Good news!") would have been more in keeping with what follows.

Let's suppose <u>we're</u> the creative team. We decide to use no. 73 as our opening. Keeping the flavor undiluted is as easy as:

> I'm going to make your day.
> I'm not only going to give a whole new personality to your bank checks. I'm going to give you a full-function desktop calculator for the privilege of doing it.

Letter openings parallel the opening of a conversation. The first sentence gets attention, or it doesn't. The next few sentences have the other person nodding yes, or they don't.

Know what I'll do?
Order these designer checks and —
— *I'll send you a* FREE CALCULATOR!

Good Morning!

I want to make your day.

You're one of a very special group of individuals we've chosen to get a **free desktop calculator** when you order a supply of the most elegant, most beautiful bank checks that ever graced anyone's checkbook.

Why you? Because the source from which your name came to us suggests you're interested in the "better-than-average" personal image, alert to new ideas. We'd like to do business with you.

Take a look at the checks in your checkbook. They're just like everybody else's checks, aren't they? Oh, the color may be pink instead of pale green or yellow, but the "personality quotient" of the typical check is <u>zero</u>.

Now take a look at the checks in the descriptive brochure I've enclosed. What a difference! These are checks with style, flair, and brightness. Some display a rainbow of colors; others have a smart executive look. Every designer check is in perfect taste. Every designer check is uniquely different from any others. Every designer check identifies the sender as someone who won't settle for the common or the ordinary.

Because we want to be your check company, **American Designer Checks will send you a free calculator** with your first order for 200 checks. Just pick the design you like, and it's a deal.

We want **you** as a customer. We believe you will enjoy your new checks so much that you'll want to reorder. If you do, you still pay the money-saving price of $5.95, $7.95 or $9.95 (depending on your selection) for a full order of 200 checks plus deposit slips!

FIG. 9–13 Letter-opening type 73: The current fashion of text before the greeting is well-founded; but synergy between an overline or a Johnson Box or a pre-greeting splash isn't automatic. In this instance, changing the line "Order these designer checks and" to a handwritten "I'm going to make your day," putting the free calculator offer in an eye-grabbing rubber stamp, and replacing the first sentence with "I really do have a deal for you" might generate more excitement. Even as it stands, the first sentence is better than most.

74. Am I right about you?

What a blessing for us is the human sense of insecurity! We feel triumph when we watch a TV quiz show and can come up with the answers two seconds before the troglodyte contestants can. We save and even frame such nonsensical throwaways as our high school diploma or a press clipping identifying us as third person from the left. We suck in our stomachs when we're in camera-range of a tourist from Latvia shooting a photograph of her fat spouse.

These reactions connect directly to our desire to be loved, to be admired, to warrant applause even by passersby whom we never saw before and who forget us six paces later.

That characteristic is the force underlying "Am I right about you?" It slams into the bulls-eye of the human psyche.

A letter from my buddy J. Peter Grace begins:

> Dear Friend:
> I hope that what I've been told about you is true.
> I've been told you are one American who understands the dire consequences for your family and our nation if we fail to eliminate the federal deficit.

J. Pete, as unpatriotic as it may seem, I'm more concerned with eliminating my personal deficit. But yeah, you have a point . . . except that (in my opinion) you're approaching it in too cerebral a manner, and you get to the point too fast. "Dire consequences" and "eliminate" aren't knockout words.

"Am I right about you," in order to build itself to maximum thrust, has to stay in the "you" mode until we've achieved that magical word <u>rapport</u>. Then you can bring in God, Abe Lincoln, and motherhood.

75. When was the last time . . .

I like this one because it's automatically reader-involving. Where danger lurks is in a mismatch between this opening and the database from whence the recipient sprung. "When was the last time you . . ." <u>has</u> to match the target, or it appears either foolish or insulting.

This isn't a major problem. After all, <u>every</u> opening should match the target, but the specificity of this one calls for unusual care.

A mailing from a book club has four printed overlines before the greeting. It begins:

GO AHEAD ... INDULGE YOURSELF!
Sample the exciting Special Club Magazine enclosed.
Take 5 books for 99¢ with membership . . . along
with valuable extras that make this a terrific deal.

Dear Reader,
   When was the last time you <u>really relaxed</u> with a good
book? I'm not talking about sneaking in a few pages between
household chores or office meetings. I'm talking about curling
up in a favorite chair and. . . .

Why am I vaguely dissatisfied? Is it because the writer underlined <u>relaxed</u> as well as <u>really</u>? Is it because the pre-greeting text gave away the play? Is it because the whole concept doesn't quite come off?

No matter. "When was the last time you . . . " does work, if it's soaked in nostalgia.

Now, when was the last time you read a flat claim like that?

10

25 More Ways to Get Right to the Point

Many of the following openings are so direct they wouldn't have been acceptable a generation ago. Directness—a marker of the last decade of the twentieth century—can bring results where dignity fails. Evaluate each of these and all letter openings—the pleasant, the personal, and the powerful—according to one criterion: Is it more likely to bring a positive response?

76. Quick: What if. . .

We're really in the provocative neighborhood with this one, which hurls down an irresistible gauntlet. "Quick: What if. . ." challenges the reader without the dangerous suggestion of superciliousness we see in other challenges.

The reader is forced to reach a <u>premature</u> conclusion, and the benefit to us is the reader's recognition, even while reaching that conclusion, that we're about to present a better solution.

A computer software company makes good use of this opening:

> **Quick.** What would happen if the power went out right now?. . .
> Would the data on your PC be safe . . . or would you have to "start all over?"
> Most people don't back up their data every day. I'll admit that I miss a few days here and there—and sort of take my chances. I'm in a hurry, or in the middle of something else—or I just plain forget. So my files sit vulnerable to all kinds of "outrageous electronic fortunes. . ."

Yep, this one sags a little after that powerhouse opening sentence. Putting "safe" before "start all over" (question mark should be outside the quotation marks here) is inside-out psychology. (You or I would have bypassed "safe" altogether or written a killer second sentence such as, "Ugh. There goes that brilliant letter or the four hours you've just spent on a financial projection.") But even with the slight loosening of the reins, it holds the reader long enough for the sales message to kick in.

FASTBACK PLUS

TigerSoftware 800 SW 37th Ave., Suite 765, Coral Gables, FL 33134   CALL TO ORDER (800) 444-3363
THIS IS A SPECIAL PRIVATE OFFER, VALID TO ADDRESSEE ONLY.   NOT TRANSFERABLE.

THE $69⁹⁰ FASTBACK WINDOWS OR DOS OFFER

<u>Dear Computer User,</u>

Quick. What would happen if the power went out right now?...

Would the data on your PC be safe...or would you have to "start all over?"

   Most people don't back up their information every day. I'll admit that I miss a few days here and there--and sort of take my chances. I'm in a hurry, or in the middle of something else--or I just plain forget. So my files sit vulnerable to all kinds of "outrageous electronic fortunes..."

   If this sounds familiar, we're both running the risk of losing the time and money we've got invested in our data--if the power went out *right now*...

   If you agree that your data is valuable enough to take care of, then we both need a copy of Fastback Plus. Through this private offer, Competitive Upgrade versions are available for DOS and Windows--you choose--at the rare, low price of just $69.90. The fastest, easiest and safest data protection available in the world today for the unheard of low price of **$69.90.**

   That's not a typo! Your choice of Fastback Plus 6.0 for DOS or Fastback Plus 1.1 for Windows--just $69.90! Plus a FREE GIFT which I'll tell you about in a moment...

<u>INTRODUCING FASTBACK PLUS 6.0 COMPETITIVE UPGRADE FOR DOS</u>

   Fastback has been the leader in backup software for years--without equal. The makers of this fine product realized the only possible way to make it better was to ask users what they thought...

   And they did.

   They got some pretty good answers, too. Those new ideas were immediately incorporated into the new version. And they're delivered to you in this special Competitive Upgrade offer. Things like an easier interface, QIC and SCSI tape drive support, virus protection, network support and the ability to back up notebooks to any device accessible to your desktop.

next page please...

FIG. 10–1 Letter-opening type 76: "Quick" is one of those magical words that, like "hot" and "grab," implicity creates excitement. The first sentence of this letter forces the reader to continue. Opinion: This letter doesn't follow up the word "Quick" with slugging force. Opinion: It should have. Isn't that why the writer chose the word in the first place?

25 More Ways to Get Right to the Point **209**

77. Isn't it nice to know
[STROKING, FLATTERING RECIPIENT]?

I'm enamored of this opening because it thrusts deep into the core of human reaction. The difference between "We love you" and "Isn't it nice to know you're loved?" is one of projected apparent sincerity. The second approach is more credible because it's a step beyond the declaration of love. Love is taken for granted, and the writer has moved beyond the statement to invite your reaction. Wonderful!

Why, then, isn't this delightfully effective opening more widely used? Simple: It isn't as universal as so many of the other openings we've discussed, such as no. 1 ("If you're like me") or no. 41 ("Visualize this scenario") or even its more mundane cousin no. 46 ("You're important to us").

A call for volunteers, from a non-profit organization, makes perfect use of this opening:

> Hi!
> Isn't it always nice to feel you're wanted?
> Well, you <u>are</u> wanted. . . .

I like "Hi!" too. It's much in keeping with the tone of the letter. . . and it doesn't require personalization to be personal. A nice touch.

78. Today I found out that you. . .

This opening is highly effective for (1) subscription renewals, (2) fund raising, and (3) highly targeted follow-up mailings.

Without the word "Today" or an evening tighter "This morning," this opening doesn't work. Here's an example:

> Dear Member,
>   This morning I learned that we have not yet received your annual Membership Renewal.

See how weak this would be if the opening were, "I recently learned that. . ."?

**Simon Wiesenthal Center**

Dear Member,

This morning I learned that we have not yet received your annual Membership Renewal.

Let me assure you that in no way do we take your support for granted.

But since you have generously demonstrated your belief in the importance of our work, <u>we are counting on you</u> once again.

This has been a momentous period for world Jewry. We've experienced war in the Middle East and, in an historic exodus, hundreds of thousands of Soviet and Ethiopian Jews have emigrated to Israel.

The world Jewish community has provided help of unmatched magnitude in response to appeals from leading Jewish organizations, and many of us contributed generously.

Yet I must remind you that there is <u>no other Jewish organization</u> that does the work of the Simon Wiesenthal Center. And it is work that <u>must</u> be done!

As I'm sure you'll agree, our enemies would like us to divert our attention from the ominous surge of worldwide antisemitism. <u>But we dare not allow that to happen.</u>

Through our global monitoring, our credibility with world leaders and opinion-makers, and our innovative educational programs, the Center -- supported by Members like <u>you</u> -- is committed to no less than preserving the future and well-being of the Jewish people.

So please...sit down and make out your tax-deductible Renewal contribution <u>today</u>. We will be deeply grateful -- as will <u>all</u> those who seek a world of tolerance and understanding.

FIG. 10–2 Letter-opening type 78: Visualize this opening with a less timely replacement for "This morning." Had the writer used "Recently" or "Not long ago" or "A few days ago," the energy would have collapsed. What if the timeliness had been even more pinpointed—"A few minutes ago"? The letter would have lost some credibility; and, worse, it would make the reader uncomfortable.

The danger of no. 78 is the occasional necessity to include <u>passive</u> <u>voice</u>, because the letter-writer is <u>re</u>acting, not acting; action, or lack of it, is on the part of the message recipient. So whenever possible, replace words such as "receive" with harder-edged verbs that are more jarring to the reader.

79. You want it. We have it.

How assumptive and straightforward can you get? The effectiveness of this opening depends on the validity of the list.

The advantage "You want it. We have it" has over no. 66 ("We can do it where others can't") is its total reader involvement. That's the key to its potency—and to its incredible ability to annoy if you're off-target. This is the stuff heavy response, coupled with heavy white mail (white mail = letters of complaint or damnation), is made of.

A subscription letter for an adult publication begins:

> YOU WANT IT, WE'VE GOT IT!
>
> Dear Reader,
>   The word is out! Gallery Magazine is not a secret anymore, and you should know what almost 4 million yearly readers have known for 20 years. Gallery is the <u>hottest men's magazine avail-</u> <u>able anywhere.</u>
>   I know, there are hundreds of magazines out there making the same claim, but only Gallery delivers, with every issue, 13 times a year.

Yes, it's mildly incoherent. If four million readers have known about this for twenty years it can't be much of a secret. (Is it number-juggling? "4 million <u>yearly</u> readers" might be a 13-issue total, which means just 307,692 readers per issue.)

This writer placed the opening above the greeting. It certainly is strong enough to justify that position. If it had been under the greeting, I'd have retained the capital letters.

If you're hung up on dignity, forget this one. If you're hung up on response, it's a perfect test against a more staid opening.

80. In the time it took you to open this envelope. . .

This venerable opening is useful for both positive and negative news. Followed with "you could have," the time could have been profitable; followed with an ongoing disaster, it's a serviceable guilt-generator.

A fund-raising letter begins:

> Dear Friend:
> In the ten seconds it took you to open and begin to read this letter, four children died from the effects of malnutrition or disease somewhere in the world.

Do you wonder, as I do, why the writer damaged specificity by including the nondescript "somewhere in the world"? No matter. The opening is automatically reader-involving. A proper gauge of the writer's talent: the ability to maintain and expand involvement.

81. Even if you. . .

What a serviceable and effective opening this one is!

"Even if you . . . " has two variations. The first has "never" as the next word—"Even if you never . . . you'll still. . . ." The intention is to overcome routine rejection of something the reader thinks isn't an improvement over what he has.

The second use of "Even if you . . . " is for the business-to-business ambience, presenting something to improve on what the reader thinks may be unimprovable. An example:

> Hello, My Friend!
> Even if you regard your market position as unassailable, your attitude, as a top executive, has to be: Is a competitor about to start breathing down the back of my neck?
> AT&T, duPont, and IBM proved <u>any</u> company can face a sudden hot and nasty competitive breath. Nobody can rest easy in the uneasy 1990s. . . .

The value of "Even if you . . . " is its unsettling effect, the demand for a second look. If you've been getting a "We don't need this" reaction to your offer, consider it.

82. Repeat a word.

This is a mechanical gimmick, so easy to implement I'm including it for those who aren't professional letter-writers. Repetition, properly handled, is like the Chinese water torture—drops keep dripping until they produce a profound effect.

Do I have to point out that the chosen word should have some guts? Do I have to point out that three is the standard number of repetitions? Do I have to point out that whatever follows should be down and dirty because the thrice-repeated word is supposed to represent drama, not quiet poetry?

An example of the repeated word:

> Dear Friend:
>   LOCATION-LOCATION-LOCATION. The three most important ingredients in a retail business are also the three most important ingredients in choosing where to spend your hard-to-come-by advertising dollars.
>   The new Colorstick provides the best location for Communicomp to advertise its goods or services. . . .

I'd have used periods instead of hyphens—"LOCATION. LOCATION. LOCATION." Some exponents of this opening add drama by intensifying each repeat: "Location. *Location.* **LOCATION!**"

What else works, other than "Die, die, die!" or "Now, now, now!"? Questions work—"Where? Where? Where?"; exclamations and invented words work—"Ycch. Ycch! YCCH!" and "Yeah, yeah, yeah!"; comparatives work—"Hotter . . . hotter . . . hotter!" which has greater impact than the progressive "Hot, hotter, hottest!"

Note that many of these end with an exclamation point. This, too, is standard dramatic technique for repetitions, whether on stage or in print.

83. You've made us unhappy.

This one is loaded with danger, even for fund raisers, because today's "me"-oriented society is crawling with latent antagonisms waiting to be unleashed. So instead of generating guilt, "You've made us unhappy" is just as likely to generate resentment.

A fine point: "You've made <u>me</u> unhappy" is less likely to create an antagonist because the recipient doesn't feel he or she is battling an army.

An example of no. 83:

> Dear Friend,
>   I am sorry to see that you've allowed your EARTHWATCH Membership to lapse. And I wanted to write you one last time to inquire why.
>   Because it's hard to imagine you've lost faith in the enterprising, hands-on brand of science that EARTHWATCH so energetically endorses and supports. I'm sure you still value these proven messages of study and personal, individual growth. . . .

Aside from the incomplete second sentence, why not add a qualifier such as "truly" between "I am" and "sorry"? This softener also is reader-involving, and "You've made us unhappy" <u>fails</u> without reader involvement.

Too, "And I wanted to write you one last time to inquire why" increases distance instead of diminishing it because past tense isn't called for here and "inquire" is as arm's-length as a supposedly personal letter can get. Better, in my opinion: "I really do have to ask why." Then, as an option if this is a long-time supporter, "Have we somehow, some way, let you down?"

A reasonably standard use of "You've made us unhappy" is <u>deep</u> in a subscription renewal series. But wherever you use it, don't make the tone accusatory unless it's a last-ditch effort after all other goads have failed.

84. Imagine this:

"Imagine this" is one of the easier workhorses, which means it doesn't carry a lot of dynamite. It lacks the punch and vigor of its better-dressed cousins, no. 3 ("What if. . ."), no. 26 ("Have you ever wished. . ."), and no. 41 ("Visualize this scenario").

That recognition doesn't suggest that "Imagine this" is useless; if it were, it wouldn't be in this group. Rather, we should save this opening for circumstances where our relationship with the reader is so tenuous we're walking on eggs.

PRENTICE HALL

Business & Professional Publishing ■ Englewood Cliffs, New Jersey 07632

Get "Madison Avenue" results with a "Main Street" budget with...

Easy-to-follow guidelines, techniques and models you can use <u>right now</u> to slash costs and boost response!

ADVERTISING MANAGER'S HANDBOOK

Examine it FREE for 30 days!

Achieve top results in these critical areas!

- A/V Presentations
- Billboards
- Brochures
- Catalogs
- Classified Ads
- Co-op Programs
- Direct Mail
- Directories
- Focus Groups
- Magazine Ads
- Newsletters
- Point-of-Purchase Displays
- Postcard Decks
- Press Releases
- Public Relations
- Publicity
- Radio Commercials
- Referrals
- Sales Promotions
- Slogans
- Specialty Advertising
- Speeches
- Telemarketing
- Television Commercials
- Trade Show Exhibits
- Transit Advertising
- Videos
- Yellow-pages Ads
- *And others!*

Dear Advertising Manager,

Imagine having a ready-to-use kit that improves your advertising almost overnight ... assures your success in marketing channels you've never tried before ... and saves you time and money on <u>all</u> advertising projects, large or small.

Well, imagine no more! Now there's a new "how-to" handbook packed with step-by-step guidelines — plus scores of easy-to-follow models, worksheets, checklists, and formulas — for creating winning advertising of all kinds. It's called

THE ADVERTISING MANAGER'S HANDBOOK by Robert Bly, noted advertising consultant to dozens of top U.S. companies

...and you're invited to use it FREE for 30 days!

Successful Advertising Made Simple

Why waste time and effort reinventing the wheel for every new campaign? The **Advertising Manager's Handbook** takes the hassle and guesswork out of advertising with detailed, expert advice at every stage of the process — from planning and budgeting to writing, designing, and producing.

Short on theory, the **Handbook** gets right down to the nuts and bolts of generating sales, leads, inquiries, publicity, consumer awareness — whatever it is you need to achieve!

CREATE ADVERTISING THAT <u>WORKS</u> Creating a postcard deck? Press release? Magazine advertisement? Point-of-purchase display? The **Handbook** shows you how to do it, <u>step by step</u>, and achieve top results. It even directs you to outside services and suppliers who can help you get the job done.

(over, please)

FIG. 10–3 Letter-opening type 84: The word "Imagine" *demands* a powerful follow-up or it falls totally flat. Falling flat is what happens here, in a too-long first sentence which doesn't follow the word with any magic or specifics.

Changing the colon to an exclamation point—"Imagine this!"—literally doubles its impact; but even doubled, it's a lightweight.

A letter from a publication begins:

> Dear Executive:
>
> Imagine the convenience of reaching for a single-source general reference publication that provides you with a wealth of information on demographics, lifestyles, consumer segment profiles, and consumer magazines/direct mail lists to help you successfully market your product or services. Imagine it costing less than the bookshelf it sits on.

Opinion: a loser in every way—too wordy, standoffish words such as "provides," a cliché in a crucial spot ("a wealth of information"), and no "grabber." But the biggest problem is the misuse of "Imagine this." What's the word "Imagine" doing there at all?

I'll repeat: No. 84 does work, but only when handled deliberately and professionally. For another example see Figure 10–3.

85. Your life is about to change.

Wow, does no. 85 fling a challenge! If you have the moxie to use this one, be sure you have a deal to match.

I've seldom had an offer strong enough or absolutely targeted enough to justify this powerhouse; and every use of it I've seen in the past few years has been damaged by the writer's desire to use it without having the backup of a proposition the reader regards as a barn-burner.

For example:

> SPECIAL NOTICE TO:
> Herschel Lewis
> Po [sic] Box 15725
> Plantation, FL 33318
>
> Your whole perspective of real estate investing is about change! I have enclosed a special invitation for you and a partner to be my guest at a unique event. . .where you will learn what I consider to be the **most important breakthrough in real estate investor history.**

See what I mean? Oh, I'm not picking it to pieces because of my misspelled name or the "Po Box" or the unindented paragraphs; no, it's because <u>nothing</u> has any impact here, including the word *perspective* when tied to *change*.

This writer would have been better off hybridizing this opening with an "If" prelude, something such as:

> If you're a serious real estate investor I'm about to change your life.
> I'm not kidding . . . and I mean a change <u>for the better</u>. No, make that a change for <u>light-years</u> better.

86. I couldn't wait!

One type of categorization divides letter openings into three varieties:

a. Aggressive.
b. Permission-asking.
c. Bubbling over with enthusiasm.

"I couldn't wait!" is the archetype of a "Bubbling over with enthusiasm" opening. And here's where the whole concept of letter-opening choice comes home to roost: Do you <u>want</u> to bubble over with enthusiasm? Do you <u>want</u> to risk being thought of as foolish by gushing over a subject your target may regard as trivial?

 You're in command of the reader's reaction. Who are you?

The only <u>professional</u> reason for choosing a particular opening: "<u>This</u> is the right opening for generating a response to <u>this</u> offer from <u>this</u> recipient."

A letter marked "Personal" (bulk mail) begins:

> Dear Linda:
> I just couldn't wait to write to you, because I have just learned that in the next few months I believe that some <u>absolutely fantastic</u> things could be coming your way. Never before in my career have I seen such powerful signs of good fortune for one individual!

ROXANNA
110 Painters Mill Road
Owings Mills, Maryland 21117

Thursday Morning

PERSONAL FOR
Linda ~~Johnson~~
~~1280 Fri Avenue~~ E.
~~Suit 4 Tarrant, SUNnnnnn-nnnnn~~

Dear Linda:

I just couldn't wait to write to you, because I have just learned that in the
next few months I believe that some absolutely fantastic things could be coming
your way. Never before in my career have I seen such powerful signs of good
fortune for one individual!

First, Linda, let me introduce myself. My name is Roxanna, and I am one of
America's leading astrologers. I have advised and helped people all over the
world, including TV and movie celebrities, political leaders, and millionaires.

Many have listened to me and suddenly become luckier than you can possibly
imagine in the lottery, on sports events, through some totally unexpected
source, or experienced other good fortune beyond their wildest hopes. Some
chose not to follow my advice and encountered severe misfortune.

Here are some examples:
I accurately predicted the success of Richard Nixon and he became President of
the United States. I also predicted Roseanne Barr's rise to fame, and today she
is the hottest star on TV. Sean Penn didn't listen to me and his marriage to
Madonna ended. Leona Helmsley didn't listen to me and was sentenced to jail.

I have helped many others to achieve riches beyond any possible expectation and
to avoid pitfalls and tragedies they never imagined could be in store for them.

How do I do this? I study their individual astrological configurations and
devise exclusive Progressive Revelations Forecasts for each of them to live by.

Just a day or two ago, while studying the stars and the planets for my
personal client list, Linda, I discovered your Golden Opportunity Days; the
beginning of your Forecast.

I was given your name as someone who could use my help. And, we can both thank
the stars for that! Because, as soon as I uncovered the beginning of your
chart, I KNEW I MUST CONTACT YOU RIGHT AWAY!

Your Golden Opportunity Days (GODs) are days that I believe can change your life
...not slightly, not gradually - BUT DRAMATICALLY, AND IMMEDIATELY!

And, according to your Progressive Revelations Forecasts, your Golden

---

FIG. 10–4 Letter-opening type 86: "I couldn't wait!" has to be followed by a burst
of spontaneous enthusiasm. This letter does just that, with phrases such
as "absolutely fantastic" and "powerful signs of good fortune." You can
see why this opening requires a perfect match of unsophisticated offer
and trusting target individual.

25 More Ways to Get Right to the Point **219**

Hilarious? To us jaded marketers, sure it is. This was bulk mail, which means, "Never before in my career have I seen such powerful signs of good fortune for one individual!" is pure hogwash. And "I have just learned that in the next few months I believe that . . . " qualifies for the Department of Utter Confusion.

But before we damn this opening, let's once again go back to the professional basis for choice: *"This is the right opening for generating a response to this offer from this recipient."*

So the correctness and effectiveness of "I couldn't wait" should never be linked to what we, the uninvolved scornful critics, opine; it's tied to the hopes and dreams of the Lindas of this world.

87. Do me a favor (I need a favor from you).

Ben Franklin said—well, may have said—"If you want to make a friend, have him do something for you." Old Ben (or whoever) spoke pre-psychiatric wisdom there. The person who does a favor for you is tied to you more closely than the person for whom you do a favor.

So why not adapt this to a letter?

A couple of reasons come to mind, pro and con. Pro no. 1: Ben Franklin was right, and affinity is the result. Pro no. 2: Curiosity forces the reader to read on. Con no. 1: Even a minor misdirection can generate antagonism instead of rapport. Con no. 2: If your target feels the "favor" is (a) stupid or (b) out of line or (c) too self-serving or (d) desperate, instead of impaling a prospect with Cupid's arrow, you've shot yourself in the foot.

This seems to be the case with the publisher of a directory, who begins a sales letter this way:

> Dear Colleague:
> I need a small favor from you. If, after reading this message in its entirety, you can think of a reason *not* to reserve your no-risk examination copy of the new **Card Industry Directory**, please drop me a line.

Sorry, buddy, you present this in a way that makes it seem too big a favor. First, what's "in its entirety" doing there? This transforms "favor" into "demand"—poor salesmanship. second, the whole concept is transparent. (Third, I still think paragraphs should be indented.)

Why didn't the writer, using the same opening, lean toward rapport instead of arrogance by writing something like this?

> Dear Colleague,
> I need a small favor from you.
> The favor is simple for you and means much to me. I'm quite convinced you'll quickly see the benefit of owning the new **Card Industry Directory**. But obviously what matters is what <u>you</u> think. So if, after reading my reasons in this letter, you don't agree, will you be my friend and tell me why?

The difference in reader interpretation between the original and our revision is one of <u>intent</u>, not <u>content</u>.

88. Get ready!

This bright opening is best-used when you're positive of the demographic/psychographic match between your offer and your reader . . . and your offer is manifestly either amusing or vigorous.

A variation of "Get ready!" is "It's coming!"—but you can see the difference: "Get ready" is loaded with <u>you</u>; "It's coming" leaves <u>you</u> as a spectator.

A letter from a rock music source has this overline:

> **Ready to rock?**
> **This is your special invitation to personally audition the world's greatest guitar bands in your house for 10 days . . . free!**

The letter then begins in high gear:

> Dear Rocker,
> Call your friends . . . check your fuse box. . .and get ready to rock. . .because we're planning to bring the world's loudest, heaviest, most awesome guitar rockers to your house for 10 days. . .free.

Nice piece of writing. I'd have said "we're bringing" instead of "we're planning to bring"; but the writing is so sprightly it—well, it rocks!

89. Time has passed since. . . (It's been a while since. . .)

This is the sedate second cousin of no. 31, "We've missed you," and a first cousin of no. 56, "I'm surprised I haven't heard from you."

No. 31 is a generic, an all-purpose opening for contacting inactive customers or donors. No. 56 and no. 89 are more specific. Both have a powerful place in fund raising. The difference is in apparent pressure. No. 56 tries to superimpose guilt; no. 89, far gentler, attempts to generate guilt.

The definition itself proves that the writer of "Time has passed" needs greater communicative ability than the more bald approach—"I'm surprised I haven't heard from you." Want proof? Visualize these as telephone openings rather than letters.

A fund-raising letter begins quietly:

> Dear Friend and Supporter,
> It's been a while since you last sent a gift to Greenpeace. Your past support helped make Greenpeace a unique force on the world scene. You know what I mean. . .[*Ellipsis theirs, ending the paragraph.*]

Good writing. I don't agree with the word "gift" in the first sentence of a "Time has passed" letter, and no, I don't know what they mean; but these are the mildest of flaws in an oh-so-gentle reminder.

90. We've all been waiting (striving) for this.

In no way is "We've all been waiting for this" parallel to no. 23, "Good news," which is aimed <u>outward</u>. The very word *We've* says to the reader, "You <u>and</u> I."

One problem with this opening—as with many—is the possibility of including outsiders who will scoff. But is it really a problem? This opening is reserved for co-thinkers. And for cold lists (outside names) the writer has every right to depend on respectable list selection to eliminate those who automatically snort, "No, I <u>haven't</u> been waiting or striving for this."

A more logical problem is using this opening and then being unable to convince your co-thinkers this really is something all of you have been waiting for.

A letter begins:

> Dear Friend of Planned Parenthood,
> The moment we've all been working for is now at hand: the creation of a national system of healthcare that includes abortion and other essential reproductive health care as a matter of right for <u>all</u> American women.

Yes, it's a shade on the intellectual side, but unquestionably the writer of this letter has every right to assume the recipient, a member of the organization, will agree with the premise.

91. Who are we?

If you'll re-read "Who Are We?" in chapter 1, you'll see why this opening requires the ultra-professional touch. Asking the person who gets your message "Who are we?" can generate guffaws instead of phone calls: "These guys don't even know who they are."

The easy and obvious test of validity: If the next sentence justifies the question, it's a "grabber" opening; if it doesn't, steer away from "Who are we?"

A letter from a sweepstakes company:

> Dear H. G. Lewis,
> Who is Ventura and why are we writing to you?
>
> We're the people with a lot of first hand experience working with Direct Response agencies. We help them to help their clients:
>
> * Increase awareness
> * Increase response levels
> * Increase order size. . . .

Does this use of "Who are we?" work? In my opinion, yes and no—yes because in an introductory business-to-business communication this opening is a safe choice; no because the answer to "Who are we?"

Ventura Associates Inc.

April 19??

H. G. Lewis
President
Communicomp
PO Box 15725
Plantation, FL 33318

Dear H. G. Lewis,

Who is Ventura and why are we writing to you?

We're the people with a lot of first hand experience working with
Direct Response agencies. We help them to help their clients:

* Increase awareness
* Increase response levels
* Increase order size

You don't have to take our word for it. Ask Mark Mylan at Grey
Direct, Kevin Davies at T.C.G. Marketing, Steele Hayes at
Targeted Communications, Jane Solomon at Rapp & Collins, Joann
Schindelheim at The Direct Marketing Group.

They come to us, as do most of our clients, on a project basis.
And we provide them with the specialized promotional services
that they can't get in-house.

Ask them about our understanding of their challenges, the quality
of our input and the kind of attention their projects receive.

An innovator in the promotion arena for more than 18 years,
Ventura's special area of expertise is the imaginative use of
contests, games and sweepstakes.

One successful, extremely cost-effective example of Ventura's
innovative strength is our annual Co-op Sweepstakes. It's a
turn-key program offering over $50,000 in prizes. This is the
kind of sweepstakes your clients would expect to pay big money
for, but the cost is only $8,500.

Want to find out more? Call or fax us today.

Sincerely,

Pamela Wragg

PW/sk
DMN.SOL

1350 AVENUE OF THE AMERICAS   NEW YORK, NEW YORK 10019-4701   212 586-9720   TELEFAX 212 586-0544

FIG. 10-5 Letter-opening type 91: "Who are we?" is a safe opening when sending
an introductory letter to a business prospect who may not know who you
are. If you use this opening, tell the recipient who you are within his or
her experiential background, not your own . . . because a business
prospect cares about his or her business, not yours.

is neither specific nor potent. "We're the people with a lot of first hand experience working with Direct Response agencies" is a claim I've heard from 22,346 sources.

Incidentally, way down in paragraph 8, this company—and it really is a distinguished supplier to our industry—clarifies what it has to offer. My opinion: Move that paragraph to the top and justify "Who are we?" as a rhetorical question.

92. I won't waste your time.

This is a good expert-to-expert vehicle. We can envision Albert Einstein beginning an explanation this way.

And that's the caution. How many conversations, let alone letters, have you had in which some boor says, "I won't waste your time". . . then wastes your time?

Terseness is the key to no. 92. If you say, "I won't waste your time," then launch into a historical summary, you've chosen the wrong opening. Einstein has given way to Tolstoy, and the word-glutted reader consciously or unconsciously becomes a resentful "I thought so" outsider.

Overlines are fashionable, but they just don't go with this opening. Here's the printed overline on a subscription letter from a computer publication:

> Announcing an important NEW, LABS-BASED RESOURCE dedicated solely to helping you successfully integrate your multi-platform information systems. *One that will cost you nothing whatsoever, now or ever.*

The letter begins:

> Dear IS Expert:
>
> I won't waste your time.
> The challenge you face now is the most complex, most demanding, most important challenge in information systems today. . .
>
> **Now, you must find a way to integrate a wide range of systems into one, incredibly powerful, multi-**

**platform environment that lets your company's
technology play in concert.**

Okay, what have we learned? Nothing. So "I won't waste your time" is —well, it's a lie.

I'm not attacking the writing; I'm attacking the use of this opening for this message. It's a mismatch. Opinion: The letter would have been stronger <u>without</u> the overline. Compare that opening with this possibility:

> Dear IS Expert,
>
> I won't waste your time.
> You need us. Simple as that. We're the key to integrating your multi-platform information systems. And incidentally, we're free.

If you can't be terse, choose another opening.

93. Thank you.

How can you go wrong saying, "Thank you"?

I like <u>ending</u> a letter with "Thank you" because to me it's more logical to thank the reader for performing whatever act the letter suggests. Thanking in advance, though, has its own benefit—setting a mood of gratitude.

So the question the writer has to ask is, "What am I thanking this reader for?" If the answer doesn't make sense, the thanks doesn't make sense.

A subscription mailing for a newsletter begins:

> Dear Reader:
> Thank you for taking the time to open the envelope. Right up front, here are answers to questions you may have. . . .

I wonder about this. Thanking the reader for opening the envelope—well, for-hire communicators know such an act is certainly worthy of thanks. And it does put the reader in a receptive state of mind. So I'm not about to attack this use of the "Thank you" opening.

But this person already <u>has</u> opened the envelope. That second sentence has terrific guts to it. Did the mailer test the opening against one which opens in high gear?

94. Why do you need this?

Here we have the third "Why" opening in our list of 100 openings. (The others: No. 20, "Why are we doing this?" and no. 28, "Why do they . . . or why don't they. . . .")

You can see the logic: The first example is first person, I or We. The second example is He, Her, or They. Who's left? <u>You</u>.

Tying "Why"—an implicit reader-involver—with "You"—an explicit reader-involver—should be sure-fire. "Why do you" is considerably weaker than "Why don't you," but it's also considerably safer because it doesn't engender the "They're trying to sell me something" reaction from skeptical readers.

A mailing for a directory begins:

> Dear Marketing Planner:
> "Why would I need another print media directory?"
> That's what you may be asking yourself as you read this letter.
> After all, you've probably already got the directory that you think of as "The Bible" in the media field. . . .

This approach may be a little too cautious. "Would" and "may" are conditional, not straightforward. I have a feeling you or I might have taken a slightly more slam-bang approach:

> Dear Marketing Planner,
> I'll bet I can guess the question you're about to ask yourself:
> "WHY DO I NEED ANOTHER PRINT MEDIA DIRECTORY?"
> If that question is on-target, it's because you're used to that other directory—the one most planners use as their "Media Bible". . . .

"Why" tied to "you" has an edge over many of the other openings we've discussed: It's never a terrible way to start out.

95. Are you really sure they're giving you the right facts?

A principal value of this opening is its inference—"You're smart, but the people who are feeding you information may be neither smart nor honorable"—without making an open accusation.

Note the crucial difference between "Are you sure they're giving you the right facts?" and "Are you sure you're getting the right facts?" The first statement assigns responsibility to an outsider; the second assigns responsibility to the reader.

Note, too, the edge this opening has over a simpler but less reader-involving "Are they giving you the right facts?"

So <u>after</u> the letter establishes competitive positioning, switch to a statement saying something such as "Now you'll get the right facts about Whatever." The compromise opening, "Now you can get the right facts about Whatever," is unrelated (see opening no. 47) because it subordinates "They" to the reader's sudden capability.

An example of "Are you really sure they're giving you the right facts?":

> Dear Publishing Executive:
>   Are you comfortable—really comfortable—about the information you're using to make today's tricky business decisions?
>   You're not you say? That's not surprising.

The omitted comma in the second sentence is the writer's error, not mine, and the third paragraph is bookish; but the tone of this letter is moderately on target. "They" aren't feeding you the right information. The competitive challenge has an extra arrow in its quiver.

96. You're in my thoughts today.

Careful with this one! It's highly emotional, but it's so personal you really can tick off the recipient. For non-fund raising, save it for genuine relationships. For fund raising, be sure whoever signs the letter is somebody who <u>might</u> have the recipient in his/her thoughts. (It's especially valuable for milking prior donors.)

A respected fund raising organization mailed this holiday message:

> Dear Mr. Lewis,
>   I often ask myself what The Salvation Army would do without good friends like you.
>   The men, women and children you've helped are living, breathing proof of the good you have done for this community. You've given those in need food, clothing and shelter. And, you've brought hope into their lives.

> That's why you are in my thoughts today as we approach the
> Christmas season. Because hunger knows no season. . . .

Altogether, completely professional.

But . . .

What if the writer had <u>opened</u> with no. 96? The letter might have read . . .

> You're in my thoughts today. I'll tell you why:
> It's because I often ask myself what The Salvation Army would
> do without good friends like you.
> The men, women and children you've helped are living,
> breathing proof of the good you have done for this community.
> You've given those in need food, clothing and shelter. And you've
> brought hope into their lives. . . .

Isn't the message more powerful when "You're in my thoughts today" is the opener rather than an ancillary?

97. If I'm sure of anything, I'm sure of this.

This opening is valuable for immediate emphasis of the writer's (a) sincerity or (b) openness or (c) integrity.

This is a highly useful, dynamic opening, but just one caution: Don't let it disintegrate into a used car dealer's arm-around-the-shoulder "I'll be honest with ya" pitch.

A letter from a computer software company begins:

> Dear Registered User:
> I know one thing for sure about my computer's memory . . . it's a
> pain in the neck. Frankly, I don't want to worry about memory. I
> want enough room to do my work and that's it. I want my system's
> memory to be handled automatically! Just take care of it and don't
> bother me!

Opinion: It works, but No. 1 ("If you're like I am . . . ") might work just as well or better. The word <u>Frankly</u> damages the pitch, as does the exclamation mark after <u>automatically</u> because the message becomes shrill and car-dealer-like. Are these objections? Nope. They're <u>sugges-</u>

tions, proof that what each of us does best is criticize the creative work of others.

98. If you're worried, here's the solution.

Openings like this become more and more valid as computers and snooping give us greater and greater ability to pinpoint our targets.

A second value of this opening is its ability to <u>generate</u> a worry that may not have existed: The target thinks, "Hey, I really should be worried about this."

A letter with a big, black, printed overline—*Why hasn't your broker told you about today's most overlooked, misunderstood and <u>profitably secure</u> investments?*—begins:

> Dear Investor:
>   If you're worried about your financial future . . . worried about increasing your investment income and looking for sound diversification . . . then I ask you to consider subscribing to <u>The Laird Letter</u>.

I have a feeling half a sentence is missing here. The writer brings in The Laird Letter as a solution without justifying it as a solution. Too, worry "about your financial future" is a generalized worry. Specifics outpull generalizations. So "If you're worried that your investments won't increase and aren't diversified enough" changes no fact but moves toward specificity.

Those are comments about <u>this</u> letter, but they don't affect the worth of the opening.

99. Test yourself.

This one can't miss. People are suckers for self-testing. They try to out-guess the contestants on quiz shows; they look for trivia questions in the inflight magazines; they spend money for a by-mail I.Q. test.

The key is to have them test themselves. They resent testing from the outside. So if you use this opening, the test has to be logical, rele-

DAY-TIMERS, Inc.
One Day-Timer Plaza
Allentown, Pennsylvania 18195-1551

215-266-9000

        Send us $1.00 -- and we'll send you a Pocket DAY-TIMER®
        Sample Kit containing our three most popular pocket-size
        planner/diary formats by return mail.

Dear Friend,

According to management consultants, the single most important
asset a busy executive can possess is skill in managing time.

        Test yourself: Do you know how to free your mind for
        important decisions? How to guarantee that you get top
        priority projects finished first? Is your work organized?
        (Or are you constantly putting out brush fires?) Can you
        remember every project you must finish today, tomorrow,
        and weeks ahead? Can you remember the details of work
        you accomplished only yesterday?

If you've answered "No" to a single one of these questions, you're
sure to benefit by using what a leading business newsletter has
called "one of the best time management aids ever developed" --
a Day-Timer planner/diary system. Although available by private
subscription only, it's used by more than 4 million business
executives and professionals across America and throughout the
world to save hours a day, organize their activities, and free
their minds for creative thinking and problem solving.

        Now we invite you to put this proven Day-Timer system
        to work for you for the next 4 months for only $1.00.

Normally, you'd pay up to $28.95 for a full-year Pocket Day-Timer
set with vinyl wallet. Some pay even more for a set with a deluxe
wallet in their choice of luxury leathers! But, for a limited time
only, we've decided to make available a Sample Kit containing our
three most popular Pocket Day-Timer formats for just $1.00. So
now, everyone who has ever wanted to test the different kinds of
Pocket Day-Timer systems can do so easily... and at practically
no cost.

There's no risk for you -- or for us. Our records reveal that 93%
of those who start to use a Day-Timer system faithfully, continue
to use it as a valued partner year after year.

Your Pocket Day-Timer planner/diary will give you an automatic
memory -- it will organize everything for you as far ahead as
you need plan, as far back as you need records kept! The basic
strategy of this highly successful system is to put all your
scattered records in one place for instant reference, so that

FIG. 10–6 Letter-opening type 99: The first sentence of this letter is marching in place. How much stronger the letter would have been if the writer had 1) put the pre-greeting text in a different typeface and 2) eliminated altogether the weak sentence beginning "According to management consultants."

vant, one the reader can pass with pride or fail without dishonor, and above all <u>clear</u>.

A letter to business executives begins:

> Dear Friend,
> According to management consultants, the single most important asset a busy executive can possess is skill in managing time.
> Test yourself: Do you know how to free your mind for important decisions? How to guarantee that you get top priority projects finished first? Is your work organized?. . .

Okay, what's your opinion? Does this "test" qualify on grounds of logic, relevance, pass with pride or fail without dishonor, and clarity? I don't think so. Asking someone, "Do you know how to free your mind for important decisions?" is an unanswerable question. A muzzy question begets a muzzy answer, if any. The <u>second</u> question qualifies on all counts: "How to guarantee that you get top priority projects finished first?" Why not use that one as the key test, or even the only test?

(What is that first limp sentence doing there at all? If the writer had a mad urge to include a management, consultant reference, a better lead-in to "Test yourself" might have been: "Management consultants agree. Do you? Managing time is <u>the</u> key executive ability.")

100. I'm mad as hell.

This opening has a colossal benefit: It's contagious. Like some of the other openings we've discussed, ranging from *No. 9* ("As you know. . .") and *No. 26* ("Have you ever wished. . .") and *No. 67* ("Remember when . . .") and *No. 68* ("Isn't it sad?" and *No. 74* ("Am I right about you?"), right up to *No. 98* ("If you're worried. . ."), "I'm mad as hell" has the power to be contagious, to generate a state of mind.

Being mad as hell is obvious for fund raisers, but astute business marketers can get results with it when all 99 other openings don't seem to work. Obviously, the anger has to be directed at <u>them</u>, not you.

In this instance, the actual words aren't necessary. What's necessary is transmitting the flavor of righteous outrage. Do that by using emotional words. Attack with fire and flame, not matchsticks.

What a way to end a series! This example is from the *Nationwide Campaign to Halt Advertising Abuse*. A Johnson Box is headed:

SICK AND TIRED OF ADVERTISING CONSTANTLY JUNKING UP YOUR LIFE? HERE IS YOUR CHANCE TO FIGHT BACK AND STOP IT!

The letter proper begins:

> Dear Citizen,
>   I believe America stands for far more important values than "shop 'til you drop" and "when the going gets tough, the tough go shopping!"
>   And right now, it's high time to <u>stop</u> Madison Avenue from defining <u>our</u> core values for ourselves and our families. We are far more valuable as human beings than <u>what we consume</u>—and we must choose and fight for an American culture of responsibility and community over runaway commercialism. . . .

Uh-oh. He's lost it. I got only as far as "defining our core values" before dropping out. The signer is "Michael Jacobson, Ph.D.," and the letter has too much of the Ph.D. in it to carry the contagion we need. Remember that key—emotional words? What could be <u>less</u> emotional than <u>defining</u> (I hate that word in selling copy) and <u>core values</u> and <u>consume</u> and <u>choose</u>?

If you're mad as hell, be mad as hell. Don't be as angry as Hades . . . .Which I'd like to think you are to see this listing of 100 ways to begin a business letter come to an end.

A Concluding Thought

As we drive the golden spike into this communications railbed, the smoke has to clear away so the master key to effective letter-writing can come clear.

The master key isn't cleverness. It isn't a massive vocabulary. It isn't thorough product knowledge.

In fact, those three elements can <u>suppress</u> <u>response.</u>

No. The key is as simple, as straightforward, and as obvious as <u>matching your message to your target</u>. Add to this just a touch of professionalism—replacing boiler-plate generalizations with specifics—and you will have a winner.

Thoughtless writing is easier to generate than thoughtful writing. These 100 ways to begin a letter <u>demand</u> thoughtfulness. So by using one of the 100 ways to begin a letter—and using it properly—at once we eliminate such openings as . . .

- We have developed a wide variety of interlocking marketing services ranging from [SNORE]. . .

- If your business demands reliable communications and you demand value . . . choose [NAME OF COMPANY].
- You have better things to think about than your busy schedule.
- DON'T PAY TAXES ON MONEY YOU AREN'T USING.
- [NAME OF COMPANY] shops the world to find the finest quality designer jewelry.

See how easy it is to write a lousy opening?

The master key: writing in a style and mode that matches the reader's demographic, psychological, and attitudinal position <u>of the moment</u>.

Not easy, you say? Wonderful. If it were easy, anybody could do what we can do.

TITLES OF INTEREST IN MARKETING, DIRECT MARKETING, AND SALES PROMOTION

For further information or a current catalog, write:
NTC Business Books
a division of *NTC Publishing Group*
4255 West Touhy Avenue
Lincolnwood, Illinois 60646-1975 U.S.A.